PSYCHOLOGY AND GENDER

This book provides an understanding of how psychology and gender are closely interrelated. It examines, critiques, and debunks some of the theoretical premises from mainstream psychology while remaining mindful and respectful of their utilities. The book brings together psychological concepts, theories, and paradigms and examines how they interplay with gender studies going beyond the typical understanding of gender as merely demographic variable. The volume discusses important concepts such as gender role development and interpersonal relationships across caste, class, genders, sexualities, race, and region. It also studies the significant link between psychology and gender and with feminism, women's studies, the women's movement, the queer movement, queer studies, as well as other social movements. It uses an interdisciplinary and multidisciplinary approach all through.

This book will appeal to students, researchers, and teachers of psychology, applied psychology, gender and women studies, sociology, practitioners, activists, those working in not-for-profit organizations and those working specifically on engendering psychology. The book will also be valuable reading for those interested in South Asian studies and other interdisciplinary courses in social sciences.

Sadhana Avinash Natu did her BA (psychology) from Fergusson College, Pune; her MA (clinical psychology) from the Department of Psychology of the then Pune University; and BEd from Tilak College of Education, Pune. She secured positions in the merit list of the university during all these courses. Thereafter, she cleared her UGC NET-JRF and obtained a doctorate from Pune University. Her thesis was titled 'A Psycho-social Enquiry Into the Gender Roles and Other Related Factors of Young Males with Special Reference to Maternal Employment'. She works across multiple sectors and disciplines. She has long-standing engagement and work in academics, NGOs, community-based organizations, corporate sector, and psychotherapy. She has worked on boards of studies of psychology and women's studies in Savitribai Phule Pune University as well as autonomous colleges. She was awarded the 'Innovative Teaching Award' of Savitribai Phule Pune University for facilitative, participatory teaching which allows students to engage critically with curricula. She writes in English and Marathi, and her translation of *Social Psychology* in Marathi, where she was the first author, won the Best Book Award of Marathi Manas Shastra Parishad. She facilitates a peer support and speak-out group, DISHA, in her institution which has served as a model for institutions across the university. She believes that there is a cogent, meaningful relationship between her social action, feminism, gynagogy, research, and the students' world and that the classroom is a microcosm of the outside world and social reality. She has written for journals, chapters in books, and books as well as columns in newspapers for dissemination of ideas. She has participated in several national and international conferences and led many symposia and conducted pre-conference workshops, especially on gender and psychology, mixed methods, and gender analysis in psychological research and critical psychology. She is a Member of the Executive Committee of National Academy of Psychology, India and Honorary Director of a Non Profit Company Centre for Inquiry into Mental Health, India.

PSYCHOLOGY AND GENDER

An Advanced Reader

Sadhana Avinash Natu

LONDON AND NEW YORK

Designed cover image: © agsandrew / Getty Images

First published 2024
by Routledge
4 Park Square, Milton Park, Abingdon, Oxon OX14 4RN

and by Routledge
605 Third Avenue, New York, NY 10158

Routledge is an imprint of the Taylor & Francis Group, an informa business

© 2024 Sadhana Avinash Natu

The right of Sadhana Avinash Natu to be identified as author of this work
has been asserted in accordance with sections 77 and 78 of the Copyright,
Designs and Patents Act 1988.

All rights reserved. No part of this book may be reprinted or reproduced or
utilised in any form or by any electronic, mechanical, or other means, now
known or hereafter invented, including photocopying and recording, or in
any information storage or retrieval system, without permission in writing
from the publishers.

Trademark notice: Product or corporate names may be trademarks or
registered trademarks, and are used only for identification and explanation
without intent to infringe.

British Library Cataloguing-in-Publication Data
A catalogue record for this book is available from the British Library

ISBN: 978-1-032-51873-2 (hbk)
ISBN: 978-1-032-59243-5 (pbk)
ISBN: 978-1-003-45375-8 (ebk)

DOI: 10.4324/9781003453758

Typeset in Times New Roman
by Apex CoVantage, LLC

Dedicated to my parents, Late Nandini and Avinash Natu.

Both of you believed in, as well as lived by, pluralistic values, transcended stereotypical gender roles and gave me the wings to live 'my dreams' while helping me remain firmly grounded and socially responsible.

Dedicated to my life partner Satish and son Tanmay Sadhana Satish, who have actively helped and supported and participated in all my professional endeavours and in making this book happen.

Dedicated to my students, colleagues, and comrades who believed in me and kept me optimistic.

Sadhana

CONTENTS

List of Figures	*ix*
List of Tables	*x*
Foreword One	*xi*
Janak Pandey	
Foreword Two	*xiii*
Anagha Tambe	
Acknowledgements	*xv*

Introduction	1
1 A Prelude to Psychology and Gender Domains	4
2 Theoretical Frameworks of Understanding Gender	23
3 Gender and Social Psychology	41
4 Gender and Developmental Psychology	57
5 Gender and the Workplace	81
6 Exploring Gender and Sexualities	106
7 Understanding Feminist Psychotherapies	123

viii Contents

8 Gender and Mental Health Challenges   145

9 Psychology, Gender, and Media   165

10 Way Forward   183

Index   *194*

FIGURES

2.1	Kohlberg's Six Stages of Moral Development	30
4.1	Women in Vocational Education and Training	70
7.1	Power Processes	136
7.2	Circle of Care	136

TABLES

1.1	Some Terms Related to Gender	6
1.2	Pathbreaking Events in the Domain of Psychology and Gender	15
6.1	Some Major References on Human Sexuality	110
7.1	Some Initiatives of Feminist Therapy	126
7.2	Classic Psychoanalytic Feminists and Their Field-Defining Texts	134

FOREWORD ONE

The biological roles expected from men and women are of a complementary and equal nature. It is natural to expect similar equality between men and women in every respect of our sociocultural and economic lives. However, men take advantage of their physical strength and women's helplessness, particularly during childbearing and nurturing, except for providing token support and care. In most cultures, men structured social systems with inequality by putting their dominance, exploitation, and edge over women. Thus, men's authority and uncalled-for advantageous position over women evolved and continues in blatant or disguised forms, raising many questions that contemporary social sciences researchers attempt to explain. In response, gender studies have emerged as a new interdisciplinary subject to answer questions related to gender issues. In the last five decades or so, diverse approaches and explanations have enhanced our understanding of different gender issues such as gender socialization, identity, roles, discrimination, and exploitation. Gender studies have evolved as a significant area of courses leading to the development of theories and applications for resolution of gender-related problems.

Among the social sciences, psychology has been at the forefront to study gender issues. Although traditionally mostly men served as participants (subjects) in psychological research, women also gradually entered as participants, mainly finding evidence supporting gender differences, if any, in psychological phenomena. By the 1960s, psychological science had accumulated vast knowledge about gender differences in social, emotional, cognitive, and personality traits' developments. However, psychologists' interest had a generally limited purpose of finding gender differences in psychological processes without much attention to sources explaining such differences. Psychologists and other social scientists realized that the real issue was to search for the sociocultural, economic, and psychological causes

xii Foreword One

affecting such differences. In the 1970s, psychologists paid attention to the role women had in society and what was expected from them by the society, shaping the women's personality and abilities. The new trend of looking at gender issues led to a fresh perspective of studying gender in psychology, leading to massive research efforts and an independent sub-discipline, 'gender psychology'.

In recent decades, research on the psychology of gender has also increased in India, requiring an integrated presentation in a book for researchers and students. This new book, *Psychology and Gender: An Advanced Reader* by Sadhana Avinash Natu serves this purpose. The conceptual issues such as the meaning of gender roles, identity, discrimination, and feminism are lucidly presented. Along with psychology, biological, sociological, and anthropological perspectives together introduce an integrated picture. The book deals with gender-related activism and issues like career and work of applied importance. Each chapter covers a wide range of topics, and the overall coverage of the psychology of gender is comprehensive. A century-old, sustained struggle for gender equalities has resulted in normative changes, but the realities are far from the expected norms. Let us be optimistic that Dr Sadhana Avinash Natu's book will positively contribute to building human societies with gender equalities. Her previous book, *Psychology and Gender: An Introduction*, was well received by readers. I am sure that students, researchers, and faculty will welcome the new book too. People involved in policy will also find the book useful for solutions for gender-related issues.

Janak Pandey
ICSSR National Fellow
Former Head, CBCS, University of Allahabad
Former First Vice Chancellor, Central University of Bihar
Former Head, Department of Psychology, University of Allahabad

FOREWORD TWO

The relationship of gender/women's studies with different disciplines has been a troubled one, albeit unevenly. While feminist perspectives are securing strongholds within the disciplinary spaces of history, English literature, sociology, economics, and so on, the discipline of psychology has been among the last bastions to open itself to the enriching forces of gender studies. The field of psychology of gender, and more specifically of feminist psychology, is still only nascent in India, notwithstanding relentless struggles of the scholars like U. Vindhya, who has interrogated psychology as usual, its content, methodology, and epistemology from a critical gender lens. This latest reference book by Dr Sadhana Avinash Natu, a senior scholar, teacher, practitioner, and a persistent advocate of engendering of psychology, is significant in clearing the way for psychological engagement with gender in India.

Feminism and women's studies have generated a lot of excitement among students and researchers of psychology, as is revealed from the discussions in the national conferences of the National Academy of Psychology, for instance, or from dissertations of psychology students in various universities and colleges. Some of the key psychological enquiries informed by women's studies scholarship are around construction of gendered identities, women's mental health and well-being, work–family interface in women's lives, and gendered violence and interventions for it. Various accounts of disciplinary encounters with gender studies have revealed that this journey has been a long and tortuous one. The emergence of women's studies and women's movements in India over last three decades and more has meant an expansion and engendering of the frontiers of psychological research, as can be witnessed from disciplinary journals and books. This has produced rigorous gender critiques of male stream psychological knowledge, and gender has thus permeated the organizational and intellectual domains. However, the sanctioned gender blindness in curriculum and teaching programmes through which the disciplinary meanings and practices are reproduced has meant that the institutional spaces have continued to be regimented, and courses on gender, if included, remain on its periphery. Rather than being disheartened that the psychology of gender is placed on the academic borderlands, Dr Sadhana Avinash Natu, through this reference book, ventures into building resources for this audacious project of engendering psychology. Her innovative and student-centred pedagogies, her interventions in the field of feminist practice and organization, and her openness to take psychological knowledge to other scientific and popular fields have taken this project beyond the routine content of a reference book.

This book is thus crucial in more than one way. Going beyond the 'sex difference' and 'gender role' paradigm of a typical 'gender in psychology' work, this book encapsulates a broad range of concerns, focusing on from key and congenial psychological objects, such as roles and relationships, sexuality, work, and mental health, or on some substantive disciplinary fields, like development psychology or psychotherapy, to more fundamental strategies of seeking to transform the disciplinary frames of concepts and theories. Secondly, this is a decolonial attempt at psychology and gender, locating itself in the dominant debates centred around issues related to relevance and cultural appropriateness of the discipline to post-colonial India. Although the efforts to develop indigenous disciplinary frameworks have been long-standing in Indian psychology rooted in the Western paradigm of research and teaching, the framing on the psychology of gender largely remains embedded in the Western feminist debates, as it is in academia in general. This book is significant in drawing from the rich feminist scholarship in India to address the psychological enquiries. Third, this book evades using gender in a narrow sense, defining it in its intersections with class, caste, and community. Again, even though prejudice, stereotypes, and social attitudes towards castes and religious communities recognized as impediments to social development have emerged as central issues in the psychological field in India, the category 'gender' is often articulated in a singular, universalizing framework, grounding women in middle-class experiences. This book recognizes the contested nature of gender.

This reference book goes towards encouraging the field of psychology of gender to grow organically and reflexively, with a critical engagement with psychology and women's studies, simultaneously. Recently, the psychological investigation has become a vital resource to analyse diverse feminist questions, such as sexual violence and its trauma and suffering, humiliation, and microaggression experienced by disadvantaged social groups in education, and cultural socialization of the young in relation to technology and class. It has brought out the need to turn to psychology for more humanistic approaches and micro-level variables, like well-being, and focus on social interactions, subjectivities, and agency, in unravelling the social world. This book can play a significant role in developing knowledges and insights in the field of psychology of gender to address some of the critical questions in women's studies today.

Anagha Tambe
Director, Krantijyoti Savitribai
Phule Department of Women and Gender Studies
Savitribai Phule Pune University

ACKNOWLEDGEMENTS

Right from the beginning of my career in teaching, I have taught 'psychology' through a multidimensional, multidisciplinary, critical, feminist, and socially engaged approach. For this, I have many persons, organizations, disciplines, and movements to thank! An active engagement with community health, advocacy, women's studies, mental health, feminism, the women's movement, and teaching of psychology has helped me adopt multidisciplinary gynagogies in classrooms, research, and co-curricular endeavours. This book follows the same pattern that I use in all my engagements: reflection, questioning, critical analysis and exploring possibilities, challenges, and some solutions.

The teaching–learning exercise of the last 34 years has been a joyous one, thanks to inquisitive millennials and post-millennials who have kept me 'perennially on my toes' – students (UG, PG, research, psychology, women's studies, and other social sciences) who have accorded me the opportunity to experiment with ideas, wrestle, tease out conundrums, and reconcile and recognize the difference between theories, applications, and the challenges of lived reality. My 'diversity-driven, democratic, feminist classrooms' have given me life lessons to engage with psychology, gender, and intersectionality! I have taught various subjects at the UG and PG levels in psychology, as well as women's studies, and engaged with students of other social sciences – sociology, social work, liberal arts – and the frameworks for the nine chapters have been derived from these exchanges.

Conducting workshops on gender sensitization in schools, colleges, and universities and those on prevention of sexual harassment at the workplace in industry, academia, and NGOs through case work and training and awareness sessions has allowed me to go beyond the classroom and canons of a text. It is this multifarious experience in 'doing psychology' and 'doing gender' across subjects, students, and sectors which has allowed me to unpack many myths; test out theories; gain wisdom from diverse participants; collect anecdotes, vignettes, and case studies; and

xvi Acknowledgements

embellish my repertoire of psychology and gender. My field-based research projects on psychology and gender have taught me the interconnections and linkages between theory and praxis sometimes and exposed the disconnect between ivory-tower navel-gazing and the nuts and bolts of a sharp, piercing reality at other times. It is these insights, as well as 'knotty, complex problems', that the book lays out.

I am a practising psychotherapist trained in cognitive behavioural therapy (CBT), but after a while I moved on to feminist psychotherapy and narrative therapy, which has allowed me to engage with diverse sets of people as clients in my institution (diversity across all stakeholders and with the peer support group that I facilitate), as well as those that I work with through community-based organizations and my private practice. Three of the chapters are tied to these understandings.

While studying psychology and during my initial days of teaching psychology, especially while dealing with mainstream psychology, there was a constant feeling of unease, since at the same time I was also involved in the women's movement, women's studies, community health, and mental health. Seniors, comrades, and fellow travellers at all these locations compelled me to interrogate psychology through the prism of gender and inequalities while prudently not 'throwing out the baby with the bath water'! Teaching gender and health, mental health, feminist research methodology, feminist psychotherapy, and more at Krantijyoti Savitribai Phule Women's Studies Centre, Savitribai Phule Pune University, as a visiting professor, alongside teaching courses in psychology, allowed me to study and understand the connections, points of departure, and the myriad, contentious challenges that the field of psychology and gender has been throwing up.

Being a part of the syllabus-framing process and research, resource person in refresher courses of engendering disciplines (engendering psychology in my case), and part of a teacher fellowship programme where I could write a monograph on this process of engendering psychology and its challenges have all gone a long way in enabling me to become a generalist in women's studies and a specialist (somewhat!) in gender and psychology and to 'do critical and feminist psychology'. For this long-standing association and work, I owe my gratitude to Krantijyoti Savitribai Phule Women's Studies Centre, Savitribai Phule Pune University, and all my friends and erstwhile seniors at the centre.

Associations with various academic departments and institutions (training, research) and long-standing engagement in various capacities (research, training, impact assessment) with community-based and rights-based organizations, such as Mahila Sarvangeen Utkarsh Mandal (MASUM), Pune, and Bapu Trust for Research on Mind and Discourse, Pune (to name a few), and with colleagues and friends in these organizations and departments, have enriched my knowledge and understanding of gender issues and other social issues. Professional bodies, such as the National Academy of Psychology and Indian Association of Women's Studies, have given me and my students a large canvas of learning about work in psychology and gender studies in India through conferences and other academic endeavours, and I am thankful for these opportunities!

Acknowledgements **xvii**

It is a heady melange of bell hooks, Mukta Salve, Kimberlé Crenshaw, Savitribai Phule, Paulo Freire, Betty Friedan, Simone de Beauvoir, Uma Chakravarti, Vidyut Bhagwat, V. Geetha, Manisha Gupte, Sharmila Rege, Bhargavi Davar, U. Vindhya, Gina Rippon, and many in this pantheon who have inspired me in all my work, and I wish to express my gratitude to them.

On a personal note, I would like to thank the following people: My parents, who encouraged me and laid down the path for my engagement with feminism – Mum, who was a living example of tackling crises head-on and a socialist from a young age, and Dada, who exhorted me to 'become fearless' and was a feminist man. Both of you would have been happy that I have been able to write books based on the two worlds that I have straddled: psychology and gender. Both of you were 'tough and tender', the perfect androgyny that I was enamoured of in the 1990s and would have been proud that I have let go of those frames and moved on to intersectional feminism and its impact on psychology.

My partner, Satish, who has been a sounding board, technical support, and unkind critic, who egged me on to prioritize writing over the umpteen other things that I do, and my son, Tanmay, who has been encouraging and informative and given me a bird's-eye view from a young reader's point of view.

How can I forget my publishers and the editorial team – Amit Kumar, for his belief in my ability to write this book and do justice to it, and Angelin Joy and the rest of the team for their inputs and support. Thank you, all! I am grateful to my institution, colleagues, my departmental colleagues, and all my wonderful students, present and past, across disciplines. I am grateful to Professor Janak Pandey and Dr Anagha Tambe for their forewords and validation of the book.

I hope that readers of all sorts – students of different disciplines, such as psychology, women's studies and social sciences; researchers; activists; NGO workers; lay readers; students in general – in India, South Asia and across the world, find the book engaging both academically and critically!

INTRODUCTION

There is a tradition of excellent text and reference books on psychology and gender (also called 'psychology of gender' or 'psychology of women') from the West (particularly EURAM, i.e. Europe and the Unites States). However, we do not have books on psychology and gender which speak to both the global and Indian contexts. It is this gap that the present book aims to fill. Courses on psychology and gender are emerging and are being taught in some universities, and it is hoped that this book will be found useful by both faculty and students. Some of the universities have courses in 'psychology and gender' on some of the sub-topics of various chapters, and this book will be appropriate for them as well. Various non-governmental organizations (NGOs) that work on gender issues, as well as those working on mental health, would find this book handy. Students of women's/ gender studies also study gender and psychology, and the book is meant for them too. Many people are conducting workshops on 'gender sensitization', and they would find a lot of important questions and issues that need to be addressed delineated here.

The book talks about the impact of gender on various branches of psychology and the way in which engendering psychology and all its work – academics, psychotherapy, research, and other applications happens. These areas have been a long-term project in the West and a non-linear project at that. In India, however, this process is still at its nascent stage. While research and work in psychology do acknowledge the broad category of 'women', 'gender' is often treated as a demographic variable and without looking at the complexities and contestations that monoliths, categories, and binaries, like 'men and women', have fielded vis-à-vis the rich research on and insights from women's studies.

Against this backdrop, the rationale of this book is to examine, critique, and debunk some of the theoretical premises from mainstream psychology while

DOI: 10.4324/9781003453758-1

2 Introduction

remaining mindful and respectful of their utility and purpose. Hence, there is a genuine attempt in all the chapters to bring together psychological concepts, theories, and paradigms and see how they speak to gender.

Almost all branches of psychology have been impacted by the gender perspective. Keeping this in mind, a few branches, such as developmental psychology, women and work, clinical psychology, and mental health, have been focused on in the book. Besides this, important concepts, such as gender role development and interpersonal relationships, have been explored through the multidisciplinary mode. In all the chapters, gender has been decoded through the intersectional axes of caste, class, genders, sexualities, and region (and race and nation as well), instead of equating gender only with women, and that too middle-class women. Intersectionality is an aspect that cannot be bypassed while studying psychology and gender, and the author has been mindful of that in all her work, as well as while writing the book.

Chapter 6 on 'Exploring Gender and Sexualities', navigates the difficult terrain of discussing heterosexuality with all its issues, as well as looking at queer sexualities and psychological problems that queer persons continue to face. Chapters 7 and 8 on 'Understanding Feminist Psychotherapies' and 'Gender and Mental Health Challenges', respectively, underscore all the challenges that exist and discuss the ways in which these challenges can be overcome. Chapter 9 deep dives into the interconnections between psychology, gender and media in an interesting fashion. This will be useful for students and practitioners, as well as those working on engendering psychology.

The chapters have been written eschewing a pedantic mode in discussion form. The concepts and theories have been illustrated with examples, tables, and so on. Some debates and controversies related to specific concepts, theories, and paradigms have been explained. In many of the chapters, mainstream theoretical approaches have been interrogated from gender and intersectional perspectives, unpacking some of the contentious issues. All these efforts are important to genuinely engage with psychology and gender.

The chapters are interspersed with informative 'boxes' with collated information, points to ponder or some trivia related to the topics. The exercises at the end of each chapter consist of summative and formative evaluative questions, as well as questions that will prompt critical thinking. Within each chapter, case studies, vignettes, and illustrations have been used to underscore the complexities and nuances of various concepts and theories. Although relevant research studies have been quoted, the emphasis has been on explaining and discussing various approaches and angles and making the writing accessible to all.

All the chapters delve into some aspects that have been put on the back burner in mainstream psychology, and while the focus is on psychology and gender, intersectionality is not lost sight of while discussing any concept. This is the major strength of the book, and it is hoped that this will help the readers understand the challenges of 'doing psychology and gender'. It is hoped that the book would be relevant for curricula, as well as reaching out to those who are interested in this field, who can use it as a resource for training.

While focusing on Western and Indian studies, care has been taken that the arguments and logic are not reductionist and that the emphasis remains on illustrating the sub-topics. Since women's/gender studies is an independent academic field and a multidisciplinary one, many of the concepts in psychology and gender also need to be understood from a multidisciplinary perspective. Social and cultural differences have also been illustrated in all the chapters. Most of the examples are used keeping young student readers in mind, but all other readers will also be able to relate to them.

The website accompanying the book will include slides and notes that will help educators use the book as a pedagogical tool. While the chapters flag the main concepts, themes, theories, and some research studies related to the nine topics, it is hoped that readers will refer to other books on the subject for a broader and more comprehensive understanding.

1
A PRELUDE TO PSYCHOLOGY AND GENDER DOMAINS

Chapter Highlights

Learning Objectives

After reading this chapter, the students would be able to

- Understand the basic difference between sex and gender.
- Understand the meaning of basic terms used in gender studies.
- Recognize the key features of various gender-related movements across the world.
- Gain knowledge about the working of academic organizations in the field of psychology and gender.

Introduction

In our everyday life, we often use the terms 'sex' and 'gender' interchangeably. This chapter begins with explaining the difference between them and then moves on to how we assume our gender roles and how they get played out at home, in public spaces, offices, colleges, and universities. There is so much 'received knowledge and information' about these roles that we rarely question them. However, a thorough understanding of gender roles and gender and psychology will help us to understand the nuances and the impact gender roles make in our everyday lives. Therefore, the chapter foregrounds all these basic concepts against academic disciplines, namely psychology and women's studies, as well as social movements. The complex concept of 'intersectionality', which interacts with and has an impact on all the other concepts, is also explained. There is also some basic information on the accommodation or lack of it among the professional and academic bodies of

DOI: 10.4324/9781003453758-2

psychology on incorporating research and interventions in the domain of psychology and gender in their broad framework.

1.1 Difference Between Sex and Gender

While the terms 'sex' and 'gender' are often used synonymously, there is a difference between the two. For the last several decades, the term 'gender' has come into common usage, particularly in women's studies. While 'sex' is based on what anatomical structure one has, 'gender' is a socially constructed condition. John Money and his colleagues in the 1950s (Money, 1955) used the term 'sex' to refer to individuals' physical characteristics and the term 'gender' to refer to individuals' psychological characteristics and behaviour. Two decades later, Unger (1979) argued that the widespread use of the term 'sex' implies biological causes and promotes the idea that differences between women and men are natural and immutable (do not change). She proposed the use of the term 'gender' to refer to the traits that are culturally assumed to be appropriate for women and men. Her work was influential in prompting a widespread shift from the use of the term 'sex' to the use of the term 'gender' in psychological texts.

Also, instead of 'sex', the term 'sexuality', that is, biological persona, sexual relationships, desire, and the expanse of one's sexual life, captures the essence much better and has linkages with gender as well; hence, a lot of academicians and researchers are opting to use the term 'sexuality'. The narrow interpretation of 'sex' as related to the act of intercourse also limits its use.

Over a century of research on the nature–nurture question has produced an explosion of new methods and definitions. Sex refers to biological differences: chromosomes, hormonal profiles, and internal and external sex organs. Butler (1990) argues that sex is natural and comes first. Gender is perceived as a secondary construct which is imposed over the top of this natural distinction. Some theorists suggest that the biological differences between men and women also result in their mental and physical differences. They argue that biologically, men are physically and mentally superior to women. Other theorists suggest that the biological differences between men and women are exaggerated. The differences are socially constructed by the patriarchal system of society by which men are described as superior to women. Therefore, women become subordinate to men in the society. We discuss this at length in Chapter 2. De Beauvoir (1964), in her book *The Second Sex*, says, 'One is not born, but rather becomes a woman.' She explains that gender differences in the society make the man superior through his role as the breadwinner. It gives him a position of power in the society and family.

For a long time, in the teaching–learning and academic world of psychology (as well as other social sciences), 'gender' has been treated as a demographic variable, so 'gender' equals women. This was happening when women's/gender studies as a discipline was looking at 'gender' as an analytical category and looking at multiple axes of exploitation (race, class and gender; caste, class and gender). This

6 A Prelude to Psychology and Gender Domains

tokenism, called the add 'women and stir approach' in Gender Studies parlance, has helped neither our academics nor our research and practice, that is, the way in which we teach, learn, research, and treat issues, themes, and concepts related to psychology and gender.

Gender and psychology are not merely 'of women, by women, for women'. All over the world, multiple factors of identity which influence psychology and gender are being studied and understood, and that is the course we must follow. Intersectionality (how various intersections, including genders and sexualities, constitute, reconstitute, interact with, and impact/influence one another) has a tremendous impact on psychology and gender. Hence, we are going to discuss and understand this concept too. Both gender and feminism (as we shall see subsequently) are about dealing with power structures and structural inequalities and about questioning and critiquing them.

In an interesting way of looking through the lens of gender, Judith Butler's theorization of gender introduces the notion of performativity, the idea that gender is involuntarily performed within the dominant discourses of hetero-reality. Butler asserts that all identity concepts are in fact those that are effects of institutions, practices, and discourses with multiple and diffused points of origin. She further states, 'Sex/gender distinction suggests a radical discontinuity between sexed bodies and culturally constructed gender.'

The earlier understanding that 'sex' is biological and a given is now obsolete, since some individuals are going for a sex-change surgery, also called sex/gender reassignment surgery. That even 'gender' is socially constructed is acceptable in contemporary times. We also understand that the connection between sex and gender is not straightforward; that is, not all who look 'manly' identify with the male gender, and some are intersex – a mix of male- and female-gender sexual organs and/or secondary sexual characteristics (Table 1.1).

TABLE 1.1 Some Terms Related to Gender

Cisgender	A person whose biological or birth sex and gender identity match
Transgender	A person whose biological or birth sex and gender identity do not match
Gender fluid	A person whose gender identity does not remain the same throughout their life
Gender queer	A person who does not subscribe to conventional gender distinctions but identifies with neither, both, or a combination of the male and female genders
Intersex	Those born with any of the several variations in sex characteristics, including in chromosomes, gonads, sex hormones, or genitals, which do not fit into typical definitions for male or female bodies
LGB	Lesbian (women attracted to women)
	Gay (men attracted to men)
	Bisexual (those attracted to both men and women)
Heterosexual	Cis men attracted to cis women, and vice versa

Source: The author.

Some of the age-old stereotypes such as effeminate boy or man, sissy boy and tomboy girl (highly sexist and pejorative terms) persist, and the gender binaries of male and female are being questioned, since there are many sexualities (earlier termed 'sexual orientations') and many genders. We are also revisiting our outmoded, unfair, and discriminatory (homophobic/transphobic) understanding about sexual minorities/alternative sexualities, a category that psychology has not focused on much. This chapter, and the book, intends to be gender-inclusive and gender-just and shine a light on the psychology of all sexualities and genders, besides the binaries of male and female.

Against this backdrop, some terms that have now become part of academic and everyday vocabulary are given in Table 1.1.

1.2 Meaning of Gender Roles, Gender Role Attitude, Gender Role Stereotype

Now that we understand the many ideas, debates, and discourses (narratives) around the terms 'sex' and 'gender', let us move on to understanding three interrelated concepts. Gender roles, as defined by Matsumoto (1996), refer to the 'degree to which a person adopts the gender-specific and appropriate behaviours ascribed by his or her culture' (p. 206). Consequently, gender roles are largely a product of the cultural contexts in which all of us are socialized.

As we grow, we learn how to behave from those around us. In this socialization process, children are introduced to certain roles that are typically linked to their biological sex. The term 'gender role' refers to the society's concept of how men and women are expected to act and how they should behave. These roles are based on norms or standards created by the society (Little, 2013). The phrase 'boys will be boys' is often used to justify the behaviours such as pushing, shoving, or other forms of aggression by young boys. The phrase implies that such behaviour is unchangeable and something that is part of a boy's nature. Aggressive behaviour of boys and men, when it does not inflict significant harm, is often accepted because it is congruent with the cultural script for masculinity.

Cis men learn to take on 'masculine' roles. They are socialized to think and act in masculine ways. Cis women learn to take on 'feminine' roles. They are socialized to think and behave in feminine ways. As the feminist writer Simone de Beauvoir puts it, 'one is not born a man but becomes one', and 'one is not born a woman but becomes one'. Learning and internalization of gender roles start with socialization at birth. Even today, societies everywhere are quick to dress male infants in blue and girls in pink, applying these colour-coded gender labels even while a baby is in the womb, so much so that in later life too, cis men avoid pink and its shades!

The drive to adhere to masculine and feminine gender roles continues later in life. Men tend to outnumber women in the professions such as law enforcement, the military, and politics. Women tend to outnumber men in care-related occupations, such as childcare, healthcare, and social work. Following such unwritten,

8 A Prelude to Psychology and Gender Domains

implicit cultural norms demonstrates fulfilment of social expectations but not necessarily personal preference (Diamond, 2002).

We can say that professions are 'gendered', and within professions, again, there is 'gendering'. For instance, that girls should opt for social sciences and boys for natural sciences and science, technology, engineering, mathematics, and medicine (STEMM) has been the cultural norm! Within social sciences, economics and political science are considered hardcore and, therefore, better suited for boys, while sociology, psychology, and literature are thought to be more 'feminine' and suitable for girls, and personal preference is set aside. Similarly, at one time, mechanical, civil, and instrumentation engineering were considered unsuitable for girls! Fine arts, dance, and culinary arts are also considered 'feminine' or 'unmanly' domains, and the military, heavy vehicles, and fast sports, like squash, are considered unsuitable for girls.

Gender roles, gender role attitudes, and gender role stereotypes are concepts that are interlinked, and they also have an impact on each other. Let us understand them in detail. Gender role attitude refers to one's belief about socially desirable roles for men and women (Spence, 1993), ranging from egalitarian to traditional. Egalitarian individuals believe that the same roles are acceptable for both women and men, while traditional individuals believe that differing roles are appropriate for men (e.g. breadwinner) and women (e.g. childcare giver). Spence (1993) suggested that gender role attitude consists of self-images associated with an individual's position and how the individual would act in a social structure. As such, gender role attitudes would serve as motivational factors related to self-concept and self-esteem and would point to rewards and punishments earned through the enactment of roles.

Gender role attitudes are typically based on stereotypes, oversimplified notions about members of a group. Gender stereotyping involves overgeneralizing the attitudes, traits, or behaviour patterns of women or men, as well as those of lesbian, gay, bisexual, transgender, intersex, queer/questioning, asexual (LGBTIQA+) communities. For instance, there is an almost universal stereotype that 'tough men don't cry, crying is for sissies'. Stereotypes and caricatures of gay men (barring rare exceptions, such as *Brokeback Mountain* and films made by directors from the community) abound in popular films from Bollywood, as well as Hollywood, where they are depicted as 'effeminate'. Roles and attitudes, as well as stereotypes, are shaped by agents of socialization.

Gender role socialization occurs through four major agents of socialization: family, education, peer groups, and mass media. Each agent reinforces gender roles by creating and maintaining normative expectations for gender-specific behaviour, that is, following the unwritten rules and norms of the society. Exposure also occurs through secondary agents such as religion and the workplace. The factors such as socio-economic status and race in the Western context and socio-economic status, caste and religion in the Indian context also have an impact on all three. Repeated exposure to these agents over time leads all the genders into a false sense that they are acting naturally rather than following a socially constructed role (Little, 2013). This is discussed in detail in Chapter 2.

The adjectives that denote gender roles (expected behaviour) with respect to girls and women are 'shy', 'quiet', 'submissive', 'tolerant', 'hard-working', 'docile', 'obedient', and so on, while those associated with boys and men are 'aggressive', 'confident', 'brave', 'controlling', and 'ready to take on the world!' Girls should not laugh loudly, so they giggle, and boys and men can laugh loudly, so they guffaw! In fact, 'alpha male', 'machismo', 'bravado', and 'braggadocio' (boastful or arrogant behaviour) are terms that cater to the masculinity lessons that young boys are made to learn from early on. Advertisements on all media often reinforce such traditional gender roles.

In most households, if a young boy aged 5 years comes home from the playground or school crying and narrates that he was beaten up or harassed by older playmates, how do most families react? 'You should have beaten them up and retaliated', 'Boys don't cry', 'Don't cry like a girl', 'You should take lessons on how to fight back', and so on. In this way, families normalize and reinforce violence and retaliation in the minds of young boys. Also, the subliminal message that boys should not cry and girls can cry as much as they want paves the way for gender discrimination, as well as reinforcing gender stereotypes: strong men and tender women!

Traditional male, female, and other-gender role stereotypes still prevail, to a great extent, the world over. But things are changing, and some people are questioning, defying, and transgressing. Spence's egalitarian roles are also followed in certain families and societies where all the tasks are shared and performed in turn by all the members. But such families are more the exception than the rule. There is no segregation of men's work (breadwinner tasks, tasks outside the home) and women's work (cooking, nurture, care, and tasks inside the home). Bem's concept of 'androgyny', a mixture of the so-called masculine and feminine roles, laid the path in the 1970s for stepping outside the restrictions and pressure of traditional roles. It meant that a person could be 'tough' and 'tender', regardless of gender.

Over the next decades, the world over, feminists succeeded in creating awareness about 'patriarchy', a system that results in the subordination of women and people of other genders and is also restricting for cis men. Patriarchy glorifies wifehood and motherhood and does not let 'parenting' or co-parenting flourish. This places the burden on wives and mothers, who are glorified as 'homemakers', and employed women end up with 'double drudgery' or the double burden of professional work and housework. 'Work–life balance' becomes something that women alone must juggle. An interesting study showed that men rarely (10 per cent of their leaves) take leave from their workplace for any family emergencies in their career whereas women take as much as 80 per cent of their leaves for family emergencies.

Since children emulate and copy their parents (their first role models), we see these roles and stereotypes being perpetuated and reinforced. For instance, if sons grow up watching their fathers beating up their mother and them, they learn to

10 A Prelude to Psychology and Gender Domains

'normalize' domestic violence and are highly likely to indulge in intimate partner violence in later life. Similarly, those who are socialized by egalitarian parents are more likely to transcend traditional and stereotypical gender roles and become skilled in all kinds of tasks without feminizing or masculinizing them (cooking, childcare, sewing, and so on are feminine tasks; changing a bulb, finance, repairs, and so on are masculine tasks) (Natu, 2002).

Mid-chapter Exercise

Since/if you are a girl/boy/non-binary person

1 What would you wear?
2 Which toys would you play with?
3 What would be your dreams and ambitions?
4 How would your behaviour and safety on the road be?
5 What would be your views on love, dating, marriage, and sexuality?
6 Violence and pleasure
7 Career and work

Do you think that things would change for you because of your gender, or would they remain the same?

To create a gender-just society, it is essential that labelling of tasks as 'masculine' or 'feminine' stops and that all tasks are shared equally by all, whether at home or at the workplace. Very often, the stereotypes spill over to the workplace too. The tasks like arrangement of refreshments for meetings and conferences are often delegated to female employees, and the main decision-making – on finance, policy, and so on – remains with the men. Whether it is in the board of directors in the corporate sector or committees in the education sector, tokenism is reflected very often (i.e. women are token members; their opinions do not count). A funny word has emerged which captures this beautifully: 'on a talk show/committee on an important topic there is one token woman' – such panels are called 'manels'!

1.3 Gender Discrimination and Gender Identity

Following the earlier discussion on role, attitude, and stereotypes, the concept of gender identity needs to be understood and redefined. Gender discrimination happens all the time in our everyday life. It also includes sexism in language, research, and everyday behaviour.

The terms 'sexism' and 'sexist' are often used to refer to discrimination against women. Gender stereotypes form the basis of sexism. Sexism refers to prejudiced beliefs that value one sex over another. Sexism varies in its level of severity. In parts of the world where women are strongly undervalued, young girls may not be given the same access to nutrition, healthcare, and education as boys. Further, they would grow up believing that they deserve to be treated differently from boys (Thorne, 1993). It should be noted that discrimination based on sex occurs at both the micro and macro levels. Many sociologists focus on discrimination that is built into the social structure; this type of discrimination is known as institutional discrimination. Much discrimination is based on stereotypes and misinformation (Little, 2013).

Let us look at examples from everyday life: In a lot of middle- and upper-middle-class households in India, women and girls eat last, and in a lot of poorer households, they eat what is left. Preferences given to the son(s), female infanticide, and sex preselection (though it is banned by law) are also testament to gender discrimination and inequality. Even in education, the dropping-out rates of girls in general and boys from poorer and vulnerable groups are more. Our advertisements in India are still talking about bank loans for a boy's education or business and a girl's marriage. Hence, gender discrimination at subtle and obvious levels is persistent.

According to Glick and Fiske (1996), sexism refers to any bias against an individual or a group of individuals based on the individual's or group members' sex. Sexism is of three types: hostile, benevolent, and ambivalent. Directly negative attitudes towards women are called hostile sexism (women are bad drivers, they cannot read maps, and so on), somewhat pleasant attitudes that are indirectly demeaning and patronizing are called benevolent sexism (compliments paid to a colleague about appearance and clothes instead of professional skills), and a combination of the two is called ambivalent sexism.

Female employees of all types, in all sectors and at all levels – from daily wage labourers to bank employees to government-sector and private-sector employees – all get paid lower salaries/emoluments for the same work that men do. Some sectors and professions have more female employees – nursing, teaching, and service sectors – but the top-level management has more men, even in these sectors. Sexual harassment at the workplace and assault are also gruesome forms of gender discrimination. Misogyny, a deep-rooted hatred for women, is the highest form of sexism, and gender discrimination, combined with toxic masculinity, is lethal.

Persons from the LGBTIQA+ community also face gender discrimination at home, on the streets, in public places, in educational settings, and at workplaces: It ranges from ragging and bullying to assault and stigmatizing behaviour. They are deprived of the opportunity to get education and fulfilling employment.

When we examine why women are not at the senior-management level in organizations, it is observed that this is a result of many factors. One of them is gender bias at the hiring stage and at the stages of annual appraisals and promotions. Gender stereotypes prevail both in normative expectations about women's behaviour at the workplace and in expectations about their performance. It is a double-edged sword: If they succeed, they are denied credit, and if they do not, they face derision. Highly competent professional women are also 'penalized' for their competence!

12 A Prelude to Psychology and Gender Domains

The glass ceiling is called so since it sets limits to a woman's achievement at the workplace. The odds are stacked against women, so they must work twice as hard as men just to prove their competence. Even when they jump through these initial hoops, there is never a guarantee that they will achieve leadership or decision-making positions in organizations. In fact, women in professional spaces often face the double bind of 'fear of failure', which is natural, since they lose their self-esteem by the time they exhaust themselves in getting to the middle-management level. But many of them also experience 'fear of success' (a term coined by Matina Horner), since they are afraid of outperforming their male colleagues and male bosses, as well as their husbands!

If one does not fit within the dominant gender schema, then the naturalness of one's gender identity is thrown into question. Transgendered and transsexual individuals experience discrimination based on their gender identity. People who identify as transgendered are twice as likely to experience assault or discrimination as are non-transgendered individuals; they are also one and a half time more likely to experience intimidation as are the latter (National Coalition of Anti-Violence Programs, 2010). Various organizations hope that by educating the public about gender identity and empowering transgendered and transsexual individuals, such violence can be ended (Little, 2013).

Gender identity is an individual's self-conception of being male or female based on his or her association with masculine or feminine gender roles. A person's sex, as determined by his or her biology, does not always correspond with his or her gender. Therefore, the terms 'sex' and 'gender' are not interchangeable. A baby boy who is born with male genitalia will be identified as male. As he grows, however, he may identify with the feminine aspects of his culture (Little, 2013). While genetics and biology are considered the main determinants of one's gender identity, the other end of the spectrum finds its identity in nurture. There are three points of view in the nature versus nurture debate. One school believes that nature (genetics) alone influences personality and behaviour. Another school believes that nurture (environment) is the only factor that has an impact on personality and behaviour. The third view is that the society creates stereotypes about acceptable behaviour, and these are ever changing and evolving. This view explains normative patterns of gendered behaviour. This is also called person (genetics) and situation (environment) interaction approach.

These debates dominated our understanding of socialization, as well as gender roles, for a long time, but over the last 20 years, we have come to agree that there are many genders beyond the binaries of male and female and, therefore, many gender identities, including gender fluid and gender queer.

The social processes of acquiring a gender and sexual identity, or of 'having' a gender or a sexuality, are essentially the same – the degree to which the society accepts the resulting identities is what differs (Little, 2013). The lives of transgender and intersex persons, in terms of gender identity, are rarely understood by the society. Transphobia is quite common, and transgender persons rarely get family and social support. An intersex person is treated as a social outcast and is compelled to join groups that give him or her support and empathy. (The preferred pronoun – he, she, or they – is chosen by the person, and it is best to ask how one would like to be addressed.)

Very often, we do not understand the difference between gender identity and sexual orientation. While male, female, and transgendered are genders, heterosexual, gay, lesbian, and bisexual are sexual orientations, and some persons prefer to be described as gender fluid, gender queer, or pansexual.

1.4 Meaning of Intersectionality and Intersectional Feminism

'Intersectionality' is a concept and a term that helps one understand the interconnections between caste/race, class, gender, sexuality, abilities, and region. It is important to link intersectionality with all the concepts we have discussed so far. Therefore, let us try to understand its meaning and implications for psychology and gender.

Intersectionality has to do with the dynamics of power in all societies, and it also challenges the mainstream feminist notion of 'women' as a homogeneous category (middle-class women in the second wave of feminism). In the West, several Black feminists were foremothers of intersectionality and intersectional feminism. Sojourner Truth, who is the epitome of intersectionality, exemplified the term in her speech in 1851 'Ain't I a Woman'. She was a former slave who understood race and gender and questioned both. Anna Julia Cooper in 1892 explained that Black women were the agents of social change. This brought the understanding about the intersections of race and gender. Audre Lorde famously called herself 'black, lesbian, warrior, poet', thereby naming the intersections of race, sexuality, and gender. Civil rights activist and popular poet Maya Angelou's work also added to the growing body of work on gender and race.

All of them preceded Kimberlé Williams Crenshaw, who in 1989 added a lot of heft to narratives around intersectionality. This brought a realization about the various overlapping categories of oppression besides gender. Intersectional feminism is therefore an important concept, in both theory and practice. The dominant ideas of white/heterosexual/ableist/upper caste/upper class were challenged by intersectional feminism to unpack the exploitation of the marginalized in a more nuanced (multilayered) fashion. For instance, it is important to understand that the oppression of marginalized persons is not merely more than that of privileged men or women, nor is it an addition of oppressions of caste/race, class, gender, sexuality, abilities, and location. These oppressions are different from each other and must be understood from their unique contexts.

In the Indian context, a lot of pathbreaking work on intersectionality and intersectional feminism has been done by Savitribai Phule, Fatima Sheikh, Mukta Salve, Uma Chakravarti, Sharmila Rege, Mary John, Nivedita Menon, V Geetha, and so on, and it needs to be comprehended well to see the linkages between

14 A Prelude to Psychology and Gender Domains

intersectionality and feminism and between structures of power and oppression in the Indian context.

What implications does intersectionality have for psychology and gender? Let us consider them one by one. First, there is no such category as 'all men or all women'; women are different from each other in terms of age, sexuality, race, caste, ability, and religion, and so are men. Second, when we are trying to study and understand issues, for example, beauty treatment for women, age, class, sexuality (various intersections), and the like will make a difference. An upper-class or upper-middle-class old woman might dye her hair, use cosmetics that make her look younger, and so on, whereas a poor woman would not be able to afford any of these embellishments.

Third, many people have several identities, and which one must be given primacy depends on the social context. For instance, a gay, Dalit, poor man is far below an upper-middle-class or upper-class woman in terms of access to resources, and he is also juggling three identities. Here, his being a 'man' does not give him privilege over women. Hence, when we study psychology and gender, the nuances that the lens of intersectionality and intersectional feminism bring in are crucial.

1.5 Feminism and the Women's Movement in the West and India and Its Effect on Psychology and Gender

Feminism is defined in many ways. The simplest way of understanding it would be that feminists believe in 'gender equality' – that all genders are equal. In fact, first-wave feminists coined the phrase 'different but equal' – men and women are different but equal. Feminism, the women's movement, and women's studies (academic discipline) are interrelated. Feminism is a political ideology; the women's movement is the struggle on the ground to bring about social change; and women's studies is a subject that builds theories, research, and policies based on the ideology and the struggle, integrating both of them. Psychology as a discipline, both in the West and in India, has been impacted by all three strands quite late, in comparison to other social sciences, such as sociology, political science, and economics. Nevertheless, the impact is noteworthy.

The three waves of feminism in the West brought forth discourses and scholars who contributed hugely to the field of psychology and gender. Some of the milestones, in terms of books based on pathbreaking research and organizational breakthroughs, are listed in Table 1.2.

In India, the Committee on the Status of Women in India published the *Towards Equality* report in 1975. This report was an eye-opener, since it tabled the status of Indian women since 1947 with respect to health, education, employment, and rights. This was followed by 1975 being declared the International Year of Women and 1975–1985 the United Nations Decade of Women. This led to the formation of many autonomous women's groups all over India, as well as the strengthening of mass-based women's organizations. The First National Conference on Women's

A Prelude to Psychology and Gender Domains   **15**

TABLE 1.2 Pathbreaking Events in the Domain of Psychology and Gender

National Organization for Women, 1966	*Founded*
Karen Horney, 1967	*Feminine Psychology*
Kate Millett, 1968	*Sexual Politics*
Germaine Greer, 1970	*The Female Eunuch*
Boston Women's Health Book Collective, 1972	*Our Bodies, Ourselves*
Phyllis Chesler, 1972	*Women and Madness*
Maccoby and Jacklin, 1974	*The Psychology of Sex differences*
Jean Baker Miller, 1976	*Toward a New Psychology of Women*
Carol Gilligan, 1982	*In a Different Voice: Psychological Theory and Women's Development*
bell hooks, 1981	*Ain't I a Woman? Black Women and Feminism*
Susan Faludi, 1991	*Backlash: The Undeclared War against American Women*
Mary Whiton Calkins, 1905	First female president of APA
Margaret Floy Washburn, 1921	Second female president of APA
Anne Anastasi, 1972	Third female president of APA; psychometrics
Sandra Bem, 1974	Bem Sex-Role Inventory
Simone de Beauvoir, 1953	*The Second Sex*
Betty Freidan, 1963	*The Feminine Mystique*
Melba Vasquez, 2011	First woman of colour elected as APA president
Nancy Chodorow, 1978	*The Reproduction of Mothering*
Dorothy Dinnerstein, 1976	*The Mermaid and the Minotaur: Sexual Arrangement and Human Malaise*

Source: Loosely based on Psychology's Feminist Voices www.feministvoices.com

Studies was organized in 1981, and the Indian Association for Women's Studies (IAWS) was established in 1982.

The mass-based groups focused on land rights, economic rights, price rise, the informal sector, and poor and working-class women in rural and urban areas. The autonomous groups and later several NGOs worked on dowry deaths, rape, domestic violence, female infanticide and health and opposed population control policies and measures, and so on. In current times, the women's movement in India has taken up critical issues related to caste, religion, citizenship, various forms of violence, and post-globalization economic problems, to name a few. Most of the social science disciplines, including psychology, however, have resisted the impact of the women's movement and women's studies, as well as gender, for long (Natu, 2002).

Indian Council of Social Science Research surveys on research in psychology have been published for a long time. They have been regular and offer information on the state-of-the-art developments in different fields of psychology. The

16 A Prelude to Psychology and Gender Domains

first three survey publications (1972, 1981, 1988) were silent on the issue of gender. It was only in the fourth (1992) and fifth surveys (2011) that gender was included and addressed. The sixth survey published in 2019 has also not addressed gender directly.

Since both feminism and gender are political concepts and psychology as a science has been apolitical in its stance for a long time, the reluctance to incorporate feminism and gender is understandable. Thus, despite an active and vibrant women's movement in India and a strong presence of women's studies centres in most Indian universities, there are just a handful of courses on psychology of women or psychology and gender in a few universities, whereas in the West this branch blossomed long ago. However, after the year 2000, topics on gender and psychology are being included in a variety of curricula across universities in India, and this is certainly a good sign. As we discussed earlier, blending the concept of intersectionality with psychology and gender in the Indian context is a huge challenge, since it means taking on board sexualities, class, religion, caste, and region and adopting a multidisciplinary approach in teaching, learning, research, and practice.

1.6 Feminism and the Men's Movement in the West and India (and Its Effect on Psychology and Gender in Brief)

There are two opposite forces that have been working the world over: a positive force – pro-feminist men's groups and an academic discipline called men's studies – and a force of organizations opposed to women's organizations and feminism. Let us understand these two forces in brief.

The men's movement has been classified into four categories: mythopoetry, men's liberation, pro-feminism, and men's rights. The mythopoetic movement believes in retelling myths, legends, and folk tales and working on self-help. The men's liberation movement works to help men 'move out of their stereotypical masculine gender roles' and explore their emotions and recognize other possibilities. Pro-feminism groups believe that men can work as allies in the transformation of traditional masculinity and bring about a change in patriarchal societies (Flood, 1996; Mudge, 1997). These three categories are working in tandem with the women's movement and feminist ideologies.

Men's rights groups, however, are a backlash against the women's movement. These men believe that they are the 'victims' and that feminists have gone too far and harmed men! They are working on men's health and education and perceived injustices and biases against men in family laws (Flood, 1996). There is ample evidence that the men's movement in the West was made up of white, heterosexual, middle-class men who were not willing to acknowledge their class privilege. It was identitarian politics at its best, where middle-class men were portrayed as 'victims' trying to turn patriarchy on its head, as it were (Connell, 1995; Flood, 1997).

The women's movement in the West began to question 'mechanical and automatic assumptions of sisterhood', thanks to the parallel discourses of intersectionality and intersectional feminism. In simple words, 'all women are not the same and are socially stratified'. In contrast, 'masculinity' became a contested category, where a collective identity as men was presumed by the men's movement, and this meant privileged men's coming together.

Many self-help books for men are promoting an authentic masculinity whereby men are in touch with their feelings, as well as those of their partners and children. Critics are questioning whether these are expressions of idealized desires or a ploy for calling out the so-called aggressive feminists who have succeeded in wounding men!

Against this backdrop in the West, in the last 20 years in India, men's rights groups have evolved around the following points: rampant misuse of pro-women laws that are used to demonize men, their leading to the destruction of fathers and husbands and, ultimately, the destruction of Indian families! Metro and mini-metro cities, such as Calcutta, Mumbai, and Lucknow, saw the groups such as Pirito Purush Pati (Persecuted Man), Purush Hakka Sanrakshan Samiti (Committee for the Protection of Men's Rights), and Patni Atyachar Virodhi Sangh (Group Protesting Torture of Wives) coming up in the mid-1990s.

The main complaint was against the alleged misuse of Section 498A of the Indian Penal Code (IPC). This law allows for immediate arrest of a husband for harassment of his wife in their marital home, and it is a non-bailable, cognizable offence. The men's rights groups demanded that a category of 'harassed husbands' be coined, which was not in the law. The mother organization that energizes these groups is the Save Indian Family Foundation (SIFF), Bengaluru. SIFF claims that both men and women undergo similar social pressure and hence demands 'gender neutrality'. It has expanded its branches all over India and has created networks where men who are arrested in cases of domestic violence and through Section 498A show camaraderie towards each other and seek help and advice from SIFF.

Such groups have been counterproductive to the women's movement and gender rights. They have turned a blind eye towards patriarchy and privilege that allows impunity to most men. Their impact on gender and psychology is that it is important to tease out these differences between the false propaganda unleashed by men's rights groups and the pro-feminist men's groups who are steadfastly working as allies of the women's movement.

Pune has pro-feminist men's groups, such as Samyak (which works on male sexuality) and Samatesathi Amhi Pursush (working on gender equality), and in Mumbai MAVA (Men Against Violence and Abuse) has been working relentlessly since 30 years. These groups are aware that patriarchies create challenges for both men and women, and hence, it is important to work on gender equality without castigating feminists but in fact in collaboration and solidarity with the latter. They have also underscored through awareness-building and gender-sensitization workshops all over Maharashtra and other states in India that patriarchies are harmful for men and that toxic masculinity takes away their humanity. Men's studies/

18 A Prelude to Psychology and Gender Domains

masculinity studies as a discipline is well established in the West, while very few universities in India run courses in this discipline. As students of psychology and gender, we must examine the challenges and solidarity that the men's movement, men's groups, and men's studies bring to the fore.

1.7 Queer Movement in the West and in India (and Its Effect on Psychology and Gender in Brief)

Although the queer movement in the West does not have an even, chronological history, some of its signposts are distinct and important. Social movements and organizing around the acceptance and rights of gay and queer persons began in response to discrimination and persecution by the Church, state, and medical authorities. The terms that were used were 'deviant' and 'abnormal', and it took a long time and a lot of battles to throw away such stigmatizing vocabulary (this is discussed in detail in Chapter 7). Although activists, researchers, and both queer persons and other liberals have carefully demonstrated evidence of LGBTIQA+ persons existing since time immemorial, the persecution of homosexual, lesbian, bisexual, and trans persons continued, and homophobia and transphobia were at their peak during the Holocaust. Along with the civil rights movement, the gay rights movement also gained momentum in the mid-1960s. Things came to a head in 1969 at Stonewall Inn in New York's Greenwich Village when gay rights groups protested police raids of gay bars. June is celebrated in the United States and now the world over, to commemorate Stonewall, as Pride Month.

Ever since the 1970s, all over Europe and the United States, several organizations working for LGBT rights came up and took up several rights issues. The 1980s saw HIV/AIDS rates spiralling, and once again homophobia and transphobia raised their head, but individuals, as well as organizations, showed a lot of resilience, and now all spaces – education, the entertainment industry, research, defence forces – have been compelled to review and rethink their biases, prejudices, and anti-queer stances. Many countries and states have legalized same-sex marriages, adoption rights for queer couples, and more. Intersectionality within queer communities – that sexuality, gender, race, and region are also intertwined – is also recognized. Thus, while the queer movement in the West has come a long way, the fight for legitimacy, respect, and equality is far from over.

India, in the 1980s, saw the HIV/AIDS pandemic from close quarters, and it was the first official recognition of gay persons albeit as a vulnerable group. The circuitous recognition of gay persons was similar to the approach of the West: discrimination and persecution from the state, religions and health and medical authorities, as well as non-acceptance from families. Several organizations came up initially to address HIV/AIDS but eventually became places of support and strength for the queer community. Humsafar Trust in Mumbai, Naz Foundation in New Delhi, Sappho in Kolkata, LABIA in Mumbai, and Sangama in Bengaluru, for instance, took up the issues of health, employment, and other pressing problems that the community had to face. Protests questioning the government's stance against homosexuality and those denouncing the attack on cinema halls exhibiting Deepa Mehta's film *Fire* marked the 1990s. The fight against Section 377 of the IPC criminalizing homosexuality, which gained momentum in 2000, brought several queer groups from all over India together (details are discussed in Chapter 7). Magazines, pride marches, parents' support groups, and queer film festivals have come up all over India. Decriminalization of Section 377 was a resounding victory for queer groups in India. But equal rights and inclusion in higher education and employment, adoption rights, access to housing, and a life without discrimination and stigma, characterized by dignity and respect are still elusive, especially for queer persons from rural areas and disadvantaged communities.

The significance of these struggles of queer persons all over the world should leave its imprint on psychology and gender academically, in the practice of psychotherapy, and in research. This challenge is spelt out in the consecutive chapters, and the way ahead is also laid out.

1.8 International and Indian Academic Organizations of Psychology and Panels on Gender

Brief outlines of professional organizations of psychology (worldwide and in India) from the point of view of incorporating gender are presented in the following sections.

1.8.1 International Union of Psychological Sciences

Professor Pam Maras from the University of Greenwich is the current president of the International Union of Psychological Science (IUPsyS). Professor Maras is the first female to hold this position in the organization's history, which dates to the very first International Congress of Psychology that was held in August 1889 in Paris, France. Professor Maras is a former president of the British Psychological Society and is the director of Research and Enterprise and professor of social and educational psychology at Greenwich.

1.8.2 American Psychological Association

Division 35 of the American Psychological Association (APA), later called Society for the Psychology of Women, was formed in 1973. It had special task forces to bring Black and Hispanic women into its fold. It brings out two journals: *Psychology of Women Quarterly* and *Feminist Psychology*. In 1974, Division 44, a society for the study of lesbian, gay, and bisexual persons, was established. In 1997, Division 51, Society for the Psychological Study of Men and Masculinities, was established. In 1999, a society for the study of LGBT persons was formed. This indicates that APA overall has taken gender, as well as intersectionality, into cognizance over a period of time.

20 A Prelude to Psychology and Gender Domains

The first issue of the journal *Sex Roles* was published by APA in 1975. *Psychology of Women Quarterly* was first published in 1976. In 1990, the first issues of the *Journal of Men's Studies* and *Feminism and Psychology* were published.

1.8.3 Association of Psychological Sciences

Established in 1988, the Association of Psychological Sciences has organized symposia on history of women in psychology and given importance to issues of race, nationality, ethnicity, and so on.

1.8.4 British Psychological Society

The British Psychological Society has a Psychology of Women and Equalities Section (POWES), started in 1988.

1.8.5 Canadian Psychological Association

The Canadian Psychological Association has a Section on Women and Psychology (SWAP). There are three major professional organizations of psychology in India.

National Academy of Psychology: Founded in 1989, the National Academy of Psychology (NAOP) does not have a division on gender/psychology of women. It has seen five female presidents over the past 32 years. It has sub-themes, with symposia, presentations, and posters on gender being presented at the annual conventions. There are pre-conference workshops dedicated to gender analysis in psychological research and gender psychology. *Psychological Science*, the journal published by NAOP, also encourages and publishes research papers on psychology and gender. *Psychology and Developing Societies*, another reputed Indian journal, also encourages and publishes research in the domain of psychology and gender. In its 32nd Annual Convention, a sub-theme was dedicated to gender, diversity, and challenges, and a special invited lecture of an Indian and Western scholar working in the field of psychology and gender was organized.

Indian Association of Applied Psychology and Indian Association of Clinical Psychology: Founded in 1962 and 1968, respectively, neither the Indian Association of Applied Psychology nor the Indian Association of Clinical Psychology has a division on gender or women. Both have had some female presidents. Journals published by both associations do publish a few research papers related to gender issues.

Indian Association of Women's Studies (IAWS): Founded in 1982. Its annual conferences give space for sub-themes related to mental health. A special issue of the IAWS newsletter dedicated to gender and psychology and mental health was published in 2003, and the author was a member of the editorial collective – as guest editor. *Indian Journal of Gender Studies* also publishes research on psychology and gender.

A Prelude to Psychology and Gender Domains **21**

However, there is a need to build more significant academic spaces and a need for continuity and consistent work in the field of psychology and gender with the help of these organizations. A cross-pollination of ideas and collaborative academic and research projects between women's studies and psychology and gender need to be initiated (in regions and states of India where there are none) and strengthened, where efforts are already being made.

Review Questions

1 What are the differences between sex and gender?
2 What is the difference between gender role, gender role attitude, and gender role stereotype?
3 Describe how gender discrimination is practised at home and in workplaces.
4 How have the women's movement and feminism contributed to the field of psychology and gender?
5 How have the men's movement and men's studies contributed to the field of psychology and gender?

Critical Thinking Questions

1 The good woman/bad woman and good man/bad man stereotypes have been perpetuated through mythology, folklore, fairy tales, fables, proverbs, and sayings. List out some of them.
2 Biologically, cis men and cis women have more similarities than differences. List out such similarities.

Bibliography

Bem, S. (1974). The measurement of psychological androgyny. *Journal of Consulting and Clinical Psychology, 42*, 155–162.
Buchbinder, D. (1998). *Performance anxieties: Re-producing masculinity*. Allen and Unwin.
Butler, J. (1990). *Gender trouble*. Routledge.
Cole, E. R. (2009). Intersectionality and research in psychology. *American Psychologist, 64*(3), 170–180.
Connell, R. W. (1995). *Masculinities*. Allen and Unwin.
De Beauvoir, S. (1964). *The second sex*. Bantam Books.
Diamond, M. (2002). Sex and gender are different: Sexual identity and gender identity are different. *Clinical Child Psychology & Psychiatry Special Issue, 7*(3), 320–334.
Farrell, W. (1986). *Why men are the way they are: The male-female dynamic*. McGraw Hill.
Farrell, W. (1993). *The myth of male power: Why men are the disposable sex*. Simon and Schuster.
Febbraro, A. (2003). Alpha bias and beta bias in research on labour and love: The case of enhancement versus scarcity. *Feminism & Psychology, 13*, 201–223.
Flood, M. (1996, Spring). Four strands. *XY*, 21–23.
Flood, M. (1997, Spring). Responding to men's rights. *XY, 7*(2), 37–40.

22 A Prelude to Psychology and Gender Domains

Ford, M. R., & Widiger, T. A. (1989). Sex bias in the diagnosis of histrionic and antisocial personality disorders. *Journal of Consulting and Clinical Psychology, 57,* 301–305.

Glick, P., & Fiske, S. T. (1996). The ambivalent sexism inventory: Differentiating hostile and benevolent sexism. *Journal of Personality and Social Psychology, 70*(3), 491–512.

Goldberg, H. (1976). *The hazards of being male: Surviving the myth of masculine privilege.* Nash.

Grimshaw, J. (1986). *Philosopher feminist thinking.* University of Minnesota Press.

Hare, M. R. (1987). *Gender and meaning of difference: Alpha and Beta bias* [Paper presentation]. Paper presented at the Annual Convention of APA (p. 19). APA, New York.

Hoffman, M. (1975). Altruistic behaviour and the parent – child relationship. *Journal of Personality and Social Psychology, 31,* 937–943.

Indian Council of Social Science Research. (1981). *A survey of research in psychology.* Popular Prakashan.

Indian Council of Social Science Research. (1988). *Psychology in India: State of the art.* Sage.

Indian Council of Social Science Research. (1992). *Psychology in India revisited: Developments in the discipline.* Sage.

Indian Council of Social Science Research. (2011). *Psychology in India, volumes 1 to 4.* Pearson.

Indian Council of Social Science Research. (2019). *ICSSR Research surveys and explorations.* Oxford University Press.

Little, W. (2013). *Introduction to sociology* (1st Canadian ed.). BC Campus Open Publishing.

Lupton, D., & Barclay, L. (1997). *Constructing fatherhood: Discourses and experiences.* SAGE Publications.

Matsumoto, D. (1996). *Culture and psychology.* Brooks/Cole Publishing Company.

Melucci, A. (1995). The process of collective identity. In H. Johnston & B. Klandermans (Eds.), *Social movements and culture* (pp. 41–63). UCL Press.

Melucci, A. (1996). *Challenging codes: Collective action in the information age.* Cambridge University Press.

Messner, M. (1995). 'Changing men' and feminist politics in the United States. In M. Kimmel (Ed.), *The politics of manhood: Pro feminist men respond to the mythopoetic men's movement (and the mythopoetic leaders answer)* (pp. 97–111). Temple University Press.

Mitra S K (Eds) (1972). A Survey of Research in Psychology. Popular Prakashan. Bombay.

Money, J. H. (1955). *An examination of some basic sexual concepts: An evidence of hermaphroditism.* John Hopkins Hospital Bulletin.

Mudge, B. (1997). *Sexism and stoicism: Theorizing pro feminist strategies* [Unpublished honours thesis, Women's Studies Department, Faculty of Social Sciences, Flinders University, South Australia].

National Coalition of Anti-Violence Programs. (2010). *Hate violence against lesbian, gay, bisexual, transgender, queer and HIV-affected communities in the United States.* www.avp.org/storage/documents/Reports/2012_NCAVP_2011_HV_Report.pdf

Natu, S. (2002). *A psychosocial enquiry into the gender roles and other related factors of young males with special reference to maternal employment* [Unpublished PhD thesis, Pune University].

Rosenthal, R. (1966). *Experimenter effects in behavioural research.* Appleton-Century-Crofts.

Shields, S. A. (2008). Gender: An intersectionality perspective. *Sex Roles, 59*(5–6), 301–311.

Spence, J. T. (1993). Gender related traits and gender ideology: Evidence for a multifactorial theory a multifactorial theory. *Journal of Personality and Social Psychology, 64,* 624–635.

Thorne, B. (1993). *Gender play: Girls and boys in school.* Rutgers University Press.

Unger, R. K. (1979). Towards a redefinition of sex and gender. *American Psychologist, 34,* 1085–1094.

2

THEORETICAL FRAMEWORKS OF UNDERSTANDING GENDER

Chapter Highlights

Learning Objectives

After reading this chapter, the students would be able to

- Understand various theories of gender role development.
- Identify the key features and differences between these theories.
- Recognize how psychological theories apply to gender constructs.

Introduction

Till the 1990s, we were using the terms 'sex differences' and 'sex roles' in psychology. Popular books, such as *Men Are From Mars and Women Are From Venus*, were being consumed with great interest. In research too, these terms continued. Since the late 1990s and 2000s, we have been using the terms 'gender roles' and 'gender differences', and Chapter 1 has already detailed out how closely and intricately sex, sexuality, gender, intersectionality, and psychology are interlinked. Against this backdrop, in this chapter, we will look at mainstream psychological theories about gender role development, the feminist critique and response to them, and new theorizations; that is, we will be reviewing mainstream theories through the gender lens.

While the 'nature' theories emphasize biological factors, the 'nurture' theories lay emphasis on psychosocial and cultural factors that influence gender role development. This nature versus nurture, as well as the heredity versus environment, debate has been going on for a long time. Before we explore all the theories and approaches, it is important to note that feminist scholarship and research have

DOI: 10.4324/9781003453758-3

24 Theoretical Frameworks of Understanding Gender

demonstrated that there are more similarities between men and women than differences. Hyde (2014) proposed that men and women are similar on most psychological variables. She called this the 'gender similarity hypothesis'. Also, Tavris (1993) wisely concluded in her book *The Mismeasure of Woman*, 'Women are not the better sex, the inferior sex, or the opposite sex,' which is important in terms of understanding the debates and points of view.

All in all, various social sciences, biology, and medicine have had different points of view about sex, sexuality, and gender, as well as gender role development. It is important to understand the similarities, differences, and gender critique of all these theories. The present chapter aims to give a bird's-eye view of these theories.

2.1 Biological Approach

Hormones, the nervous system, and neurotransmitters are some of the biological influencers of gender role development and behaviour. Let us understand these aspects one by one. Male hormones are androgen and testosterone, and female hormones are progesterone and oestrogen. Male and female hormones are found in and are important for both males and females. The idea that hormones have gender is a myth (Crocetti, 2013). That testosterone levels are related to aggression has also been proved to be a myth; testosterone powers the drive to achieve social dominance, whereas societal factors and a congenial cultural atmosphere normalize male violence. In fact, interestingly, aggressive behaviour leads to an increase in testosterone levels in males and so does interaction with a gun! This means that the explanation that high levels of testosterone make males behave aggressively is not true. The latter has more to do with socialization (the way they are brought up in homes; Bussey, 2013), cultural acceptance (males must be aggressive!), and normalization of violence (men will be men). We shall understand this in detail through the social learning theory.

To study the effects of prenatal hormones on gender roles, scientists have studied children suffering from endocrine disorders: It was observed that girls exposed to abnormally high levels of androgens during prenatal development exhibited more stereotypically male behaviour (e.g. choosing masculine toys, like guns and balls) than other girls did. Moreover, boys exposed to abnormally low levels of androgens during prenatal development exhibited more stereotypically female behaviour (e.g. choosing feminine toys, such as dolls and doll houses) than other boys did. These findings suggest that prenatal hormones shape gender differences in humans. However, there are several problems with this evidence (Bussey, 2013).

First, behaviour is impacted by socialization after birth. Second, it is always dangerous to draw conclusions about the general population based on small samples of people who have rare conditions. Third, most of the endocrine disorders studied have multiple effects (besides altering hormone levels) that make it difficult to isolate actual causes. Finally, most of the research is necessarily correlational, and it is always risky to draw causal conclusions from correlational data.

After birth, the hormone testosterone plays an important role in 'sexual desire' for both, men and women. This means that reduced levels of testosterone lead to reduction of sexual desire in both, and increased levels of testosterone lead to an increase in sexual desire in both (Petersen, 2011). However, we cannot conclude that sexual desire is controlled solely by testosterone levels, since there is a lot of research evidence that indicates that social and cultural factors have a huge role to play in both the experience and expression of desire. In fact, in many cultures all over the world, expression of sexual desire by women is taboo and a sign of a 'bad woman'. Hence, in the gender roles of men and women, with reference to expression of sexual desire, we see a lot of double standards. For instance, a woman who is freely expressing desire is considered a 'loose' woman, and her character is judged, whereas a man who does so is celebrated as a 'Casanova', 'Don Juan', or 'cool, macho guy!'

Is there a gender difference in the functioning of the brain and the nervous system? Does that lead to differences in gender roles among males and females? Biologists, neurologists, and geneticists have recorded that the brain size differs – men have larger brains – and lateralization differs. There have been several studies on who is more left-brained and who is more right-brained among men and women, since left- and right-brain functions are different. Meta-analysis tells us that these differences are not significant! There are no major differences between men and women with respect to verbal and spatial skills (functions of the left- and right-brain hemispheres, respectively).

The other important aspect is that the most significant brain development happens in the first 5–10 years after birth. We have humungous data that show that girls and boys are socialized differently. The brain responds to the environment, so what are thought to be solely biological differences may be a result of socialization and environmental factors too! In fact, male and female brains are more similar than different. Fine (2013) argues that we must be wary of engaging in 'neurosexism' or using these biological findings to support our pre-existing gender stereotypes. Neural plasticity also helps dispel the nature–nurture binary.

In her book *The Gendered Brain*, Rippon analyses the data on sex differences in the brain. She admits that she, like many others, initially sought out these differences. However, she could not find any beyond the negligible, and other research was also starting to question the very existence of such differences. For example, once any differences in brain size were accounted for, 'well-known' sex differences in key structures disappeared. This was when the penny dropped: Perhaps it was time to abandon the age-old search for the differences between the brains of men and the brains of women. Rippon unpacks the myths about differences between men's and women's brains, asking 'Are there any significant differences based on sex alone?'

She argues that the idea of the male brain and the female brain suggests that each is a characteristically homogenous thing and that whoever has a male brain, say, will have the same kind of aptitudes, preferences, and personalities as everyone

26 Theoretical Frameworks of Understanding Gender

else with that 'type' of brain. We now know that is not the case. We are at the point where we need to say,

Forget the male and female brain; it's a distraction; it's inaccurate. It's possibly harmful, too, because it's used as a hook to say, well, there's no point girls doing science because they haven't got a science brain, or boys shouldn't be emotional or should want to lead (Rippon, 2019).

This tells us what a long way we have come from the biological determinism followed by Freud, many neurologists, and evolutionary biologists in decoding gender roles.

Mid-chapter Exercise

'Biology/anatomy is destiny' – Sigmund Freud's contentious quote implied that a woman's role was circumscribed by reproduction. She always had a dependent identity of being someone's daughter, mother, sister, wife, daughter-in-law, and so on. Feminists strongly contested this 'biological determinism'.

- How do you view the biological differences between genders?
- Do you think we can segregate men's work and women's work? For example, are household work, cooking, and looking after children women's work, and driving and working outside the home men's work?

2.2 Psychological Theories: Psychoanalytic, Social Learning, Cognitive

Gender role development is a very crucial aspect of the socialization process. The concept of socialization has been developed in the discipline of sociology and social psychology. It refers to the process of deliberate shaping of an individual, by conscious and active training of the individual, to imbibe and adapt to the mores, values, and expectations of society. Jahoda and Lewis (1988) presented the core meaning of the varied definitions of the term 'socialization' as 'the process whereby the children become effectively functioning members of a particular society'. The universality and the importance of the process of how girls get to be girls and boys get to be boys are reflected in the prominence that gender role has received in the psychological theories of gender role development. Several psychological theories have been advanced to explain the process of gender role development.

2.2.1 Psychoanalytic Theory

Freud (1931), the pioneer of the psychoanalytic theory, emphasizes the child's identification with the same-sex parent as the primary mechanism whereby a child becomes gender-socialized. This identification results from the child's discovery of genital sex differences, and hence the girl identifies with her mother and the boy with the father. This discovery, according to Freud, creates penis envy among girls and castration anxiety in boys. Freud also talks about the Oedipus complex, that is, the son's attraction towards the mother, and the female Oedipus complex, or Electra complex – the daughter's attraction towards the father. The identification with the same-sex parent is also a result of the successful resolution of the Oedipal conflict, which Freud describes as competing with the same-sex parent for the affection and attention of the parent of the opposite sex. The concepts such as 'penis envy' and 'castration anxiety' have been countered with 'womb envy' by Karen Horney, who declared the idea of castration anxiety or emasculation as irrational.

The psychoanalytic theory has been criticized by those within psychology (e.g. Karen Horney) and by feminists too (e.g. Mitchell, 1974). Juliet Mitchell saw Freud's asymmetrical view of masculinity and femininity as reflecting the realities of patriarchal culture and sought to use his critique of femininity to critique patriarchy itself. She tried to reconcile psychoanalysis and feminism. Also, many psychologists thought that generalizing this theory to all cultures was not possible.

Since no empirical evidence for the Freudian view has been found, the feminist critique and recasting of Freudian theory has been gaining ground. Freud's theory has had some revival and revision in the works of Chodorow (1978) and Lerman (1986). Chodorow re-conceptualized Freudian views in the spirit of the feminists who regarded the sexes as different in nature but as having equally important and valid experiences, behaviours, and attitudes. Lerman has been critical of the emphasis on the resolution of the Oedipal complex and the scant attention paid to Freud's female patients' narratives.

Chodorow disagreed with Freud that gender identification began at the phallic stage; she argued that it began at infancy. She opined that initially, both male and female infants identified with their mother, but since a mother and her daughter belonged to the same sex, their identification was stronger than that between a mother and her son. This identification then makes daughters merge with mothers and relate more to motherhood, whereas boys steer away from mothers and femininity later and denigrate femininity, thereby establishing their separateness and individual identity. However, empirical findings do not support either Freudian psychoanalysis or Chodorow's theory. There is also no evidence that the mother–daughter bond is stronger than the mother–son bond. Women's sense of self-esteem is also not enhanced by motherhood!

Further, a girl's sense of self is profoundly determined by this early relationship, which is never entirely broken. Girls never separate themselves from their mothers and therefore define themselves throughout life in relational terms. Boys, on the other hand, begin with the same intense attachment but must smash it to form a distinct, masculine identity. Masculinity, according to Chodorow, involves denying feminine maternal attachment. Men's identity, then, is defined not in relational terms but rather in terms of individuation and independence. It is also defined

28 Theoretical Frameworks of Understanding Gender

by rejection and devaluation of the feminine. However, as indicated earlier, this assumption could not be empirically tested and established.

Chodorow's theory focused not only on the consequences of the child's early attachment to the mother but also on male dominance in society. Taking note of the fact that social psychologists' research showed that men fall in love romantically and women sensibly and rationally, she concluded that this was a result of women's economic dependence on men. 'Women's displays of romanticism, then, may simply be a way of making sure that they and their future children are provided for.'

Both these theories indicate that many assumptions about gender role development have been put forth and tested since a long time ago.

2.2.2 Social Learning Theory

Bandura (1977) suggested that behaviours are learnt through observation and imitation of others and that similar principles are applied to acquisition of gender-appropriate behaviour, which means that children observe, imitate, and model their behaviour on the lines of that of their same-sex parents.

Mischel (1966) focused on the rewards and punishments that children receive for sex-appropriate and sex-inappropriate behaviours. He also highlighted the vicarious learning that observation and modelling can provide. His theory located the source of gender role typing in the gender-differentiated practices of the socializing community. It means that when a boy displays 'courage', which is thought to be a masculine attribute culturally, he is praised, and if he does not, he is ridiculed or, worse still, called a 'sissy'. This reinforcement can happen at home, in school, or among peers and sometimes in all three locations. Hence, social learning takes place through the process of 'identification' (generally with the same-sex parent, teachers, peers, role models) and later 'imitation' (think of girls dressing up like their mothers, trans persons cross-dressing, boys imitating the swagger of their favourite hero or sportsman, and so on) and 'internalization' (we end up unconsciously copying the gestures, facial expressions, and vocabulary of our role models in the private and public spheres).

This theory has received both acceptance and criticism – acceptance due to its generality, since the theory posits that there is nothing special about gender. Hence, feminists argue that if there is nothing special about gender, then the phenomenon of gender role typing is neither inevitable nor unalterable. At the same time, this theory is criticized because it depicts the child as a passive recipient and observer of culturally transmitted information. In fact, research has revealed that be it rules of gender or rules of syntax, the child is not a passive recipient; she or he is actively constructing rules to organize and thereby to comprehend the vast array of information in his or her world (Bem, 1993).

While applying the social learning theory to gender differences in aggression and sexuality, we understand how useful it is. For example, in a household where aggression and violence are normalized, a boy is likely to internalize such behaviour and not question it, whereas a girl is likely to observe the passive–aggressive behaviour of the women in the family and imitate it. While picking up the dos and don'ts of expression of sexuality too, children are likely to observe, imitate, and model their behaviour on family members, peers, relatives, and depictions on media and social media. Hence, with respect to understanding gender differences in both socialization practices and cultural double standards and perpetuating gender role stereotypes, this theory gives us a lot of insight. It also assures us that 'what is learnt can be unlearnt'. This principle is used in anger management, questioning of domestic violence, and instigation of both behavioural change (individual) and social change.

2.2.3 Cognitive Development Theory

The hallmark of the cognitive development theory is the role of the child as an active processor of culturally transmitted information. It postulates that because of the child's need for cognitive consistency, self-categorization as male or female motivates him or her to value or devalue oneself based on gender. This gender-based value system, in turn, motivates the child to engage in gender-congruent activities, to strive for gender-congruent attributes, and to prefer gender-congruent peers (Kohlberg, 1966).

Kohlberg explained how moral development, which is an important part of cognitive development, takes place in six stages. He based his theory on the earlier work of Jean Piaget. Kohlberg's stages, further divided into three stages, are called pre-conventional (avoiding punishment, self-interest), conventional (good-boy attitude, law and order morality), and post-conventional (social contract, principle). They run through the developmental stages of infancy, pre-schooling, schooling, and teenage, up to adulthood.

Kohlberg's theory has been so popular since its inception that many psychologists now seem to accept almost as a given that a young child would spontaneously develop a gender-based self-concept and gender-based value system, even in the absence of external pressure to behave in a gender-stereotyped manner. Though the formal theory does not dictate that any category should have primacy, the implicit assumption is that gender is more perceptually salient. The theory fails to explain why gender would have primacy (importance and priority) over other potential categories of the self, such as race, religion, or caste. The assumptions of this theory also do not have cross-cultural validity.

Carol Gilligan worked with both Erikson and Kohlberg. She felt that Freud, Erikson, Piaget, and Kohlberg all followed 'the women as deficient model'. She argued that Lawrence Kohlberg's stages of moral development were male-oriented, which limited their ability to be generalized to females. In her pathbreaking book *In a Different Voice*, she explained the backdrop of this work – a time when several movements, such as the civil rights movement, anti-war movement, opposition of nuclear weapons, the movement to end poverty, the women's movement, and the gay liberation movement, were taking shape in the United States.

30 Theoretical Frameworks of Understanding Gender

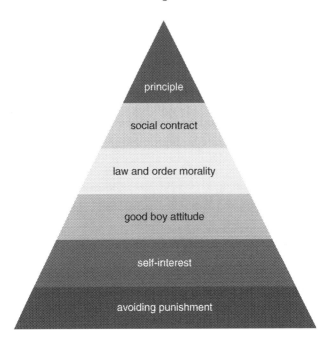

FIGURE 2.1 Kohlberg's Six Stages of Moral Development
Source: www.pngwing.com/

Gilligan swam against the tide of 'men as the norm of rationality, morality, humanity and morality'. She used the interview method to demonstrate moral development, experience of conflict, and concepts of self and morality among a cross-section of men and women of different ages. After analysing the data from the interviews, she proposed her theory of stages of female moral development. She propounded that Kohlberg's theory prioritizes the 'male voice' that accentuates rights, justice, individualism, and logic. Her study highlights the 'female voice' signalling 'interpersonal relationships and care'. This study was a springboard for her 'Ethics of Care Perspective'. She also believed that androgyny (integrating masculine and feminine characteristics) is the best way to achieve self-actualization.

Kohlberg argued that women were 'lacking or deficient in morality'. Gilligan corrected him saying that 'women view things contextually and look at them as conflicting responsibilities rather than as competing rights or moral absolutes'. For instance, many employed women often reach their office late, not because they do not respect the value of punctuality but because they need to complete their household chores, drop their children at day care/school, take care of guests, and so on. It is comparatively easier for male employees to be punctual, since they do not prioritize household tasks (or do not need to in a patriarchal society). Gilligan's work helped the researchers who followed her to tease out many of the factors of the ethics of care.

In her 2011 book *In a Different Voice*, Gilligan says she has made a distinction, that she has come to see as pivotal to the understanding of ethics of care. Within a *patriarchal* framework, care is a feminine ethic. Within a *democratic* framework, care is a human ethic. A feminist ethic of care is a different voice within a patriarchal culture because it joins reason with emotion, mind with body, self with relationships, and men with women, resisting the divisions that maintain a patriarchal order.

She calls the different moral approaches 'ethics of care' and 'ethics of justice' and recognizes them as fundamentally incompatible. Her theory has come in for criticism from feminists who argue that this is a false binary, since both men and women are governed by the same patriarchal rules in each culture and society. It would be more worthwhile to examine why relations becomes more important for women while men are compelled to seek a 'just goal'. It was pointed out that the theory was 'essentialist', meaning it focuses on essentializing men and women and ascribing to them qualities that are different, saying that women are more caring and men follow rules more, thereby reinforcing and perpetuating the same stereotypes that feminist psychologists were struggling to deconstruct and dismantle. However, it cannot be denied that Gilligan's theory made a major contribution at that point of time and led to a lot of churning among mainstream psychologists, as well as feminist psychologists, about gender development models and theories.

2.2.4 Sociological Perspective: Social Role Theory, Sociobiology

2.2.4.1 Social Role Theory

Parsons and Bales (1955) discussed social roles in the family as instrumentality – provision of protection and discipline – and expressiveness – nurturing, mothering, and caregiving: Work outside the house is for men, and family responsibility is for women. They were inspired by Freud's theory and saw these social roles of men and women as immutable and unchangeable, though they understood that these roles would create a lot of hurdles for women in their careers. Sociologists have also given a lot of importance to the relationship between role, status, and the resultant role conflicts. For instance, women face role conflicts among their multiple roles as daughter, wife, mother, and/or daughter-in-law at home and, if employed, a role clash with their role as an employee. Men in patriarchal households face fewer role conflicts. A higher status is accorded to men, and women experience a secondary status at home and in society.

Sociologists also place a lot of emphasis, as do social psychologists, on the 'agents of socialization' as influencers of gender role development: parents, peers, school and college, media and social media. The impact of agents of socialization varies from culture to culture. 'Parents' are the first and the most powerful agents of socialization. They influence the way in which the gender role is shaped in direct

32 Theoretical Frameworks of Understanding Gender

and indirect ways, through food, clothes, toys, books, schools, education, communication, career choices, friends, marriage/intimate relationships, and values. Several studies have shown that the self-concept and self-esteem of children and young adults of all genders are influenced greatly by parent–child interactions.

If parents reinforce stereotypical masculine and feminine behaviour for a long time, it would be difficult for their children to make out-of-the-box choices, and sometimes, the latter cannot make such choices at all – a boy who wants to paint or become a dancer or chef, or a girl who wants to take up boxing or bodybuilding or become a pilot. Division of labour among parents at home influences children's ideas of what constitutes men's and women's work. When gender equality is not practised by parents, then it is extremely difficult for children to recognize day-to-day sexism at home and outside.

Since the schooling age, the life of children is dominated by 'peers' (friends, classmates, acquaintances). The latter dictate what are gender-appropriate and gender-inappropriate behaviours – in terms of clothes, hobbies, entertainment, games, and so on. Very often, they reinforce gender stereotypes. Till adolescence, same-gender friendships are preferred, and by late adolescence, opposite-gender friendships are pursued. Gender-atypical behaviour comes in for ridicule, teasing, and at times ragging and bullying. Queer children and young adults face a lot of trauma due to such behaviour of peers, and so do those who cannot 'fit in to such sub-cultures' in the Indian context – those who come from smaller towns or rural areas. Peer pressure works both ways; at times conformity is rewarded, and sometimes non-conforming children and young adults end up defining gender roles, rewriting social rules, and subverting the social sphere, but the latter is rare.

Schools, colleges, teachers, and education also have a great influence on gender roles. Very often, these institutions and individuals reinforce gender-appropriate behaviour in classrooms and in career choices; the lack of encouragement for girls in STEMM sectors is evident at the school level. They also perform the role of moral police in terms of regulating sexuality and interaction between genders: even in co-education schools and colleges in India, there is segregation of genders, conversations between students of opposite genders are strongly discouraged, and barriers to advancement in higher education which come in the way of rural, disadvantaged girls, as well as boys, are rarely understood. Exceptional schools, colleges, and education promote healthy, normal interaction among members of all genders on campus and encourage gender harmony. Enrolment and encouragement to students from the LGBTIQA+ community in schools and colleges are still a long way off.

'Media', which includes mass media and social media, is also an important influence. It depicts men, women, and members of the LGBTIQA+ community in films, serials, advertisements, and memes, and currently, OTT (over-the-top) platforms have a humungous impact on children and young adults. Commodification of women and misrepresentation and caricatures of or slurs on the LGBTIQA+ community, as well as on black people and ethnic minorities in the West and persons from the Northeast, Dalit Bahujan people, tribal communities, and religious minorities in India, are also causes for concern. Studies show that watching or binge-watching such content leads to violent behaviour, harassment, and a warped perception about gender equality. Social media content, such as on Facebook, Instagram, Pinterest, and Twitter, is creating complex problems related to sexting, sexual cyberbullying, and hypermasculine and toxic masculine behaviour. For example, the film *Kabir Singh*, which valorized toxic masculinity, was appreciated by young men and women who found the character relatable, as against offensive! This also ties up with the premise that gender is socially constructed by parents, family, relatives, peers, school, college, media, and society, in general. Social expectations, social pressure, and conformity are expressed through unwritten rules and codes.

Girls are supposed to speak softly, laugh softly, and be seen, not heard. This is laid down as feminine behaviour. On the other hand, boys and men can talk loudly, guffaw, and are encouraged to behave in an aggressive and confident manner. There are restrictions on the movement of girls, and parents, schools, colleges, media, and society at large constantly monitor them. Boys are not scrutinized so much. Members of either gender grow up imbibing these values from their families and the larger society. There are cultural differences – between urban and rural communities within countries, between countries and between the Global North and the Global South.

In her work, Alice Eagly has revisited the social role theory and offered different insights (Eagly, 2000). She says that societal role structures shape behaviour, making men more agentic and women more communal. Since men are breadwinners, they get a lot of freedom and agency. Women, even when they earn, are considered responsible for the household and hence have a communal orientation. These social structures of the public and the private define their gender roles; women try to be more accommodating and relation-oriented, and men can afford to be non-conformists. Men also get to play roles in business and community at a wider scale, which women must struggle to play even in the 21st century. This creates more confidence among men, and women end up showing more agreeableness and conformity.

2.2.4.2 Socio-biology and Evolutionary Psychology

Evolutionary psychologists suggest that gender differences in behaviour reflect different natural-selection pressures operating on the genders over the course of human history (Byrd-Craven & Geary, 2013), that is, natural selection favours behaviours that maximize the chances of passing on genes to the next generation (reproductive success). To support their assertions, evolutionary psychologists look for gender differences that are consistent across cultures. Despite some fascinating exceptions, gender differences in personality, cognitive abilities, aggression, and sexual behaviour 'are' found in many cultures (Lippa, 2010). However, these

34 Theoretical Frameworks of Understanding Gender

differences are not significant, just as we saw earlier in the case of genetic and biological differences.

According to evolutionary psychologists, these consistent differences have emerged because males and females have been confronted with different adaptive demands. For example, males are thought to be more 'sexually active and permissive', because they invest less than females in the process of procreation and can maximize their reproductive success by seeking many sexual partners (Webster, 2009). The gender gap in 'aggression' is also explained in terms of reproductive fitness. Because females are more selective about mating than males are, males must engage in more competition for sexual partners than females do. Greater aggressiveness is thought to be adaptive for males in this competition for sexual access because it should foster social dominance over other males. Evolutionary theorists say that gender differences in 'spatial abilities' reflect the division of labour in ancestral hunting-and-gathering societies in which males typically handled the hunting and females the gathering. Males' superiority in most spatial tasks has been attributed to the adaptive demands of hunting (Newcombe, 2010).

Evolutionary analyses of gender differences are interesting but controversial. Although it is certainly believable that evolutionary forces could have led to some divergence between males and females in typical behaviour, evolutionary hypotheses are highly speculative and difficult to test empirically. In addition, the evolutionary theory can be used to claim that the status quo in society is the inevitable outcome of evolutionary forces. Thus, if males have a dominant status over females, natural selection must have favoured this arrangement. The crux of the problem is that evolutionary analyses can be used to explain almost anything. For instance, if the situation, through mental rotation, were reversed – if females scored higher than males – evolutionary theorists might attribute females' superiority to the adaptive demands of gathering food, weaving baskets, and making clothes – and it would be difficult to prove otherwise. Hence, this perspective does not yield conclusive findings about differences in gender roles.

2.3 Anthropological Understanding

2.3.1 Psychological Anthropology

In a historical study of 11 cultures, the authors conclude that 'we are the company we keep'. If we interact with infants, it brings forth nurturing responses, whereas peers and older individuals elicit different behaviours. The authors suggest that since young girls are given childcare responsibilities while young boys are not, girls are more likely to become nurturing (Whiting & Edwards, 1988). However, this does not explain why girls are given this responsibility. This theory does not explain why some domestic tasks are thought to be men's work and some are thought to be women's work (gendered). Why is this hierarchy of tasks created? For instance, the tasks of cleaning up after meals, cleaning the house, and helping

Theoretical Frameworks of Understanding Gender **35**

an infant clean up after ablutions are performed by women and are also thought to be 'dirty, secondary, unwanted tasks', whereas tasks that are glorified, like buying expensive things for the household, are performed by men.

This notion that 'we are the company we keep' is also congruent with Maccoby's idea of 'self-socialization' (Maccoby, 1974). Self-socialization means that children know intrinsically, and later through observation, how males and females should behave. This self-socialization helps them make choices about clothes, hobbies, goals, and so on. It does not answer, however, the question of why one makes specific choices. This perspective deserves further exploration.

Anthropological understanding, about hunting and food-gathering societies of various cultures, tells us that at one time men and women shared these tasks and that as we moved towards agricultural and industrial societies, men tended to step outside, whereas women stayed tied to the hearth and home (this is discussed further in a later chapter). Cultural and traditional practices show interesting insights, like the *ghotuls* in the tribal belts of India, where girls and boys live together and can decide whether and when they want to choose a specific life partner. Gender roles and the freedom to choose intimate partners were not circumscribed by moral and religious restrictions in earlier times in India. Mythology tells us about the Rishi Vishwamitra and the apsara Menaka who had a Gandharva *vivaha* (exchanged garlands and 'started living together'). We also have the principles of duality and complementarity among men and women in Chinese culture, called the 'yin-and-yang' principle, which in Indian culture is called 'purush and prakruti'. There is also the intriguing concept and myth of '*Ardha Nari Nateshwar*' co-existence of the so-called masculine and feminine elements in one entity. It is akin to Jung's '*anima and animus*'.

2.4 Other Theories

2.4.1 Gender Schema Theory

The gender schema theory is a sophisticated version of the cognitive development theory and social learning theory. In this theory, 'a schema' is a set of ideas that helps an individual organize information and filter new information (Bem, 1981). This theory proposes that gender role typing is derived from the generalized readiness on the part of a child to encode and organize information (including of the self) according to the culture's definition of maleness and femaleness. It is mediated by the child's own cognitive processing, which is derived from the gender-differentiated practices of the social community. It is a learnt phenomenon, hence neither inevitable nor unalterable.

The compelling features of this theory are its ability to explain the primacy of gender as schema and the subtlety of information processing regarding males and females. It is a theory of process, not of content. Sex-typed individuals are seen to differ from other individuals, not primarily in the degree of femininity or

36 Theoretical Frameworks of Understanding Gender

masculinity they possess but in the extent to which their self-concept and behaviours are organized on the basis of gender rather than on the basis of any other dimension.

By the mid-1980s, Bem began to feel 'theoretically hemmed in', partly because of her own overly narrow focus on how gender stereotypes in the head constrain both sexes. This left out the social institutions that pushed women or men into different and unequal roles, and the fact that because most societies are male dominated, women are a lot more constrained by these social institutions than men are. In her later work, therefore, Bem proposed another theory.

The enculturated-lens theory is a theory that arose to re-conceptualize Bem's views on gender role development in her book *The Lenses of Gender*. In this book, she argues that there are hidden assumptions embedded in cultural discourses, social institutions, and individual psyches which shape not only perceptions of reality but also the material aspects of reality itself (e.g. unequal pay and inadequate day care facilities for children; Bem, 1993).

These assumptions take the form of three kinds of lenses. One is 'androcentrism' (male-centeredness) which considers the male norm as standard. The second is 'gender polarization', which superimposes a male–female dichotomy on almost every aspect of human experience (e.g. modes of dress, social roles, ways of expressing emotions, and experience of sexual desire). The third lens is 'biological essentialism', which rationalizes and legitimizes the other two lenses by treating them as inevitable consequences of the intrinsic biological nature of men and women. This theory goes beyond the gender schema theory and tries to explain how we both acquire culture's lenses and construct a conventional gender identity or construct a gender-subversive identity. This is also called the 'social construction of gender'. Social construction of gender roles explains why some characteristics are thought to be feminine and others masculine (so-called). Social control, norms, and social pressure define masculinity, femininity, and queerness. Those who do not follow these normative gender roles are thought to be abnormal, labelled, stigmatized, and alienated (this has been discussed in Chapter 1). Another aspect is that there are a lot of cultural differences regarding conformity and non-conformity of gender roles, and this acts as a defining factor in gender role development.

Finally, the gender schema theory and the multifactorial gender identity theory have been hallmarks of social psychology. Both these theories give us schemas or conceptual frameworks to understand the linkages between gender and culture, and between society and consumers and buyers. The former theory helps individuals identify masculine and feminine gender identities (socialization practices aid this process) and assign meanings to life events and experiences, as well as their surroundings (think of school and college gatherings, Valentine's Day celebrations, the experience on a first date, wedding ceremony, and so on). All these gendered experiences are socially constructed. The latter theory, as Palan (2001) posited, states that gender identity is a complex mesh of gendered personality traits, interests, roles, and behaviours. All these factors are acting together.

Theoretical Frameworks of Understanding Gender **37**

Now, let us understand some of the in-built and inherent biases among the theories. They are listed in the subsequent sections.

2.4.2 Alpha and Beta Bias

How Is It Linked to the Understanding of Gender Roles and Psychology and Gender in General

An alpha or type I error involves claiming a significant difference when one does not exist, and a beta or type II error involves overlooking a significant difference when one does exist.

Using constructivism as a conceptual framework, gender theories can be considered as representations that either exaggerate or minimize male–female differences. The tendency to exaggerate differences is called 'alpha bias', and the tendency to minimize differences is called 'beta bias'. Alpha bias can be seen in psychodynamic theories, in Parson's sex role theory and in feminist psychodynamic theories. Beta bias can be seen in psychological research on men which is incorrectly generalized to women, in theories that view male and female roles as complementary, in some systems approaches to family therapy, and in recent social policies. All current representations of gender involve alpha and beta bias. The constructivist view holds that the true nature of gender is undecidable (Hare, 1987).

The view of males and females as having mutually exclusive qualities transcends Western culture and has deep historical roots. Ideas of male–female opposition are present in Eastern philosophy and in the works of Western philosophers, from those of Aristotle, Aquinas, Bacon, and Descartes to the liberal theory of Locke and the romanticism of Rousseau.

Febbraro (2003) observed that these biases are evident in research literature on women and work and family studies. Alpha bias is at play when it is posited that women experience more stress as compared to men in families and workplaces. Beta bias is at work when it is stated that multiple roles at home and at the workplace impact men and women in similar ways. Within Western cultures, alpha bias is more predominant than beta bias. For example, Freud wrote that girls identify less with the same-sex parent (mother) than boys, and hence their superegos are weaker than boys! He did admit that men were also falling behind in ideal superego achievement. Hoffman (1975) showed that there was no gender difference in the doing of forbidden tasks – that in fact girls were better than boys at resisting temptations (this was a test of the strength of the superego, which works on the morality principle).

Parsons' sex role theory, which dominated the social theories of the 1950s and 1960s, also exaggerates male–female differences. The very language of the sex role theory conveys the sense that roles are fixed and dichotomous, as well as separate and complementary.

38 Theoretical Frameworks of Understanding Gender

Alpha bias is evident in the hypothesis of mental disorders favouring males over females (males are more likely to develop mental disorders). This is substantiated by arguments about females exhibiting excessive emotionality – a characteristic of histrionic personality – and males exhibiting more hostility and aggression – traits associated with an antisocial personality. It is now accepted that these are stereotypes and hence have the alpha bias.

Androgyny is thought to be a perfect example of beta bias. Having a combination of masculine and feminine characteristics is supposed to be psychologically healthier and is observed more in women. This is a result of studying individuals in isolation from their contexts, which leads to such erroneous findings. Another aspect is that researchers are friendlier, warmer, and more encouraging with female participants than males (Rosenthal, 1966), and it is this differential treatment (beta bias) and the assumption that there are no differences which is problematic. In fact, a male or androcentric bias dominated the entire format of research for a long time.

Mid-chapter Exercise

Search for these forgotten female psychologists on the internet: Anna Freud, Mary Whiton Calkins, Mary Ainsworth, Leta Hollingworth, Karen Horney, Melanie Klein, Mamie Clark, Christine Ladd-Franklin, Margaret Floy Washburn, Eleanor Maccoby, and Thelma Gwinn Thurstone.

Review Questions

1 What do the studies on biological differences between men and women prove?
2 How has the Freudian theory been questioned and refashioned by feminists and feminist psychologists?
3 What are the major concepts explored in sociological theories of gender role development?
4 What are the major concepts explored in anthropological theories of gender role development?
5 What is Bem's contribution to the study of gender roles?

Critical Thinking Questions

1 Explain alpha and beta bias with the help of examples.
2 What are the problems with Freud's biological determinism (biology/anatomy is destiny)?
3 How do cultural factors contribute to our understanding of gender roles?

Bibliography

Bandura, A. J. (1977). *Social learning theory*. Prentice Hall.

Bem, S. L. (1981). Gender schema theory: A cognitive account of sex typing. *Psychological Review*, *88*(4), 354.

Bem, S. L. (1993). *The lenses of gender: Transforming the debate on sexual inequality*. Yale University Press.

Bussey, K. (2013). Gender development. In M. K. Ryan & N. R. Branscombe (Eds.), *The SAGE handbook of gender and psychology* (pp. 81–99). SAGE Publications.

Byrd-Craven, J., & Geary, D. C. (2013). An evolutionary understanding of sex differences. In M. K. Ryan & N. R. Branscombe (Eds.), *The SAGE handbook of gender and psychology* (pp. 100–114). SAGE Publications.

Chodorow, N. (1978). *The reproduction of mothering: Psychoanalysis and the sociology of gender*. University of California Press.

Crocetti, D. (2013). Genes and hormones: What make up an individual's sex. In M. Ah-King (Ed.), *Challenging popular myths of sex, gender and biology* (pp. 23–32). Springer. https://doi.org/10.1007/978-3-319-01979-6_3

Eagly, A. W. (2000). Social role theory of sex differences and similarities: A current appraisal. In T. Eckes & H. M. Trautner (Eds.), *The developmental social psychology of gender* (pp. 123–174). Erlbaum.

Febbraro, A. (2003). Alpha bias and beta bias in research on labour and love: The case of enhancement versus scarcity. *Feminism & Psychology*, *13*, 201–223.

Fine, C. (2013). Is there neurosexism in functional neuroimaging investigations of sex differences? *Neuroethics*, *6*(2), 369–409.

Freud, S. (1931). Some psychological consequences of the anatomical distinction between the sexes. *The Psychoanalytic Review*, *18*, 439.

Hare, M. R. (1987, August–September). *Gender and the meaning of difference: Alpha and Beta bias* [Paper presentation]. Paper presented at Annual Convention of American Psychological Association.

Hoffman, M. (1975). Altruistic behaviour and the parent–child relationship. *Journal of Personality and Social Psychology*, *31*, 937–943.

Hyde, J. S. (2014). Gender similarities and differences. *Annual Review of Psychology*, *65*, 373–398. https://doi.org/10.1146/annurev-psych-010213-115057

Jahoda, G., & Lewis, I. (1988). *Acquiring culture: Cross cultural studies in child development*. Croom Helm.

Kohlberg, L. (1966). A cognitive-developmental analysis of children's sex-role concepts and attitudes. In E. R. Macoby (Ed.), *The development of sex differences* (pp. 82–173). Stanford University Press.

Lerman, H. (1986). From Freud to feminist personality theory: Getting here from there. *Psychology of Woman Quarterly*, *10*, 1–18.

Lippa, R. A. (2010). Sex differences in personality traits and gender-related occupational preferences across 53 nations: Testing evolutionary and social-environmental theories. *Archives of Sexual Behavior*, *39*(3), 619–636.

Maccoby, E. E. (1974). *The psychology of sex differences* (Vol. 1). Stanford University Press.

Mischel, W. (1966). A social-learning view of sex differences in behavior. In E. Maccoby (Ed.), *The development of sex differences* (pp. 56–81). Stanford University Press.

Mitchell, J. (1974). *Psychoanalysis and feminism: Freud, Reich, Laing, and women*. Pantheon Books.

40 Theoretical Frameworks of Understanding Gender

Newcombe, N. S. (2010). On tending our scientific knitting: Thinking about gender in the context of evolution. In J. C. Chrisler (Ed.), *Handbook of gender research in psychology* (Vol. 1, pp. 259–274). Springer.

Palan, K. M. (2001, January). Gender identity in consumer behavior research: A literature review and research agenda. *Academy of Marketing Science Review*, 1–25.

Parsons, T., & Bales, R. F. (1955, December). Family, socialization and interaction process. *Social Forces*, *35*(2), 181.

Petersen, J. L. (2011). Gender differences in sexual attitudes and behaviors: A review of meta-analytic results. *Journal of Sex Research*, *48*(2–3), 149–165. https://doi.org/10.10 80/00224499.2011.551851

Rippon, G. (2019). *The gendered brain*. Vintage.

Rosenthal, R. (1966). *Experimenter effects in behavioural research*. Appleton-Century-Crofts.

Tavris, C. (1993). The mismeasure of woman. *Feminism and Psychology*. https://doi. org/10.1177/0959353593032002

Webster, G. D. (2009). Parental investment theory. In H. T. Reis & S. Sprecher (Eds.), *Encyclopedia of human relationships* (Vol. 3, pp. 1194–1197). SAGE Publications.

Whiting, B. B., & Edwards, C. P. (1988). *Children of different worlds: The formation of social behavior*. Harvard University Press.

3

GENDER AND SOCIAL PSYCHOLOGY

Chapter Highlights

Learning Objectives

After reading this chapter, the students would be able to

- Understand various kinds of social relationships.
- Identify the impacts and effects of gender identities on various relationships.
- Recognize the connection between social relationship parameters, violence, and gender norms.
- Gain perspectives on how to induce or increase awareness or sensitize about gender harmony in the public and private spheres.

Introduction

We are born into families, and we have no choice in that, but we can choose our friends and colleagues for interaction, and love happens! All of us need people with whom we can share our joys and sorrows, besides our family – our primary group as human beings. Interpersonal relationships can range from friendships, intimacy, marital relationship, live-in relationship, and relationships with members of the opposite gender to intimate same-sex relationships. All these bonds enrich our lives and bring meaning to our existence. In this chapter, we will learn more about friendships, romantic relationships, and gender. We will also dwell on professional relationships and the complex aspects of violence experienced in relationships, as well as the efforts, mechanisms, and conduciveness essential for creating gender harmony in all our spaces. It is also important to identify the challenges that exist in creating equal, positive, and mutually enriching relationships and nurturing them,

DOI: 10.4324/9781003453758-4

42 Gender and Social Psychology

as well as helping them thrive and flourish. We will attempt to do so in the chapter. Close relationships are often long-lasting and help create positivity and harmony in a person's life. In contemporary times, these encompass real-time bonds, as well as online contacts on social media. Internet and social media have a deep impact on close relationships, and that is here to stay. Gender has a huge impact on the way in which all these relationships develop and culminate or continue.

3.1 Friendships and Gender

In early childhood and late childhood, same-gender friendships with classmates or playmates due to proximity, similarity, or complementarity are a frequent occurrence. After adolescence, friendships with and attraction towards members of the opposite gender begin. One's choice of a friend depends on familial background, parental approval, and the benefits and liabilities of that friendship. There are a lot of restrictions to opposite-gender friendships from parents, families, teachers, and the larger society. Girl–boy friendships are looked at with suspicion, and 'we are just friends' is thought to be a euphemism for more intimate relationships called 'affairs', 'being in a relationship', and so on. Cultural and social pressures prompt young girls and boys to view such friendships with a strong sense of foreboding. In India, while cities do offer more space and anonymity, rural heartlands are more discriminatory in nature. This creates many problems for normal, healthy, and positive friendships with members of the opposite gender. It is not just this discrimination but also differences in class, caste, region, and nationality that become influencers in one's choice of friends. Sometimes, it is not the youngsters but parents who oppose friendships with people who are 'different' in terms of status, caste and/or religious identity, region, and nationality.

In the popular parlance of post-millennials, one's BFF (best friend forever), 'bestie', or 'bae' (before anyone else, babe, baby, close one) can be of either the same or the opposite gender. *Friends*, the popular sitcom series that premiered 10 years ago and has had a long run (it has spawned series in Marathi and Hindi too), created tropes and stereotypes that the next generation continues to adhere to and emulate. For the young, upward-mobile, urban millennials, metrosexuals, and post-millennials, it has meant 'spaces to hang around' with friends, markers of urbanity to be followed, and fashion diktats from celebrities to be copied, such that one conforms to one's cliques. There is not much gender difference in these lifestyle statements about friendships either among heterosexual youngsters or even with those from the lesbian, gay, bisexual, transgender, intersex, queer (LGBTIQ) community.

There are conflicts among friends, as well as those involved in romantic relationships. There are many causes, such as competition and jealousy and differences in points of view, and people of all genders face these conflicts in friendships. Let us look at what some studies indicate about friendship and gender. Wright (1982) stated that women's friendships are more 'face-to-face', whereas men's friendships are 'side-by-side'. By this, he meant that women tend to share more intimacy in their relationships, whereas men's friendships revolve more around interdependence. Women do not hesitate in sharing their deepest secrets with their best friends. This helps them bond emotionally with their friends in a better way. Men may not engage in this form of emotional bonding with their friends.

Hall (2011) opined that women place higher expectations on their friendships as compared to men when it comes to the aspects of communication, symmetrical reciprocity, solidarity, and overall friendship expectations. Hall believed this difference in expectations from friendship between the genders could be since women place greater emphasis on gaining support from others for childrearing activities, as supported by the evolutionary theory.

Friendships with the opposite gender provide an insider perspective about the other gender, which helps in all the relationships over one's lifespan in private and public spaces (husband–wife relationship, familial relationships, relationships with colleagues at the workplace and in the larger society). The nature, process, and durability of same- and opposite-gender friendships are also different and complex and need to be explored and understood across cultural settings.

3.2 Romantic Relationships and Gender

Friendships are a crucial and integral part of an individual's life. They are also a steppingstone towards the formation of romantic relationships. An initial attraction towards pleasant qualities may turn an individual towards seeking a deeper, stronger connection with the person he or she is attracted to. In some cases, both persons experience this attraction, and they may move on from being friends to becoming romantic partners.

When it comes to romantic relationships and beliefs, men have been found to fall in love quicker and easier as compared to women (Brantley et al., 2002). This can be because there is more social acceptance for their romantic involvements. Men and women have also been found to place emphasis on different aspects of romantic relationships. Women have been found to hold the emotional aspect of love with more importance as compared to the sexual, whereas men place more importance on the sexual aspect of a relationship than the emotional (Schmitt et al., 2009).

Infatuation, love, one-sided attraction, platonic relationships, and permanent relationships (marriage, live-in relationships) are viewed differently by persons of different genders. In the Indian context, though there has been considerable change in the ways in which society views romantic relationships, a lot of taboos and inhibitions persist. Generation Z, especially in cities, is not putting up the constructs such as virginity and taboos against premarital sex on a pedestal, like previous generations of young adults did. But the gatekeeping and moral policing around romantic couples in familial and public places are still rampant.

However, in urban and rural areas, expressions of romantic love between heterosexual couples, as well as queer couples, are still looked askance. Until 2018, with

44 Gender and Social Psychology

Section 377 being in force, queer couples had to lead double lives and hide their love life from society. Since their love was decriminalized, it has not immediately led to social acceptance, but at least they are not treated as criminals!

It is very interesting to note that in many workshops that I engage on sexuality and gender, as well as diversity and inclusion (D&I), participants often ask about the age at which a queer person realizes their sexual or gender identity (pansexual and gender-queer persons often prefer the pronouns 'they', 'their', and 'them'); the simple answer is: the same age/time that a heterosexual person realizes that he/she is heterosexual! Such questions arise due to the dominant narratives of heteronormativity in society.

Gender binaries continue to dictate our lives, social interactions and ideas of love, romance, and intimate relationships. Caste, religion, region, language, and other social indicators also have an impact on romantic relationships and choices of intimate partners. Inter-caste and/or inter-religious love, marriages, and live-in relationships are also a much-contested arena.

A study conducted by Alexander et al. (2007) focused on young adults belonging to rural and urban areas in Pune district. The study put forth interesting statistics regarding the attitudes and behaviour of youth in Pune towards relationships and sexual interactions. It was found that 17–24 per cent of the men studied had been involved in a romantic relationship (past and/or present) and 20–26 per cent had engaged in physical intimacy with their partners, while 16–18 per cent had engaged in sexual intercourse. Among women, the percentage fell below 10 per cent for all the three factors mentioned earlier. An interesting finding was that among women, closeness to family was associated negatively with being in relationships. This study underscores the fact that as far as sexual intimacy and sexual activity are concerned, there are gender-based differences.

LGBT and intersex persons face a lot of difficulties in their romantic relationships, from dating to committed relationships. This happens since they must hide their sexual preferences and orientation and guard against social sanctions, hostility, and rejection. However, just like heterosexual (straight) persons, they too value friendliness, social support, love, and care in their intimate relationships.

The ways in which girls and boys view friendships and intimate relationships are quite different, and the ways in which they approach each relationship also differ drastically. A study examining friendships and sexual partnerships among youth in Mumbai city found that these relationships appeared in three major forms: platonic *bhai–behen* (brother–sister) relationships, true romantic love and sexual 'timepass' relationships. It was found that boys often took advantage of the fluid boundaries of these relationships and engaged in multiple relationships; however, girls engaged majorly in a single true-love relationship (Abraham, 2010). Whether this can be generalized to all boys and girls is a contentious issue. However, it can be said that in a patriarchal world, double standards are used to judge boys and girls indulging in intimate relationships; while boys can flaunt their multiple relationships, girls are judged as 'characterless' when they are involved in multiple relationships.

Gender and Social Psychology **45**

Hindin and Hindin (2009) assessed relationship-related statistics in the national capital – Delhi – and found that 76 per cent males would try and seek out more information about the person they are romantically interested in, while only 61 per cent females would engage in this behaviour. Also, merely 14 per cent females believed that it was okay to engage in premarital sexual relationships, whereas 33 per cent males approved of premarital sex. This study was conducted on an urban sample; the findings from rural areas would be different.

In recent years, experiencing physical attraction towards an opposite-gender friend, as well as engaging in sexual activities (hooking up) in response to this attraction, is becoming common. Individuals are now keeping an open mind about engaging in intercourse without having any strings attached or being 'friends with benefits'. They are just interested in easing sexual tension without committing to each other (Bogle, 2008). Generation Z is now realizing that sexuality and virginity are merely social constructs that they can have their own opinions and rules about and that they do not need to adhere to societal norms regarding the same.

One-sided attraction leads to several undesirable experiences and violence against women, such as physical stalking, cyberstalking, acid attacks, stabbing, and killing. Objectification and commodification of women in families, law, religion, popular media, and society, besides wrong socialization practices that do not teach boys to take no for an answer, in the consumerist, neoliberal world we live in, are responsible for violence resulting from being spurned. These cases have been occurring both in India and across the world over the last 30 years, and the nature of the violence has become more gruesome.

We also observe that close relationships online have also become the order of the day, with more and more people getting access to smartphones and other gadgets. Men and women, as well as those from the queer community, are using dating apps, engaging in sexting, trying to come close online, and ultimately trying to follow up on that in real time. Since cyber-selves can be 'constructed' at times, this leads to fudging, lying, cheating about appearance, careers, prospects, sexuality, and so on, and heartbreak.

LGBTIQ persons also desire a stable and long-term relationship like straight couples. They too want to maintain families and experience parenthood. Studies on their experiences are few and far between but indicate that the quality of the parent–child interaction, and not the parents' sexual orientation, is the key factor that influences parenting outcomes (just like for heterosexual parents). Children report stigmatization of their parents by society as the biggest stressor.

In India, just like in many other Asian cultures, arranged marriage is still the norm for most couples. Romance and love marriage are a trial by fire that few brave; some lucky couples do find 'love' in arranged marriages too. If we consider marriage and live-in relationships (cohabitation) as permanent relationships, then they are gendered. Women have fewer choices as far as decisions about when to marry, whom to marry, and whether to get married at all are concerned. Hence, in India, 'girls are married off' (families arrange their marriage) and rarely have the

46 Gender and Social Psychology

choice 'to find love and get married to a partner of their choice'. Boys have slightly better chances of braving the odds and doing so, since patriarchy gives them rights (not that they always do, since that means opposing the family and losing rights over property and the cushion of kinship networks). Unlike in the West, where choosing one's partner is the norm, in India it is still a rarity.

Live-in couples do make the brave choice of defying social norms, but after a break-up, the women in this relationship face greater social stigma than the men in such relationships. Divorcee women and single-parent women too must struggle more than men in similar circumstances. Queer couples living in and those getting married (they must go abroad to do so) also face a lot of discrimination, social ostracism, and even social boycott at times. Very few have familial support, and most rely more on LGBTIQ networks for help.

Mid-chapter Exercise

List out Bollywood songs that objectify women, such as 'Tu Cheez Badi Hai Mast Mast' and 'Mere Angane Mein Tumhara Kya Kaam Hai' and discuss how they influence the attitudes, thoughts, and behaviour of boys from a young age.

3.3 Relationships at the Workplace and Gender

Men and women are working together in all the sectors of work – government sector, private sector, NGOs, and service sector – spending 8–10 hours together; hence, there are various factors related to gender that come into play. Since a lot of women have entered the workforce in the last 30 years all over the world and some of them are at middle- and senior-level positions, organizational practices need to undergo overhaul and change. But since this is not being done, a lot of challenges are experienced: female bosses and reaction of male juniors, sexual attraction between co-workers, influence of gender stereotypes on workplace behaviour, and sexual harassment at the workplace.

While working together as colleagues, subordinates, or superiors, men and women must maintain collegiality. This in turn is connected to their socialization at home and in educational institutions. Many a time, the soft skills essential for seamless interaction with all genders is absent, since homes and educational institutions often reinforce gender role stereotypes. People do not feel comfortable with each other and face problems in communicating, due to gender barriers, and persons from queer communities face discrimination and stonewalling in hiring, retention, promotion, and relocation.

Let us understand some of these aspects. A study by Elsesser and Lever (2011) yielded some interesting findings in the context of gender and workplace relationships. The researchers observed that the male employees in their sample showed a

Gender and Social Psychology **47**

less favourable attitude towards female bosses, while the female employees judged their male bosses in a more favourable manner. Less than half of the employees also indicated a preference towards male leadership as compared to female leadership. Elsesser and Lever also found that competent male and female managers tend to have a healthy relationship with their subordinates, regardless of their gender.

Though historically typical masculinity in the workplace was viewed as desirable, since men exhibited the characteristics such as competitiveness, aggression, and control, in current times, interpersonal skills and competence are also thought to be important. More masculine men view themselves as lacking in interpersonal domains. This perception also depends and changes according to the gender of the colleagues.

Leadership in workplaces and gender is an especially important area of concern, as well as deliberation. 'Think manager, think male' is the popular notion. Hence, women must work doubly hard to make space for themselves in the upper echelons of leadership in all sectors (this is discussed further in the next chapter). Female leaders who are assertive and focused are perceived as too dominant and aggressive (masculine characteristics) and hence breaking the mould, and those that are cool, calm, and collected are perceived as too passive (not agentic or masculine enough). Thus, female leaders must navigate their way around this slippery slope and evolve their own leadership style and strategies to negotiate the patriarchal attitudes of male colleagues, as well as patriarchal structures of organizations.

Mid-chapter Exercise

We hear phrases like 'boys will be boys' and, in the context of the public sphere, 'old boys' club'. How do you relate to such terms? What message do you get when you hear and read them?

3.4 Relationships, Violence, and Gender

While friendships across gender are marked by care and closeness, romantic and intimate relationships among all genders are governed by desire, pleasure, love, and fulfilment. On the other end of the spectrum are pain, exploitation, and violence. Sometimes a loved one inflicts pain, physical, verbal, mental, or sexual, and treats it as normal. This normalization of violence in relationships of all kinds across genders is a definite cause for concern. It also underscores the need for corrective action. Let us attempt to unravel its various layers.

Anger is one of the six basic emotions that human beings experience (Ekman et al., 1972). Aggression can manifest itself in either the verbal or the physical form, both of which can be particularly hazardous. Sexual violence or violence towards a fraction of society (women, LGBTIQ individuals) which is more vulnerable than the rest is an unfortunate reality.

48 Gender and Social Psychology

Though in mythological and religious contexts women are powerful deities that are highly respected and worshiped, this respect ceases to exist when it comes to women in real life. In India, we have always lived through this paradox of treating women as 'devi' (deity/goddess) or 'dasi' (slave) but rarely as an equal human being. Due to various factors, patriarchy being the most prominent one, women are often seen as inferior beings that need to suffer all forms of discrimination in silence.

Women are expected to play a dual role. They are expected to fulfil all the duties of a mother, daughter, sister, daughter-in-law, or any other social role with strength, much like the worshipped deities, but they must also be submissive to and dependent on the males in their life (Sharma, 2015). Under these contexts, violence towards women is normalized.

Physical aggression has been found to be quite common in both adolescent and adult romantic relationships (O'Leary & Slep, 2003; O'Leary et al., 1989). Aggression in a relationship can be used to assert dominance over the partner. A vast majority of adolescent couples report experiences of physical aggression in their relationship within a span of six months (Gray & Foshee, 1997).

Burk and Seiffge-Krenke (2015) aimed to study the effects of reported aggression among adolescent couples and its effect on relationship functioning. They observed that more than half the sample consisted of couples that were either relationally or verbally aggressive with each other. Only 42 per cent of the couples were found to be reportedly non-aggressive.

Also, among the couples where one partner was found to be either relationally or physically aggressive, higher rates of conflict, less adaptive coping and more jealousy were reported. The least adaptive functioning of the relationship was observed among couples who reported being mutually aggressive with each other. They reported higher conflicts with each other, deficits in emotion regulation and reflections during conflicts, and lack of affiliative relationship qualities. This is seen among a lot of adolescent and young adults in India too.

According to the National Crime Records Bureau report (2011), the most common crimes committed against women included cruelty by husbands and in-laws, molestation, rape, kidnapping, sexual harassment, death due to dowry, and illegal trafficking. Women may often become victims of acid attacks if they reject the advances of men that they are not interested in, or due to family disputes, revenge, or political differences, as well as dowry demands (Ahmad, 2011). Women engaged in small business or small roles at work and those of a higher economic status are at greater risk of being abused. Mentally ill women also have a higher likelihood of experiencing violence (Sharma, 2015).

In fact, the activists who were part of the women's movement in India had to lobby and petition for a long time to get a law for prevention of domestic violence passed. In 2005, the Protection of Women from Domestic Violence Act was passed. Proving that the home was not a safe place and that perpetrators of violence could be fathers, brothers, husbands, and other male relatives took a long time. We have

Gender and Social Psychology **49**

statistics telling us that domestic violence exists in all strata, busting the myth that only poor women get beaten. There are many examples of poor women offering more resistance and breaking free from violent homes, since they are wage-earners, as compared to a lot of middle- and upper-class women who hold on to the pretence and facade of a happy home. The latter also give more importance to social approval and offer less resistance. Intimate-partner violence (spouses, live-in partners, and partners of any gender) is also acknowledged separately from domestic (household) violence, and how women and people of any gender who face exploitation should resist it is another important area of focus.

Rape, sexual assault, and marital rape are issues that are often obfuscated and ignored. Often, the issue of women's consent in sexual relationships is ignored. Just because a woman is married, she is supposed to have given her consent for all future sexual interactions with her husband. Even when a woman is in a live-in relationship with a man, she is supposed to be submissive and provide herself willingly to her partner. Though people are now realizing that marital rape does exist, it is still not considered to be a serious issue. Research has found that women who wanted to leave, were attempting to leave, were in the process of leaving, or had already separated from their husband/partner admitted that pornography was a major factor that led to their being sexually abused by their husband/partner (DeKeseredy & Hall-Sanchez, 2016).

Feminist literature and research have shown that violence against women is not just 'sexual' in nature. It is also a marker of patriarchal power, caste domination, and economic power over women. Hence, while laws for prevention are necessary and help in creating mechanisms for women to seek justice, changing patriarchal attitudes that result in such heinous crimes is a difficult task. In the 1970s, the first important issues addressed by the women's movement in India were dowry deaths and rape. Feminist activists, researchers, scholars, and jurisprudence were successful in demonstrating that victim blaming (blaming the woman for the act) needs to stop, that the onus needs to shift to the perpetrator (the one who commits the crime), and that the society needs to stop calling the woman unclean or tainted and rather needs to rally for her. Over the last 40 years, the discourse around violence against women has also shifted from regarding them as victims to regarding them as survivors who have agency.

Women are also at the receiving end of a lot of blame if they have been sexually assaulted or if they had agreed to other sexual acts but not intercourse by itself. Instances where a woman has agreed to have sexual intercourse only if a condom is used but has been ignored are also considered to be rape; however, many may be unable to comprehend and accept this fact (Lanford, 2017).

It is a fact that merely defining what consent is does not guarantee a reduction in sexual assault. The way society views women and their bodies, attitudes, mannerisms, and so on is guided by misogynistic views contributing to rape culture. If a woman is 'sexually adventurous', she is often blamed openly if she is abused or assaulted, since she was 'asking for it'. Over the years, the notion that women mean

50 Gender and Social Psychology

'yes' when they say 'no' has been broadcast widely across cultures and countries. This mindset helps men justify assaulting women even if women do not necessarily consent in the first place (Lanford, 2017).

Women are not the only ones to suffer sexual violence. Individuals belonging to the LGBTIQ community often face a lot of violence just because they are 'different' or not conventionally normal. Men also experience unpleasant sexual encounters, including being raped or abused; however, they may not report such instances, fearing a tainted image or a threat to masculinity (Javaid, 2017). According to an article in *Hindustan Times* (Chaturvedi, 2017), among the men of alternative sexualities in India who were still closeted and living with their parents, about 52.4 per cent faced physical violence, 55 per cent faced sexual abuse, and 46.5 per cent faced emotional abuse at the hands of strangers or goons.

LGBTIQ youth are often bullied at school. They are victimized in middle and high school, due to which they experience tremendous stress and trauma. These youth often go on to develop serious mental health issues, like depression, as well as physical problems, like the risk of contracting sexually transmitted diseases (STDs) or HIV, apart from the issues like lower self-esteem and life satisfaction. Owing to the paucity of research on the mental health issues of LGBTIQ individuals, little is known about these. The negative environments that these youth must grow up in may have long-term mental and physical health implications (Russell et al., 2011).

A study by Bungener et al. (2017) examined sexual and romantic behaviours, such as kissing, having sexual intercourse, falling in love, and engaging in romantic relationships, among transgender teenagers. The researchers found that most of the participants reported that they had fallen in love; however, an exceedingly small proportion of them had engaged in sexual intercourse.

As compared to people of other orientations, like straight teenagers, they seemed to be much less experienced in sexual or romantic relationships. Transgender individuals are often targeted and bullied, due to which they might perhaps choose to not engage in romantic relationships for fear of being harassed.

Thus, it can be observed that regardless of gender or sexuality, individuals do have to go through traumatic sexual experiences that can be physically and mentally damaging. A change in the attitudes and mindset of the individuals and society can help reduce the occurrence of sexual crimes. The attitudes such as victim blaming, toxic masculinity, and homophobia need to be checked to arrest the rampant increase in sexual assault and harassment.

Sexual harassment at the workplace is also a major issue (this is discussed further in the next chapter). It creates a lot of barriers for the entry and progress of women in workplaces. For the queer community too, it is often an unsurmountable barrier at the workplace. Until some years ago, it was thought that the glamour industries (films, music, entertainment, modelling, advertising, and so on) were more likely to be hotbeds of such crimes. However, in recent years, the 'Me Too' campaign, which began with the Hollywood film industry, has exposed sexual harassment in

Gender and Social Psychology **51**

practically all fields of work – including journalism, academia, and of course the entertainment industry – all over the world, which has been an eye-opener. In the next chapter, we will address some of the causes of sexual harassment and identify preventive safeguards.

Mid-chapter Exercise

That the Hindi film *Kabir Singh* celebrated and glorified 'toxic masculinity' was the verdict of several feminist analysts of cinema and social science. The film fraternity and those who 'enjoyed' the film called this reaction and analysis over-intellectualization! Where do you stand in this debate?

The Hindi film *Shubh Mangal Zyada Saavdhan* conveys some key messages about gay relationships and love among queer people. Do you agree with them?

3.5 Gender Harmony

If India aims to become a developed, powerful country, economic progress needs to be accompanied with social development. All Indians, regardless of gender, sexual orientation, religion, or any other form of classification, can contribute towards the advancement of the country. Societal evolution is also necessary to achieve this goal.

Uplift of the various strata of society which are still devoid of basic human rights, such as women and LGBTIQ individuals, through provision of unbiased employment opportunities can prove to be a step in the right direction. Gender harmony can help bring down the barriers to economic, as well as personal, development which have been created through sexist thought processes.

The viewing of a woman as the primary caretaker is still widely prevalent. Women are expected to take care of parents, children, in-laws, and older members of the family while also handling the responsibility of the entire household. Many women are also now expected to work and share the financial burden of the family. Playing all these roles may lead to eventual emotional burnout.

This could be the reason why more women experience chronic depression as compared to men (Nolen-Hoeksema, 2001). Men may not be raised under these conditions and often limit themselves to the role of the breadwinner. Attending to the domestic chores of the house is still considered to be the primary responsibility of a woman (Wesley et al., 2009).

Quek et al. (2010) studied how marital harmony is interpreted and negotiated among married couples in a multicultural context and the role gender plays in this scenario. They interviewed 20 Chinese American couples and found that though harmony was sought by all the participants, two completely different forms

52 Gender and Social Psychology

of harmony emerged, namely structural and relational harmony. Social harmony refers to traditional social norms that emphasize obligation. Relational harmony is centred on the marital relationship itself. The couples did not fall entirely in either category, owing to multiple influences in their lives.

The role of gender inequality in the transmission of STDs and HIV is becoming more and more apparent. Owing to the discrimination that women face, they often do not have the authority to enforce safe sexual practices, such as use of condoms during intercourse or testing of partners for HIV. This leaves them highly vulnerable to contracting HIV through unprotected sex. Once they contract the deadly disease, they are often shunned by society and do not receive the necessary medical help. They are thus less likely to survive under such conditions (Ehrhardt et al., 2009).

Kulkarni (2014) has emphasized the importance of 'breaking the ice' between males and females so that they become more aware of and sensitive towards the issues surrounding the opposite gender. This sensitivity inculcates a sense of mutual respect towards the other person irrespective of their gender. It can also encourage equal employment opportunities at workplaces. A welcoming and supportive environment can be established at workplaces for women so that they can be more vocal about the issues like sexual harassment and abuse.

According to Bohra et al. (2015), gender sensitization is essential to preventing violence against women through focusing on sensitivities, as well as creating awareness of boundaries in the relationships between men and women. Sensitization can also be accomplished through making individuals aware of the code of conduct that needs to be followed while dealing with members of the opposite gender in various social settings. Individuals must also be made aware of strategies to prevent violence.

Sensitization is possible through teachers, parents, employers, and NGOs that can take up important issues of gender discrimination and disparity and make individuals aware of the same. Through workshops, street plays, and lectures, as well as videos presented to laypersons, an effective impact can be created regarding the issues such as handling of relationships, prevention of violence, and sex education, as well as appropriate communication skills. NGOs, welfare organizations, social activists, and government bodies, like village panchayats, as well as the police force, can play an important role in crime reduction and boosting of gender harmony (Bohra et al., 2015).

Pandey (2014) has also put forth suggestions regarding improving gender sensitivity at the workplace. The suggestions were drawn from her study with 76 women, including female students, salaried women, self-employed women, and housewives. They include mentoring by senior female employees to boost the confidence of women who wish to join the workforce after a break. Flexible work timings, as well as the option to work from home, can enable more women to contribute to the workforce.

Pandey has also suggested activities, like corporate training and strict compliance to policies, as well as sensitization of youth while in school and college, to

Gender and Social Psychology **53**

go hand in hand with the implementation of legislative acts on women's safety and equality. Equality in wages can be ensured through rotation of tasks at work, such that no gender is associated with a specific job. Also, teams consisting of an equal number of males and females can help promote gender parity.

According to Iyengar (2016), societal reformation, especially in the context of gender, is only possible through gender sensitization. She has stated that women are often seen as the weaker sex having a different role to play in the socio-economic area. Through sensitization, modifications in behaviours and thought processes can be made regarding the way in which individuals view their gender, as well as the opposite gender.

Iyengar has also stated that school is one of the primary areas where individuals can be sensitized. Minds can be sensitized while young, and the values like gender equality and mutual respect can be instilled in schools itself. This can help bring up a generation of 'aware' individuals who go on to become responsible adults. Teachers play a key role in this transformation. They can encourage free and open participation in scholastic activities regardless of a person's gender or orientation, thereby sowing the seeds of equality and a non-judgemental attitude.

The importance of sensitizing individuals towards the oppression that other individuals face daily cannot be stressed upon enough. This awareness of the hardships that other people must endure can help people make better choices considering the way they act with fellow humans at their schools or workplaces or even in their homes. Hence, it is important to study through research the effects of gender sensitization on harmony between the genders.

Once again, intersectionality cannot be forgotten. In gender sensitization, the intersections of caste, class, religion, and gender cannot be overlooked. For instance, the 2006 Khairlanji (Maharashtra) case, wherein the women of a Dalit family were paraded naked in the village and then killed, was a case of caste and gender violence. This case did not make it to the national radar for a long time since the victims were from a lower caste. This underscores the fact that the nuances of gender and violence cannot be missed. In contrast, the Delhi rape case of 2012 (which deserves all our sympathy) made media headlines all over the country, since it happened in the national capital and was a crime committed against a middle-class girl. Public apathy and sympathy are shaped not just by the injustice meted out to individuals but by the social demographic of the victim too. Feminist activists, scholars, and researchers have shone a light on these double standards of society as well.

Similarly, the Unnao rape case of 2017 is a case of gender, religion, and violence and created an uproar and cleavages in public opinion. Once again, it is essential to examine it from the complex lens of multifactorial violence (the state too was complicit in this violence) to understand its multiple hues. The suicides of Rohith Vemula in the year 2016, a research student at Hyderabad Central University, and Dr Payal Tadvi in the year 2019, a postgraduate medicine student at Nair Hospital, Mumbai, are examples of institutional violence and atrocities and an indictment of

54 Gender and Social Psychology

the higher education system. They point to the interlinkages between caste, gender, and violence, as well as their impact on a person's psychosocial health and creation of vulnerabilities – a cry that needs to be addressed (Natu, 2022).

When we think of creating gender harmony in homes and workplaces and on our streets, some more complex factors emerge. In the context of women's safety, 'protectionism' (women should come home by 7 pm/before dark – it is for their own good), 'infantilization' (we know what is best for women), and 'victim blaming' (they bring it upon themselves when assault, rape, or molestation or harassment at the workplace happens) are adopted as measures. They are detrimental for gender equality, as well as for women's agential role (decision-making and empowerment). It is the responsibility of individuals, families, the state, and the larger society to create safe and equal spaces for women, children, and the queer community.

Review Questions

1 Describe the factors that influence friendships between members of opposite genders.
2 Trace the similarities in factors that impact intimate relationships among straight, as well as queer, persons.
3 Comment on measures that can be taken to ensure gender harmony in the private and public spheres.

Critical Thinking Questions

1 How do socialization practices influence one's choice of friends?
2 Comment on the commodification and objectification of women in media and popular culture and its relationship with violence against women.
3 Think of popular films that promote equal, caring, and loving relationships and elaborate on their underlying principles.
4 List out films that speak about inter-caste, inter-religious love and queer love.

Bibliography

Abraham, L. (2010). Bhai–behen, true love, time pass. Friendships and sexual partnerships among youth in an Indian metropolis. *Culture, Health & Sexuality, 4*(3), 337–353.

Ahmad, N. (2011). Acid attacks on women: An appraisal of the Indian legal response. *Asia Pacific Journal on Human Rights and the Law, 12*(2), 55–72.

Alexander, M., Garda, L., Kanade, S., Jejeebhoy, S., & Ganatra, B. (2007). Correlates of premarital relationships among unmarried youth in Pune district, Maharashtra, India. *International Family Planning Perspectives, 33*(4), 150–159.

Bogle, K. (2008). *Hooking up: Sex, dating, and relationships on campus.* New York University Press.

Bohra, N., Sharma, I., Srivastava, S., Bhatia, M. S., Chaudhuri, U., Parial, S., Sharma, A., & Kataria, D. (2015). Violence against women. *Indian Journal of Psychiatry, 57*(2), S333–S338.

Brantley, A., Knox, D., & Zusman, M. E. (2002). When and why gender differences in saying 'I love you' among college students. *College Student Journal, 36,* 614–615.

Bungener, S. L., Steensma, T. D., Cohen-Kettenis, P. T., & Vries, A. (2017). Sexual and romantic experiences of transgender youth before gender-affirmative treatment. *Pediatrics, 139*(3), 41–41.

Burk, W. J., & Seiffge-Krenke, I. (2015). One sided and mutually aggressive couples: Differences in attachment, conflict prevalence, and coping. *Child Abuse & Neglect, 50,* 254–266.

Chaturvedi, S. (2017, July 1). 52% of gay men in India without peer support suffer violence: Survey. *Hindustan Times.* www.hindustantimes.com/india-news/52-of-gay-men-in-india-without-peer-support-suffer-violence-survey/story-HKOutVLK7YbIieafqsTrwL.html

DeKeseredy, W. S., & Hall-Sanchez, A. (2016). Adult pornography and violence against women in the Heartland: Results from a rural Southeast Ohio study. *Violence Against Women, 23*(7), 830–849.

Ehrhardt, A. A., Sawires, S., McGovern, T., Peacock, D., & Weston, M. (2009). Gender, empowerment, and health: What is it? How does it work? *Journal of Acquired Immune Deficiency Syndromes, 51*(Suppl. 3), S96–S105.

Ekman, P., Friesen, W. V., & Ellsworth, P. (1972). *Emotion in the human face: Guidelines for research and an integration of findings.* Pergamon Press.

Elsesser, K. M., & Lever, J. (2011). Does gender bias against female leaders persist? Quantitative and qualitative data from a large-scale survey. *Human Relations, 64*(12), 1555–1578.

Gray, H. M., & Foshee, V. (1997). Adolescent dating violence: Difference between one-sided and mutually violent profiles. *Journal of Interpersonal Violence, 12,* 126–141.

Hall, J. A. (2011). Sex differences in friendship expectations: A meta-analysis. *Journal of Social and Personal Relationships, 28*(6), 723–747.

Hindin, J., & Hindin, M. J. (2009). Premarital romantic partnerships: Attitudes and sexual experiences of youth in Delhi, India. *International Perspectives on Sexual and Reproductive Health, 35*(2), 97–104.

Iyengar, G. (2016). *Gender sensitization in education: A pathway to women empowerment* [Paper presentation]. National seminar on Accelerating Rural Growth: By Empowering Women Through Innovation and Technology (pp. 74–76).

Javaid, A. (2017). In the shadows: Making sense of gay male rape victims' silence, suffering, and invisibility. *International Journal of Sexual Health, 29*(4), 279–291.

Kulkarni, G. K. (2014). Need for gender neutral policy at workplace. *Indian Journal of Occupational & Environmental Medicine, 18*(2), 37–38.

Lanford, A. (2017). Sex education, rape culture, and sexual assault: The vicious cycle. *Furman Humanities Review, 27*(5), 61–77.

Morrison, R. L. (2009). Are women tending and befriending in the workplace? Gender differences in the relationship between workplace friendships and organizational outcomes. *Sex Roles, 60,* 1.

National Crime Records Bureau. (2011). *Crime in India: Statistics.* Ministry of Home Affairs.

Natu, S. (2022). Enabling spaces for and with marginalised young people: The case of the Disha peer support and speak out group. In J. Batsleer, H. Rowley, & D. Lüküslü (Eds.), *Young people, radical democracy and community development.* Policy Press.

Nolen-Hoeksema, S. (2001). Gender differences in depression. *Current Directions in Psychological Science, 10*(5), 173–176.

O'Leary, K. D., Barling, J., Arias, L., Rosenbaum, A., Malone, J., & Tyree, A. (1989). Prevalence and stability of physical aggression among spouses: A longitudinal analysis. *Journal of Consulting Clinical Psychology, 57,* 263–268.

O'Leary, K. D., & Slep, A. M. S. (2003). A dyadic longitudinal model of adolescent dating aggression. *Journal of Clinical Child and Adolescent Psychology, 32*, 314–327.

Pandey, N. (2014). Gender sensitivity in India – reality or myth. *Indian Journal of Applied Research, 4*(4), 92–94.

Quek, K. M., Knudson-Martin, C., Rue, D., & Alabiso, C. (2010). Relational harmony: A new model of collectivism and gender equality among Chinese American couples. *Journal of Family Issues, 31*(3), 358–380.

Russell, S. T., Ryan, C. Toomey, R. B., Diaz, R. M., & Sanchez, J. (2011). Lesbian, gay, bisexual, and transgender adolescent school victimization: Implications for young adult health and adjustment. *Journal of School Health, 81*(5), 223.

Schmitt, D. P., Youn, G., Bond, B., Broos, S., Frye, H., Johnson, S., & Stoka, C. (2009). When will I feel love? The effects of culture, personality, and gender on the psychological tendency to love. *Journal of Research in Personality, 43*, 830–846.

Sharma, I. (2015). Violence against women: Where are the solutions? *Indian Journal of Psychiatry, 57*(2), 131–139.

Wesley, J. R., Muthuswamy, P. R., & Darling, S. (2009). Gender difference in family participation and family demand in dual career families in India. *Vilakshan, 5*(2), 49–62.

Wright, P. H. (1982). Men's friendships, women's friendships, and the alleged inferiority of the latter. *Sex Roles, 8*, 1–20.

4

GENDER AND DEVELOPMENTAL PSYCHOLOGY

Chapter Highlights

Learning Objectives

After reading this chapter, the students would be able to

- Understand how gender norms are created from birth and infancy.
- Identify the effects of gender identities at various stages of life.
- Recognize the key challenges that young populations face due to gender constructs.
- Understand the implications of gender norms for old age.

Introduction

A lifespan, from birth to old age to death, is gendered at every step. We discussed in the previous chapter relationships and how they are related to psychology and gender. In the current chapter, we will dwell on developmental stages, in the context of how gender plays out in these stages. We all know how blue is associated with a male child and pink is associated with a girl child, and in the Indian context, laddus are distributed when a girl child is born and *pedhas* when a boy is born, signifying the difference! But this is just the beginning. From then onwards, the child's clothes, toys, games, dreams, ambitions – everything is viewed through a gendered lens. Some professions and careers are still a male bastion, out of bounds for females. An LGBTIQA+ child has trouble getting support for even basic education, leave alone higher goals and ambitions. Gender role stereotypes and social pressures are major hurdles along all these goalposts. Every stage is circumscribed by challenges pertaining to psychology and gender, and the more things change, the more they remain the same. Just as we make some progress with respect to

DOI: 10.4324/9781003453758-5

58 Gender and Developmental Psychology

choices, we must take a few steps back due to the backlash faced from society at large. For instance, while girls are getting free and compulsory education as a right and this helps us as a society to make progress, it comes at a cost, especially for those from marginalized castes who have to face discrimination and sexual harassment in the very same spaces. There are cultural and subcultural differences in how gender impacts life roles. This chapter will address all this and more.

4.1 Families and Gender

How do families as a unit respond to gender roles, gender role attitudes, and stereotypes? Let us try and understand this. Although the importance of gender role attitudes in family dynamics has been of interest to psychologists for several decades, the gender role attitudes of family members – mothers, fathers, sisters, and brothers – are typically studied in adults and children separately or in terms of mother–daughter, mother–son, father–daughter, father–son relationships or parents' relationships with children of either gender. That this approach is likely to limit our understanding of the ways in which family members' gender characteristics are connected is what researchers tell us (Marks et al., 2009).

To fully understand the processes involved in the formation of family patterns of attitudes, longitudinal studies (studies that could go on for many years) are vital. This is because relationships develop and bloom in myriad ways across a lifespan. Although it may seem logical to conclude that sibling dyads (girl–girl, girl–boy, boy–boy) exerted an influence on family patterns of attitudes rather than the other way around, a longitudinal analysis exploring the development of gender role attitudes within the family could help pinpoint the unique ways in which parents and children impact the family system. By examining family patterns of gender role attitudes, rather than just focusing on individuals or single dyads, a deeper understanding of the processes involved in gender role attitude development, among both parents and children, can be gained. Gender role attitudes are connected to the aspects of family life such as relationship quality (closeness of the bonds) and division of labour (How are the household tasks divided among the children? Are they gender based: daughters helping with cooking, cleaning, and household chores and sons with outdoor work, such as buying things and repairing? Or are they egalitarian – both sons and daughters helping with all kinds of tasks?) and are shaped by the family context (this can range from the rural/urban nature to the caste, class, and religious backgrounds of the family). Education and modernity also have an impact. There are no clear-cut equations: A rural, less-educated family could be egalitarian, and even a family where the parents are highly educated could be very traditional and restrictive, insist on gender-based division of labour, and discriminate between sons and daughters. The worldview of the family about gender is important.

Overall, findings suggest that when parents and children show marked discrepancies in cultural values and attitudes, they report more conflicts and a poorer

Gender and Developmental Psychology **59**

relationship quality. Comparable consequences may occur when parents and children have different views on gender roles. Like dissimilar couples, dissimilar parents and children may need to negotiate and redefine their roles in the family, which may, in turn, compromise parent–child relationships. However, it is important to recognize that in some instances, children's divergence from their parents' attitudes is encouraged by parents (Acock, 1984), and thus incongruence may not always result in problematic relationships.

This has a direct bearing on gender roles. For instance, when parents support the aspirations and ambitions of young girls and boys even when they defy the norms, they are saved from conflicts, distress, and a lot of struggles. When boys choose to become artists, dancers, and other non-alpha-male occupations with their parents' blessings, the discord on account of conforming to gender roles does not overpower the relationship. However, this is more the exception than the rule. If young adults have divergent views on career choices and/or choice of life partner from those of parents, the boat of the parent–child relationships is rocked! The areas where discord is evident are all subtle and lie below the surface: Does the daughter get an equal opportunity to continue with higher education as the son does? Why are we still advertising bank loans for a son's higher education and a daughter's wedding? Does this not exhibit the gender discrimination in families? Even upper-middle-class and upper-class families would rather 'invest' in a daughter's marriage than in her education! This just shows that we have miles to go before families become gender-egalitarian.

When cis men and women face blatant discrimination in families, the fate of queer youngsters in their families is even bleaker, barring rare and notable enlightened exceptions. It is extremely difficult for parents and families to accept that their child is queer and different. Hence, for queer young adults, attainment of education, employment, and acceptance and support is often an ordeal. The continued importance of parents in the lives of young adults is indisputable: beginning at birth, extending through adolescence and even into emerging adulthood, affecting all relationships beyond those with the parents and determining the individual's own sense of self-worth. Attachment accounts for this vast impact and influence of parents (Katz-Wise et al., 2016). Forsaken by their family, very often, queer young adults are compelled to find social support from friends, peers, and groups where they can belong.

Famous Chief Justice Leila Seth writes in her memoir that it was a huge challenge for her to accept that her son, famous author and poet Vikram Seth, was bisexual. She writes movingly and poignantly about wholeheartedly embracing her son's sexuality and personhood. Both went on to support the removal of Section 377 from the IPC. Her journey from not understanding her son's sexuality, thinking of societal pressures of conformity to wholeheartedly supporting her son, is narrated with a rare honesty. Parents who are involved in a similar struggle should really read this book.

It is not surprising that queer sexuality and its lack of acceptance by family and society lead to distress, trauma, and ill mental health among queer youth. Families

60 Gender and Developmental Psychology

and society stigmatize LGBTIQA+ persons and their identity, and this pushes a lot of queer youngsters towards depression and suicide. Coping with this familial and societal rejection and facing the dilemma of whether to 'come out or not', as well as facing the consequences of coming out, are recurring sources of distress.

According to Bowlby (1980), attachment to the primary caregiver guarantees survival because the attachment system is activated during stress and concerns the accessibility and responsiveness of the attachment figure to the child's distress and potential danger. The pattern or style of the attachment that develops is based on repeated interactions or transactions with the primary caregiver during infancy and childhood. The possible parental responses to a child's sexual orientation, gender-related behaviour, or identity when these deviate from parental expectations are linked to the child's attachment. It is therefore terrible for queer persons when their primary caregiver forsakes them or constantly forces them to 'become straight'!

Most sexual minority youths are born to heterosexual parents. These parents may not commonly possess implicit or explicit negative attitudes towards homosexuality and expect their children to be heterosexual. Parents may not only be surprised that their child may be or is a sexual minority, but they may also respond negatively to the child. Similarly, the vast majority of transgender and/or gender-non-conforming youths are born to cisgender and/or gender-conforming parents who often possess negative attitudes towards those who violate societal expectations for gender identity, expression, and roles and expect their children to be cisgender and gender-conforming. The negative responses from parents to LGBT youth may range from anxious concerns about the child's well-being and future to abuse and even banishment of the child from the home (Katz-Wise et al., 2016). We see these responses across cultures.

Youth homelessness is linked with numerous threats, such as violence, substance use, and mental health problems. Although discrimination and victimization related to a minority sexual orientation status are believed to be important causal factors, research is needed to improve our understanding of the risks and protective factors for homelessness and to determine effective strategies to prevent homelessness among this population (Corliss et al., 2011).

As with stigma attached to sexual minorities and transgender individuals, gender nonconformity is also stigmatized in and of itself, particularly among boys. Connell's theory of hegemonic masculinity sheds light on this stigma, as it suggests that one form of masculinity, with the features such as aggression, limited emotionality, and heterosexuality, is culturally desired (hegemonic masculinity is a practice that gives a dominant position in society to men). For this reason, deviation from this level of masculinity among boys can be stigmatized. Like stigma related to sexual minorities and transgender individuals, stigma related to gender nonconformity is often enacted through prejudice, discrimination, and victimization (Connell, 1995). The process of sexual-orientation disclosure in families may be shaped by the values of the family system. In one study investigating traditional values and family acceptance of sexual minorities, families with a strong emphasis on traditional values (e.g. importance of religion, emphasis on marriage, emphasis on having children) were perceived as less accepting of a sexual-minority orientation than less-traditional families. Parental responses to youths' disclosure of a sexual-minority orientation may also differ based on race/ethnicity or cultural levels of acceptance of sexual-minority individuals, though research is lacking in this field (Merighi & Grimes, 2000). In most Asian cultures, including India, there is truly little research available on this topic. *Manachiye Gunti* (Marathi), or *Beautiful People* (English), a compilation of stories of parents of LGBT youths published by Samapathik Trust, Pune, tries to fill this void, and this effort is commendable.

Gilbert (1993) described a three-dimensional theoretical structure of gender: gender as difference, gender as structure, and gender as process. Gender as difference broadens our understanding of behaviour in the social context but obscures inequality by masking the differences in power between men and women. Gender as structure refers to the way in which attitudes towards men and women become institutionalized within societal structures. For example, a male employee who has a child is perceived as male; a female employee with a child is a mother. Gender as structure is evident in the workplace when the assumption is made that women will provide care for dependants and is demonstrated by the dominance of one gender or the other in certain occupations. Gender as process refers to the patterns of interactions among men and women based on assumptions about gender roles. Women are seen as nurturers and providers of emotional care, whereas men are seen as providers of economic support. These processes define the relationship between families and gender (a more detailed discussion on gender-based division of domestic labour will follow in the next chapter).

Chatterjee (1987) was of the opinion that 'discrimination begins with the fact that a girl is unwanted and therefore eliminated even before she can emerge into the world'. Incredibly early in life, children begin to experience gender-based differentiation and discrimination in their relationships with others, in the distribution of family resources, and in their entitlement to family membership: in nutrition, healthcare, education, and so on. Female feticide, infanticide, and son preference in families speak eloquently of the discrimination. Moreover, within families, girls/women were neither expected nor encouraged to develop a sense of autonomy or control. It is a fact that female feticide, infanticide, and son preference prevail in families, across all strata, castes, religions, educational backgrounds, and regions.

In India, gender exceptionalism is seen in its religious and cultural institutions that give families economic incentives to have fewer girls and to invest less in them. However, economic rationales seem unable to fully explain the level of gender discrimination in India. For example, investments in girls' health and education ought to have financial returns for parents in the form of lower dowry payments or a higher-quality son-in-law. Thus, in addition to differing incentives, preferences might be systematically different in India. A preference-based explanation might explain, for example, why Indian women are more likely to say that a husband beating his wife is justified compared to women in other equally poor countries.

62 Gender and Developmental Psychology

Insofar as these preferences are deeply held and difficult to change through the pro-girl policies in place today, such as financial incentives to have daughters and to educate them, they may represent a significant challenge to erasing discrimination against women (Dhar et al., 2014).

The bonds between the members in a family have always been glorified in Indian family life and culture. However, violence against women, and in some cases even against young girls and aged women, in the family is one issue that challenges the cultural notions of family as a 'haven' in India (Chowdhury, 2007). Notwithstanding the gradual shrinking of the larger family constellation, accompanied by various transformations within the family structure, the lives of many women rest on a continuum of unsafe spaces (Stanko, 1990).

We have also witnessed this vividly during the recent Covid-19 (coronavirus disease 2019) pandemic, with 'Stay Home, Stay Safe' proving to be a myth. The number of cases of child sexual abuse and domestic violence has spiralled all over the world, bearing testimony to the fact that homes and families are many a times violent, unsafe, and exploitative.

4.2 Birth, Infancy, Childhood, and Gender

As expressed in the introduction, the very birth of a girl/boy/intersex child marks the beginning of the process of gendering and continues through the lifetime of the child. The birth of a girl is greeted sombrely and grudgingly, with son preference being the prevalent norm. Even now, it is rare for parents to desire a girl child and rejoice at her birth. In Maharashtra, girls are named 'Nakusa' or unwanted and carry that name forever. This is not the case of just one state; several other restrictive and discriminatory practices exist across states which demean a girl child right at her birth. A boy's birth, on the other hand, is treated with jubilation, and he is thought to be the one who carries the family legacy forward, heir and the one who will light the funeral pyre. The desire for one or more sons can be simply understood by the number of progeny a couple has! Even an educated family rarely follows the one-child norm (especially when the firstborn is a girl)! The birth of an intersex child throws the family into turmoil and anguish, since the fear of stigma far outweighs the love for the child.

Society and parents give boys entitlement over their sisters from early childhood. Boys are raised in a way that provides them with a feeling of authority over women and makes them expect women to accept their superiority. They react violently when they feel that their authority is being threatened, mainly because they are brought up in a violent environment and have learnt to deal with frustrations in a violent manner. When looking at the characteristics of a child that made his or her parents proud of him or her, the more frequently cited reasons for parental pride were gender-specific characteristics: Parents were proud of their boy if he was tough and strong, brave, more of a 'man', and his 'father's son', and because he carried the family name. On the other hand, parents were proud of their daughters if they were helpful with household chores, obedient, and beautiful (Hamieh & Usta, 2011).

In this way, families reinforce and perpetuate gender stereotypes, very often. This may lead to toxic masculinity being reinforced knowingly or unknowingly among young boys who have 'never taken no for an answer', with all their demands being met in the family. We see this behaviour playing out in 'one-sided attraction', 'stalking', 'cyberstalking', and 'harassment', where some boys have not learnt that 'no means no'. This is embedded in the deep-rooted patriarchal and socially stratified structures, and 'boys will be boys' is touted by the larger society. Gender sensitization since childhood, with the caste, religion, region, and sexuality intersections, then becomes imperative in families and schools and through media and civil society engagements.

The socialization process can be divided into primary and secondary socialization. Primary socialization occurs when a child learns the attitudes, values, and actions appropriate for individuals as members of a culture. This is mainly influenced by the immediate family and friends. Secondary socialization is the process of learning what is the appropriate behaviour as a member of a smaller group within the larger society. It involves the behavioural patterns reinforced by socializing agents of society, like schools and workplaces. All through infancy and childhood, children are exposed to gender role stereotyping in terms of choice of toys, games that they play, hobbies, playmates, and later their choice of careers and occupations.

It is thought that boys should be given toy guns, football, bat, ball, and the like by their parents and should be encouraged to play outdoor games, whereas girls are expected to play with dolls (albeit new and fancy versions of Barbie dolls!) and doll houses and play indoors. When they break these gender binaries in play, they are called sissies (boys) and tomboys (girls). These gender-discriminatory social sanctions and social control play a major role in defining, shaping, and restricting the choices of play and games of children. What starts as play-acting or role-play in childhood for girls, boys, and gender-non-conforming children translates into adult roles. A sensitive portrayal of this was depicted in the Hindi series *Paatal Lok* on an OTT platform. Two young 'boys' who are street children indulge in petty thieving in Mumbai local trains for their livelihood. One of them is a cis boy, while the other is discovering and exploring 'his' trans identity. The transgender 'boy' picks up a compact and a lipstick from a woman's purse that they have robbed and tries on both and admires 'himself' in a wayside mirror, while the cis boy is happy buying snacks with the cash. In a remarkably simple way, this depiction illustrates how the transgender 'boy' explores and wrestles with 'his' identity from a really young age.

4.3 Adolescence and Gender Disparity

According to WHO (2017), when children move into early adolescence, they begin to take on new gender roles associated with femininity and masculinity, often

64 Gender and Developmental Psychology

reinforcing socially and culturally conventional gender norms related with being women or men. These gender roles have an impact upon the decisions that young people take in early adolescence and, therefore, upon their health and well-being. They have an impact on the choices young adolescents make in relation to sexual and interpersonal relationships, which can influence their health and well-being throughout the rest of their lives. To ensure health throughout people's lives, it is therefore crucial that countries address gender inequality, particularly unequal gender norms in early adolescence.

Unequal gender norms develop early in childhood and intensify in early adolescence. There are some similarities and differences in how unequal gender attitudes and norms manifest across different geographic and sociocultural contexts. Societal expectations of boys and girls differ, and so do their own gender attitudes – across all contexts, puberty is associated with an expansion of boys' worlds and a shrinking of girls' worlds. Boys do not always recognize their own privilege, and when they do challenge norms, they are punished. Girls recognize their own disadvantage and are more willing to challenge norms but need support to exercise their agency. Race, ethnicity, class, and immigration status influence gender norms and attitudes – these norms and attitudes can vary within sub-populations of the same geographical area. There is compelling evidence that peers and parents are influential in shaping gender norms and attitudes. There is some evidence that schools and teachers also shape norms and attitudes. Evidence on the influence of the media is beginning to emerge.

There is a lot of peer pressure, along with societal pressure, on adolescents to conform to stereotypical gender roles, such as watching certain types of movies or serials and reading chick lit for girls and watching action movies and reading macho literature for adolescent boys. Adolescent girls face several issues related to body image, body shaming, weight, norms of fashion, beauty, skin colour, and so on, while adolescent boys are compelled to go to gyms, develop six-pack abs, look muscular and macho, and conform to the alpha-male norm by the time they reach youth. LGBTIQA+ adolescents are trapped in a limbo with respect to their body image, self-image, and self-esteem.

Depression in adolescents is more common among girls; this gender disparity becomes more apparent during the teen years when girls face close to twice as much depression as do boys. Vulnerability–stress models help explain these differences, and a tendency towards rumination may play a role in both the development and the continuation of depressive symptoms (McGuinness et al., 2012). In India, one of the causes of vulnerability and distress being more among girls than boys is that social pressure and social conformity restrictions are more on girls than boys. Until childhood, in most homes, girls and boys are treated as 'children', but the moment they step into puberty, girls are given several instructions; these range from 'sit properly' and 'do not play with boys' to 'do not wear such clothes'. Both the family and the larger society start their surveillance and moral policing, whose forms are different between rural and urban locales. In rural settings, since there are more community settings, everything is out in the open, and parents are distressed by 'what will people say' (*log kya kahenge*). In urban settings too, this prevails, but there are more insidious comparisons and surveillance as well. All of this creates burdens for young adolescent girls.

Some of the bones of contention and double standards that start in late adolescence and continue into youth within families are these: at what time boys and girls should return home (girls have to be back before it is dark!), their pocket money, who their friends should be (this demonstrates restrictions based on not just gender but also caste and religion, exposing biases and prejudices), and their ideas and opinions about love, friendship, intimacy, and sexuality. A boy gets to denote his 'cool index' and 'swag', whereas a girl who is an extrovert, popular, and outgoing and demonstrates this in the public space is called names ('loose', 'characterless', and worse). This shines a light on societal hypocrisy and double standards and illustrates how gender discrimination circumscribes the freedom and security of youngsters.

The other factor that cleaves the life of young adolescents is the physiological changes: menarche (beginning of the menstrual cycle) among girls and the onset of secondary sexual characteristics among boys. In many parts of the world, menstruation tends to be a taboo topic, surrounded by silence and shrouded in myths. Yet menstruation and menstrual hygiene are emerging as pivotal issues for gender equality, human rights, and development (Patkar et al., 2016). Indeed, menstruation perpetuates humanity and should be celebrated today and every day, rather than hidden behind shame and disgust. It starts with incorrect information, misinformation, superstitions, and social practices, such as keeping away from others and not touching food, entering the kitchen or religious places of worship. Many girls do not understand what is happening when they start menstruating and have limited knowledge on biological processes. Due to a lack of facilities at school, at work, and in public spaces, women often prefer to manage menstruation at home, meaning they are unable to participate in cultural, educational, social, and income-generating activities. Poor practices and unsafe materials compound this problem. In addition, many women and girls lack access to safe and hygienic materials.

One of the most significant barriers for women is the social restrictions, beliefs and myths that influence the management of menstruation and, as a result, affect the daily lives of women and girls. When menstruating, women and girls are subjected to various religious, food-related, domestic, or sexual prohibitions, which often lead to further isolation or stigmatization. Finally, perceptions of menstruation affect how many cultures perceive girls. Starting to menstruate is often viewed as a sign of maturity, meaning girls have reached a potentially marriageable age. Yet early marriage significantly increases the risk of child pregnancy, repeated pregnancy without adequate birth spacing, and complications, like obstetric fistula.

Many of the world's major religions – such as Islam, Christianity, Judaism, and Hinduism – refer to menstruating woman as unclean and suggest they be segregated during their period. Even today, in some communities, women are banished

66 Gender and Developmental Psychology

to sheds during their period because of so-called impurity during menstruation, despite the ancient practice being outlawed (Wills, 2017). Given that menstruation is still overwhelmingly considered women's secret business, young girls are taught from an early age that they must manage it privately and discreetly. This shame, Professor Ussher argues, affects not only how women feel about menstruation but also how they feel about their bodies. This can impact their sexuality and their knowledge about the sexual body. This shame has 'massive knock-on effects' for how women understand their whole reproductive system. Data show us how little women understand that menstruation is just part of a cycle and that when one is not on a period, there are just as significant and dramatic changes happening in one's hormonal profile. Women would benefit greatly from really understanding the highs and lows of their reproductive cycles.

Some women's organizations in India that work on gender and reproductive health have demonstrated through their research, as well as intervention work, that along with the biological understanding about menstruation and reproductive cycles, it is important to engage on the psychological and sociological understanding of menstruation with adolescent boys and girls. For example, workshops on fertility awareness for adolescent and young girls which help them understand the bio-psychosocial factors of menstruation and reproduction empower them with facts and the perspective to question the stigma attached to 'what is natural, normal and biological'. Sexuality education and awareness workshops for adolescent boys and girls also go a long way in addressing fears, myths, curiosity, and taboos with a scientific and holistic approach.

My experience of conducting interactive sexuality education workshops for mixed groups of late-adolescent and young boys and girls has been full of insights. Since they are from a truly diverse, heterogeneous range (urban and rural poor, middle- and upper middle class, from different states, upper class, and a few international), the workshops have offered me a rainbow of learning. Their information, discussion, questions, and interactions covered the entire gamut: lack of awareness and knowledge on the subject, misinformation, misconceptions, and a lot of scientific information, as well as experimentation and exploration. On the experiential base too, they range from naive, inhibited, and curious to sexually active. Some of the rural students and urban poor who have had more community experiences, where lack of resources has led to their living in confined spaces, have seen and known more about sexual aspects of life than their urban, well-to-do counterparts. The uber-rich students have experimented, been adventurous/mis-adventurous and sexually active online and/or offline since it is cool. Hence, the sexual repertoire of late adolescents and young adults is not homogeneous. While the naive are still asking questions about how a girl gets pregnant, some want to discuss misconceptions about masturbation and BDSM (bondage, discipline, sadism, masochism). Discussion of the nuances of sexuality such as desire, pleasure, pain, exploitation, violence, love, passion, and their importance in interpersonal and intimate relationships gets foregrounded in the workshops.

For LGBTIQA+ adolescents at the cusp of youth and adulthood, dealing with sexuality and gender is a critical issue. Since their sexualities and genders do not always conform, an adolescent boy who identifies with the male gender, is not heterosexual, and identifies as gay (sexual orientation) may be attracted (sexuality) to males, to both males and females, to transgender persons and to all of them (gender-fluid/pansexual). Since there is no simplistic one-to-one correlation between sexualities and genders but rather a complex intertwining, it is exceedingly difficult for families and the larger society to understand them.

Family acceptance of LGBT adolescents is associated with positive young-adult mental and physical health. Interventions that promote parental and caregiver acceptance of LGBT adolescents are needed to reduce health disparities. A study in the West found that across all grades, LGBT students were about 91 per cent more likely to be bullied and 46 per cent more likely to be victimized compared to their heterosexual peers. Lack of policies and practices that affirm and support LGBT youth – and a failure to implement protections that do exist – means that LGBT students nationwide continue to face bullying, exclusion, and discrimination in school, putting them at physical and psychological risk and limiting their education. Areas of concern include bullying and harassment, exclusion from school curricula and resources, restrictions on LGBT student groups and other forms of discrimination, and bigotry against students and staff based on sexual orientation and gender identity. While not exhaustive, these broad issues offer a starting point for policymakers and administrators to ensure that LGBT people's rights are respected and protected in schools. LGBT students have also described persistent patterns of isolation, exclusion, and marginalization that have made them feel unsafe or unwelcome at school. Students have described how hearing slurs, lacking resources relevant to their experience, being discouraged from having same-sex relationships, and being regularly misgendered made the school a hostile environment, which in turn can impact their health and well-being (Dwedar, 2016).

While there are few studies in India on depression among the LGBT community, a 2012 study of men who have sex with men, conducted in Chennai and Kumbakonam, showed that many of the participants reported moderate to severe depression scores (Hamid, 2015). The contributing factors are lack of acceptance by family and society, fear of prosecution under the laws like Section 377, and the perception of queerness as a disease to be 'cured'. The confusion begins at adolescence. The notion that being homosexual is wrong is present all around us. Thus, teenagers begin to think there is something wrong with them. When they are older, they begin to read and learn more. But often, this leads to a breach with the family – they either leave or hide their sexuality, both of which can cause problems. In their 20s, it gets more difficult – either there is pressure from the family to get married or they may be looking for a partner but be unable to find one. A break-up too can lead to depression – there is no one they can talk to, and no form of social support offered. Those living in rural areas do not have access to resources of information and support groups.

68 Gender and Developmental Psychology

> **Key Insight**
>
> The question asked by straight persons all the time is, when does a queer person know or realize that one is not heterosexual? The counter-question is, when does a heterosexual person realize that he/she is heterosexual? If that starts from childhood/late-childhood/adolescence/youth through attraction/infatuation/crush/obsession/love and is explored till an 'aha' moment comes, then it is exactly the same across the same life stages for LGBTIQA+ persons!

Section 377 is no longer in force, but social ostracism, discrimination, and isolation and alienation of LGBTIQA+ adolescents and youth have not ended. Although being 'queer' is no longer abnormal (from the revised DSM-III onwards, thanks to the protests and petitions of LGBT groups the world over, being queer is no longer a diagnostic category), it is still seen as such by many psychiatrists and clinical psychologists. Hence, wanting to 'cure' them and make them 'normal' continues unabated. Few mental health professionals are gender-sensitive and use or practise queer-affirmative therapy. Hence, parents bring LGBTIQA+ adolescents or youngsters to these professionals for treatment, and aversive therapy is still practised! Though we in India claim to be modern, the taboo around and social ostracism of queer individuals continue, and the social pressure makes a lot of parents of queer adolescents and youth succumb to it. Educated parents also force their queer children to undergo treatment and get married and push them towards leading dual lives. It is not education, then, that transforms, but it is acceptance of 'difference' which helps parents embrace their children regardless of the latter's sexuality (and disability).

Closing gender gaps across all stages of childhood and adolescence and eliminating gender discrimination – whether against girls or against boys – are fundamental to inclusive and sustained progress for countries around the world. In addition to the harmful and often tragic effects of gender inequalities on children and adolescents, the kinds of persistent inequalities that we continue to see through the available data, especially during the adolescent years, are major barriers to the efforts of many nations to move out of long-term poverty and achieve their development aspirations (Rao, 2011). Trying to give girls, boys, and LGBTIQA+ youngsters access to all the axes of development (health, education, employment) and love, acceptance, security, and encouragement in the private (family) and public (school, street, society) spheres would help countries across the world achieve sustainable development.

4.4 Youth and Adulthood Challenges and Gender

It is well known that young adults try to train and acquire skills for gainful employment and move on to these domains as adults. Is there a gender gap, and are there gender differences vis-à-vis educational fields and work sectors? Yes, there are huge gaps and differences. Although women have made important entries into the science and life science industries over the years, both fields still face large gender differences when it comes to the career advancement of men and women. STEMM is still a male bastion the world over, with women trying to get a foothold, a step in. (The next chapter on workplace and gender will discuss many factors related to this in greater detail.)

Higher education in India (and all over the world) is deeply gendered. Two examples are: more girls opt for social sciences, humanities, languages, and literature (some make a genuine choice, while others are forced and compelled by the popular gender stereotype that these are soft disciplines (another myth!) and hence better for them – and they cost less too! (most families want to spend less on a girl's education)); and more boys overall opt for natural sciences and professional courses than girls (some because it is prestigious and their families are willing to spend on their education, and others because they are genuinely interested). Hence, even though in India girls outperform boys in X and XII standard exams, their dropout rates are higher, and very few can move to higher education – a small proportion of those who can become career professionals. The same is the case with young adults (all genders) who are from poor strata and/or marginalized castes, Adivasis, and/or sexual minorities. Pursuing higher education is a distant dream for many of them.

Even within specific streams, choice of courses is gendered: In medicine, softer specialties (so-called) are for women (paediatrics, obstetrics, gynaecology, ENT (ear, nose, throat) and so on), while surgery remains a male bastion, and women must struggle to get into the latter and survive. In engineering too, civil, mechanical, and instrumentation engineering are considered 'masculine' branches, and females wanting to make this choice must struggle in a classroom and a field where they are a minority. In social sciences too, more boys opt for economics, political science, and geography, since sociology, psychology, and anthropology are considered feminine pursuits! Language and literature are still infra dig for many boys! These examples illustrate that the choice of courses, streams, and careers for young adults is circumscribed by gender stereotypes, as well as gendered reality.

Another case in point is the option for girls to join the armed forces. The Women Special Entry Scheme for Indian Army, Navy and Air Force started way back in 1992. Women got recruited for a maximum of 14 years (short-service commission). Only women in law and medicine were allowed permanent commission. In March 2019, women were allowed permanent commission in 10 branches of the army but not all. Thus, this highly contentious issue of whether women should work in all three branches of the defence with permanent commission (in all sub-branches) in India, like in 16 other countries that employ women in combat roles, remains unresolved.

Later, as young adults, women also lose out on the potential employability gains related to vocational education and training (VET). In most countries, more men than women attend VET courses, despite VET providing exceptionally good employment prospects, particularly when not pursuing tertiary studies or when compared to dropping out of education before the end of high school (Quintini, 2016). Overall, women stand to gain from undertaking studies in traditionally male-dominated sectors, both in terms of employability and in terms of earnings. However, such a switch would require action on various fronts: high-quality career guidance based on sound labour market information on skill requirements to inform girls on promising careers in growing economic sectors; information campaigns promoting diversity in workplaces and encouraging employers, particularly in shortage occupations, to tap into under-represented socio-demographic groups – such as women in male-dominated professions; and the identification of female role models in male-dominated careers to promote interest among girls and their families, as well as employers. All over the world, vocational and career guidance for young girls and boys is not pitched at out of the box or gender bender careers, and there is still no familial and social support for it. The focus is still on 'typically status- and prestige-oriented fields', such as medicine and engineering in the metro cities and administrative services in two-tier, mini metro cities and rural areas (UPSC (Union Public Service Commission), State Public Service Commission).

Post-structuralist feminist critique considers gender not as biological but as performative – in terms of learned behaviour and beliefs that become embodied; 'women' (insofar as the word denotes a common identity) tend to embody discourses considered feminine, and 'men' masculine because they learn to 'do

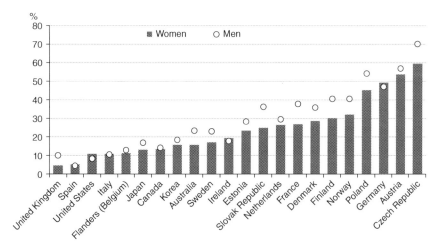

FIGURE 4.1 Women in Vocational Education and Training

Source: Quintini (2016)

Note: Share attending VET (vocational education and training) or holding a VET qualification as the highest educational credential.

gender'. Importantly, this is not to say that men cannot ever embody feminine discourses, nor that individuals can only embody either masculine or feminine discourses. Indeed, men do embody, and operate within, feminine discourses, and women masculine – we have hugely successful male paediatricians and female surgeons as evidence. However, what we do suggest is that in a domain where masculine discourses predominate, like surgery, feminine qualities have less cultural worth and are therefore more marginalized. It therefore follows that it is harder for those who have constructed a feminine identity for themselves – more usually, though not exclusively, women – to imagine, access, and engage in such a practice, especially when they simultaneously compare it (imaginatively or otherwise) to a practice like paediatrics which discursively embraces and values those same aspects of their identity (Holmes & Marra, 2010).

In 2010, education rights advocates from around the world united to push for recognition of gender identity and expression as protected grounds in international human rights legislation – and succeeded. Research and activism in transgender education is not an easy prospect because you become known; murder and rape, and discrimination are a reality also for transgender adults, not only for students. The transgender community, one of the marginalized and vulnerable communities in the country, is seriously lagging on human development indices, including education (Rajesh & Aslam Naved, 2013). What is appalling is that despite affirmative action (reservation policies, right to education, and so on), the disparities remain substantial among the transgender community in India. Most of the population is uneducated or undereducated, thereby being excluded from participating in social, cultural, political and economic activities. Along with teachers' apathy towards the transgender community, exclusion from society, poverty, continued discrimination, and violence are some of the crucial factors to which can be attributed the poor participation of transgender persons in educational activities. Transgender people face prominent levels of stigma in almost every sphere of their life, such as health, schools/colleges, employment, social schemes, and entitlement. Extreme social exclusion diminishes one's self-esteem and sense of social responsibility.

Transgender persons in India are shunned by family and society alike. They have restricted access to education, health services, and public spaces (Rajkumar, 2016 [2011]). Until recently, they were excluded from effectively participating in social and cultural life. Politics and decision-making processes have been out of their reach. Their fundamental rights are not acknowledged. Reports of denial of services to and harassment, violence, and unfair treatment against transgender persons have come to light. Formal education for transgender persons is not popular in the Indian context. They are deprived of the family and school environment; they discontinue their education and risk their future career opportunities. A close analysis of various reports and discussions with the community and stakeholders suggests that transgender persons are mostly uneducated or undereducated and become reluctant to continue schooling. It is because of this that they take up begging and sex work. It is mandatory for the government to provide inclusive

72 Gender and Developmental Psychology

education for transgender students and provide adult education to them. The term 'third gender' is a problem in itself. It treats sexuality as a ladder-like structure in which the lowest rung is occupied by the queer community. Although it provides them with legal recognition, it does not alleviate them of their conditions, as they continue to be part of the marginalized and excluded section of society and are not considered equal to the rest of the Indian population.

I want to share a very heartening anecdote here. It is from an educational context. A young girl who is studying in a college in a small town was referred to me for counselling. She is a lesbian who is struggling with her identity and still unsure whether she is a transgender (she relates to being a boy better). She was infatuated with a female teacher, and the restrictive atmosphere of the educational setting was not supportive or understanding at all. She came with her parents for the session. The parents come from a lower-middle-class background and are semi-educated. After having their queries and concerns answered, they were willing to accept their daughter's being 'different', changed their mind about aversive therapy and were willing to support her education. They also understood that she was not 'abnormal' and did not need 'cure', and their love for their daughter helped them take a leap of faith and be on her side, regardless of social ridicule, ostracism, and discrimination. Thus, it was not education, exposure, or an urban lifestyle but acceptance, understanding, and empathy that helped them rally around their daughter.

Another challenge for young adults is marriage, which is deeply impacted by gender differences and gender discrimination in various ways. Each social group in the Indian context, be it a caste, religion, or tribe, has its own rules and regulations that define the practices of social relations within the group and outside the group. Marriage as a social institution establishes social relations between the members of two families. It is largely regulated by the norms and values of the groups and society. In the same way, choice of marriage is also much influenced by caste and religious norms and values. Here, individual preferences are constrained by the groups' norms. At this juncture, higher education has a potential role in shaping the marital choices of students (Ramshenna & Gundemeda, 2015).

Marriage patterns are changing through much of the developing world. Young men and women are waiting until they are older to marry, they are marrying someone closer to their own age, and they have more say about whom they marry. However long they wait, almost everyone marries or enters a marriage-like relationship. For many, the marriage is a key component of the transition to adulthood. As health and longevity improve and women become more financially independent, partnering trends also appear to be changing. Growth in female education and economic activity and rapid cultural changes in family norms have been taking place alongside a postponement and decline in marriage. The decline in early marriage is quite widespread, lending support to the notion that global changes are having widespread effects on personal behaviour. Not only is reduction in early marriage occurring in many settings, it is also occurring, in some regions, over a relatively wide age span. This suggests that policy shifts, like increases in the legal age at marriage; social shifts, like the expansion of education; or ideological shifts, like a change in norms regarding very early marriage, all contribute to the changes observed.

Marriageable age is an important factor, governed by social control as is the compulsion of marriage. While sociologists think of marriage as a social institution, psychologists regard it as the most intimate relationship (just like live-in). In India, young adults are caught in this psychosocial trap! If it is indeed a matter of intimacy, then in love and attraction, choice should be crucial. However, if it continues to be a social institution where families marry families (like they do in India), then family, relatives, and kinship networks control marriage, with youngsters having nominal or almost no say in the matter. It is not surprising that most marriages in India continue to be arranged and endogamous (within the same caste, sub-caste, and religion) and have spawned and sustained a marriage industry! The challenge for young adults comes in when they want to or do defy norms, fall in love, and choose a partner on their own. There is severe familial and social opposition when it comes to inter-caste, inter-regional, religious, national love! It means battling it out with kith and kin, facing estrangement (more for girls) and losing property rights and rights over familial wealth and social support, besides facing social sanctions and death threats. Very few youngsters muster the courage to defy social norms and strike out on their own financially, socially, and psychologically and choose their loved partner.

On the other hand, the choice to not get married and stay single, live-in relationships, and premarital sex too continue to face more severe censure in most Asian cultures, including India, as compared to the West. LGBT youngsters are forced into heterosexual marriages and end up facing several mental health issues. Since Section 377 was decriminalized, queer youngsters and older adults have been able to breathe more freely, but several rights, such as the rights to same-sex marriage, ownership of property, employment, equal and dignified treatment at the workplace, parenting, adoption, and social acceptance as equal citizens, are still far away from the horizon. (More information on this will follow in the chapter on exploring sexualities and gender.)

The problems faced by transgender persons are many. Since their sexual and gender identities are non-normative, it has been difficult to find a legal category for them since laws operate within the gender binaries of male and female! It is instructive to understand what psychosocial challenges they face the world over. For example, in the 2015 U.S. Transgender Survey, nearly half the respondents reported being verbally harassed in the past year for being transgender. Nine per cent said they had been physically attacked. Hui Liu, a professor of sociology at Michigan State University, suggests it is likely that having a legally recognized marriage is especially important for transgender people because they are more likely to lack economic, social, and psychological resources relative to the general population. In this sense, the marriage-equality movement and resulting policies to increase transgender people's access to legal marriage should be effective in

74 Gender and Developmental Psychology

reducing trans persons' experiences of discrimination (Lawson, 2017). This does not mean that marriage results in a decrease in discrimination; rather, it equips them to handle discriminatory experiences better.

In India, traditionally, Section 377 has been used to criminalize and harass the trans community. The moment one is visibly trans is when it is presumed that one is engaging in activities that Section 377 seeks to curb. Thus, gender identity and sexual orientation have a nexus. There is a vast range of laws that are all gendered in their applications, not just family laws, and there is no clarity regarding how a trans person would be able to deal with these laws – those on marriage, adoption, succession, inheritance, and so on (Bhattacharya, 2016). Hence, the challenges faced by them are manifold. Though there is some inclusion of them in education and employment, it remains more the exception than the norm. (More elaborate information on this point will be given in the next chapter.)

4.5 Old Age and Gender Differences

The last stage of development is old age. This stage is also marked by gender differences, risks, and challenges. Let us understand the situation across the world. Older adults have the highest rates of suicide of any age group in the United States, and depression is the foremost risk factor. In addition, stressors common in late life, such as loss of loved ones, relocation, health conditions, caregiving demands, change in employment status, and poverty, significantly affect the health and independence of older adults. There is increasing evidence across behavioural and neurophysiological domains that gender differences play a prominent role in modulating the effects of aging on brain function. The overall finding is that age-related decline begins earlier in men than in women. The decline is most pronounced in frontotemporal regions of the brain, associated with attention, inhibition, and memory (Gur & Gur, 2002).

The general demographic argument is that because women have greater longevity worldwide, they constitute much of the older population, although this is less so in Asia than in the West (Knodel & Saengtienchai, 1999). Moreover, because the proportion of women among the elderly increases with age, they form a particularly large share of the oldest old, to the extent that older populations experience greater poverty or health problems; women are typically assumed to experience a greater share of such difficulties (Mehta, 1997). Also, because women have greater longevity and tend to marry men who are older than they are, researchers have argued that elderly women are more likely to care for ailing spouses, more likely to experience marital dissolution through widowhood and less likely to remarry.

Even though many of the diseases or conditions common to later life are experienced by both men and women, the actual rates, trends, and specific types differ between the genders. While some of these differences are the result of physiological differences, to fully understand ageing and health, a gender perspective is required. To illustrate, almost everywhere in the world, cardiovascular diseases are

Gender and Developmental Psychology **75**

the main killer of older people of both genders, yet it is commonly thought of as a male disease and, as a result, often goes undiagnosed in women, particularly in low- and lower-middle-income countries. On the other hand, men are more likely than women to avoid seeking medical help at least until a disease has progressed. A gender analysis should be applied no matter what the issue being considered is, be it abuse, emergencies, health promotion, primary healthcare, supportive environments, or income security (WHO, 2008). Despite the enormous medical progress made over the past few decades, the fact remains that the last years of life are still often accompanied by increasing ill health and disability. The key factor in healthy ageing is the ability to maintain independent living for as long as possible. Effective programmes promoting healthy ageing and preventing disability in older people would result in more efficient use of health and social services and would improve the quality of life of older persons through enabling them to remain independent and productive.

The gender perspective on the health of men, including ageing men, builds on experience from the women's health movement, although it is much less articulated. This perspective recognizes that the health of men cannot be separated from their socially constructed roles. In turn, these roles are strongly influenced by culturally dominant views on masculinity. The social construction of masculinity, the way men are expected to behave, appears to be an important determinant of the health of men in all societies. Men's health is inevitably influenced by the nature of their social relationships. On the basis of the perceived lack of male skills in building social networks and familial ties, a substantial proportion of older men may be more isolated and less socially supported than women. It is known that appropriate social integration is beneficial to health. Of course, a global approach to the health of ageing men and women cannot neglect the health needs of older men and women living in affluent countries. However, if this global approach is to be meaningful, it must be driven by the perspectives and needs of older men and women in the poorer regions. The health of indigenous older men and women must also be considered as part of this global perspective. Many groups of older indigenous men and women are at a disadvantage from a health perspective for reasons intimately related to their experience of colonialism and ongoing experience of racism (WHO, 2008).

One of the crises that ageing adults face is 'empty nest syndrome' – the depression, loss of purpose, and crisis of identity that parents, especially mothers, supposedly feel when their children leave home. Sociologists popularized the term in the 1970s, and the media has helped make its existence part of conventional wisdom (Clay, 2003). More recently, several psychologists have begun taking a more nuanced look at this transition. They acknowledge that parents do feel a sense of loss when their nests empty, but they have also found that this period can be one of increased satisfaction and improved relationships. Some findings even challenge the notion that an empty nest is hardest on women – if anything, one research suggests, it may be men who do not fare so well when children

76 Gender and Developmental Psychology

leave home. According to Fingerman (2002), most parents enjoy greater freedom, a reconnection with their spouses and more time to pursue their own goals and interests once their children leave home. Parents in her studies report that seeing a child start on the path towards successful adulthood gives them a feeling of joy and pride. Most importantly, the parent–child relationship improves for many of them when children leave home. Other psychologists' research reveals another unexpected benefit of the empty-nest period: a renewal of ties with other family members. 'The research is very caught up in the parent/child relationship and the marital relationship, but there are a lot of other important relationships,' says Victoria Bedford, PhD, an associate professor in the School for Psychological Sciences and the Center for Aging & Community at University of Indianapolis. 'This is not to say that the parent/child relationship and the marital relationship aren't important; they're just not the whole picture.'

First introduced in 1914 by writer Dorothy Canfield, the concept of 'empty nest syndrome' was clinically identified and popularized in the 1970s as a group of symptoms, including depression, loneliness, and low self-esteem, found among mothers whose last child had recently moved out of the family home. A great deal of sociological research since then has sought to find out how the 'empty nest' relates to mothers' (and to a lesser extent fathers') well-being and how other circumstances, like being employed outside the home, may influence the experience. Helen M. DeVries, PhD, is one of the psychologists who started researching on the empty nest when her own experience did not conform to societal expectations. According to DeVries' research, it is men who are more likely to have a demanding time when their children leave home. Of course, says DeVries, all bets are off when the children fail to make a successful transition. One woman in her sample had a child who was not doing well; as a result, she felt reluctance about pursuing her own goals, guilt about her performance as a mother, and a nagging sense of responsibility.

The empty nest syndrome in the Indian context often translates into a price paid by middle- and upper-middle-class parents (especially mothers) whose primary responsibility is their children. I have seen many such mothers who have sacrificed their work and hobbies to dedicate themselves to their children (and families and kinship networks). It is when middle age and old age set in that they face loneliness, helplessness, feelings of worthlessness, and low self-esteem. Once the 'young birds' have flown from the coop, these mothers feel a deep sense of lack of achievement and accomplishment. Their life seems hollow without the chores that they did for their children, well into the latter's youth: picking them up from and dropping them at school, coaching classes, hobby classes, playground, friend's place, and so on, taking care of their studies, food, clothes, and daily routine, and supervising and monitoring their lives, and the micromanagement that goes with it. They face a terrible void in their lives and may go through distress and depression. They must learn to go back to their earlier interests, hobbies, and pursuits to get their life back to normal. Bonding with the husband/partner also has to be improved.

Perimenopause and menopause set in among women in their mid-50s or late 50s and pose a lot of physical and psychological challenges. Taking note of this, psychologists have studied this phenomenon in detail. Some, but not all, studies suggest that perimenopause and midlife are associated with the occurrence of substantially more negative life events compared to at other stages of a woman's life. For example, Greene and Cooke (1980) reported that perimenopausal women reported more negative life events than younger women. Additionally, they observed an increase in negative life events, predominantly reflected in the occurrence of events related to interpersonal losses (e.g. children leaving the home, death of parents), consistent with the construct of the empty nest syndrome. In contrast to Greene and Cooke, Dinnerstein et al. (2001) observed that empty nest–type events were neither confined to midlife nor necessarily associated with negative moods (in fact, these were more typically associated with positive mood states). Nonetheless, both Greene and Cooke and Dinnerstein found that the presence of negative life events was associated with perimenopausal moods and behavioural symptoms.

On the other hand, there have been very few studies about men in their mid-50s or late 50s and approaching old age who go through andropause or climacteric and its psychological effects. Old men and old women who were career professionals also face the reality of retirement during this life stage. This too creates a vacuum in their lives. Older men and women who superannuate or take voluntary retirement at an earlier age must prepare and plan for this minutely, beforehand, to avoid and reduce psychological pain and helplessness. They must be ready to relinquish their role of breadwinner/earner and organizational role to one of advisor/mentor/supporter in the private and public spheres. In this period of life, the relationship between the older couple is tested: Can they be companions for one another, help each other in withstanding the physical and psychological changes and challenges related to ageing and 'age together, happily and gracefully'?

Older women go through dilemmas, like whether they should dye their hair to look younger/young or whether they should resort to hormone replacement therapy (with all its side effects and drawbacks) to retain their vitality. Old men go through phases of toying with the idea of retaining their sexual energy through using Viagra and resorting to hitting the gym with a new-found fervour to clutch on to the end of youthfulness. Younger persons in the family need to understand that at this age the older persons need empathy, support, and encouragement to go through this phase of life.

Over the last 15 years or so, remarriage among the elderly has become, if not common, at least more frequent than before in India. Matrimonial portals today include several profiles of senior citizens, and services have sprung up catering exclusively to second marriages. These are seeing a steady growth in registrations of people aged 60 and above. The reasons are simple: life expectancy is up from 32 years at the time of independence to over 67 today. According to the 2011 census, 10.38 crore Indians are over 60. Many are single or divorced or have lost their spouse and are looking for a new beginning, for another shot at a relationship.

78 Gender and Developmental Psychology

Facilitating the marriages of elderly people can raise issues that are vastly different from those that concern younger couples. Health requires earnest consideration, with chronic and other ailments being causes for worry. Financial stability is also a cause for concern. Assets can indeed become a thorny issue, and the older couple must be practical about this. In recent years, children are becoming increasingly open to the idea of finding, and even actively coming forward to find, partners for their parents. Bengaluru-based Shanthi Kotresh, who conducts matchmaking events for senior citizens and for persons with disabilities, says that she sees people come to her accompanied by their children. In some cases, the children live in another city or work full-time and are not able to care for their parent and would like them to find a partner (Hamid, 2018). Live-in relationships among the upper middle class and upper class in cities are on the rise too, and acceptance for them is slowly increasing.

This is not the universal norm, however. For old persons who are poor, disabled, and/or queer, social and familial support is missing, their financial resources are meagre, they have very little or no access to health and mental healthcare, and they must depend on the government or NGOs for help and assistance in being looked after.

Review Questions

1 What are the major gender differences in the challenges faced by boys and girls in childhood, adolescence, and youth?
2 How do gender stereotypes influence career choices of young adults?
3 What are the hazards encountered by various genders and categories of old persons?

Critical Thinking Questions

1 What images do the following terms create: 'male chauvinistic pig', 'toxic masculinity', 'misogyny', 'feminazi', 'wimp', 'woke', and 'gender sensitive'? Comment.
2 Reflect on the following terms: 'gender-sensitive parenting', 'gender-equal career opportunities', and 'queer-affirmative workplaces'.

Bibliography

Acock, A. C. (1984). Parents and their children: The study of intergenerational influences. *Sociology and Social Research, 68,* 151–171.

Bhattacharya, U. (2016). *The transgender community and legal researchers on the transgender bill 2016.* www.thecitizen.in/index.php/en/newsdetail/index/7/9471/the-transgender-community-and-legal-researchers-on-the-transgender-bill-2016

Bowlby, J. (1980). *Attachment and loss: Vol. III: Loss: Sadness and depression.* Basic Books.

Chatterjee, M. (1987). *A situation analysis of women from birth to twenty (the report of the national workshop on the girl child).* NIPPCD.

Chowdhury, A. (2007). *Domestic violence against elderly women in South Orissa: A study of incidence, patterns, and perspectives (project report)*. National Commission for Women.

Clay, R. A. (2003). An empty nest can promote freedom, improved relationships. *American Psychological Association, 34*(4), 40.

Connell, R. W. (1995). *Masculinities*. University of California Press.

Corliss, H. L., Goodenow, C. S., Nichols, L., & Bryn Austin, S. (2011). High burden of homelessness among sexual-minority adolescents: Findings from a representative Massachusetts high school sample. *American Journal of Public Health, 101*(9), 1683–1689. https://dx.doi.org/10.2105/AJPH.2011.300155

Dhar, D., Jain, T., & Jayachandran, S. (2014). *Intergenerational transmission of gender attitudes: Evidence from India*. www.isid.ac.in/~epu/acegd2014/papers/DivaDhar.pdf

Dinnerstein, L., Lehert, P., Dudley, Emma, B. S., & Guthrie, J. (2001). Factors contributing to positive mood during the menopausal transition. *The Journal of Nervous and Mental Disease, 189*(2), 84–89.

Dwedar, M. (2016). *'Like walking through a hailstorm' discrimination against LGBT youth in US schools*. Human Rights Watch. www.hrw.org/report/2016/12/07/walking-through-hailstorm/discrimination-against-lgbt-youth-us-schools

Fingerman, K. L. (2002). *Mothers and their adult daughters: Mixed emotions, enduring bonds*. Springer.

Gilbert, L. A. (1993). *Two careers/one family*. SAGE Publications.

Greene, J. G., & Cooke, D. J. (1980). Life stress and symptoms at the climacterium, *The British Journal of Psychiatry, 136* (5), 486–491. https://doi.org/10.1192/bjp.136.5.486

Gur, R. E., & Gur, R. C. (2002). Gender differences in aging: Cognition, emotions, and neuroimaging studies. *Dialogues in Clinical Neuroscience, 4*(2), 197–210.

Hamid, Z. (2015). Depression stalks LGBT youth. *The Hindu*. www.thehindu.com/news/cities/chennai/depression-stalks-lgbt-youth/article7127900.ece

Hamid, Z. (2018). They are 60, 70 or 80 years of age and finding love again. *The Hindu*, 13 January. www.thehindu.com/society/love-again-they-are-60-70-or-80-and-finding-life-partners/article22429443.ece

Hamieh, C. S., & Usta, J. (2011, March). *The effects of socialization on gender discrimination and violence (Oxfam research report)*. Oxfam.

Holmes, J., & Marra, M. (2010). Introduction. In *Femininity, feminism, and gendered discourse* (pp. 1–18). Cambridge Scholars Publishing.

Katz-Wise, S. L., Rosario, M., & Tsappis, M. (2016). LGBT youth and family acceptance. *Pediatric Clinics of North America, 63*(6), 1011–1025. http://doi.org/10.1016/j.pcl.2016.07.005

Knodel, J., & Saengtienchai, C. (1999). Studying living arrangements of the elderly: Lessons from a quasi-qualitative case study approach in Thailand. *Journal of Cross-Cultural Gerontology, 14*(3), 197–220.

Lawson, K. (2017). *Marriage could offer more protections to transgender couples*. www.brides.com/story/marriage-could-offer-more-protections-to-transgender-couples

Marks, J., Bun, L. C., & McHale, S. M. (2009). Family patterns of gender role attitudes. *Sex Roles, 61*(3–4), 221–234. http://doi.org/10.1007/s11199-009-9619-3

Mcguinness, T. M., Dyer, J. G., & Wade, E. H. (2012). Gender differences in adolescent depression. *Journal of Psychosocial Nursing and Mental Health Services, 50*, 17–20. https://dx.doi.org/10.3928/02793695-20121107-04

Mehta, K. (1997). The impact of the ageing revolution on Asian women. In *Untapped resources: Women in ageing societies across Asia* (pp. 1–6). Times Academic Press.

Merighi, J. R., & Grimes, M. D. (2000). Coming out to families in a multicultural context. *Families in Society, 81*(1), 32–41. https://doi.org/10.1606/1044-3894.1090

80 Gender and Developmental Psychology

Patkar, A., Aidara, R., & Winkler, I. T. (2016). *From taboo to empowerment: Menstruation and gender equality.* openDemocracy. www.wsscc.org/2016/05/27/taboo-empowerment-menstruation-gender-equality/

Quintini, G. (2016). *Gender differences in career choices and their consequences.* https://oecdskillsandwork.wordpress.com/2016/03/08/gender-differences-in-career-choices-and-their-consequences/

Rajesh, & Aslam Naved, M. D. (2013). *Approach paper on education and employment opportunities & challenges for transgender.* Ministry of Social Justice and Empowerment Government of India. www.socialjustice.nic.in/pdf/appendix5

Rajkumar, D. (2016 [2011], November). Education of transgenders in India: Status and challenges. *International Journal of Research in Economics and Social Sciences*, 6(11), 15–24.

Ramshenna, C. A., & Gundemeda, N. (2015). Youth and marriage: A study of changing marital choices among the university students in India. *Journal of Sociology and Social Anthropology*, 6(1), 137–147.

Rao, G. (2011). *Gaps in health, protection, and education especially evident in adolescence.* UNICEF. www.unicef.org/media/media_59777.html

Stanko, E. (1990). *Everyday violence: How women and men experience sexual and physical danger.* Pandora/Unwin Hyman.

WHO. (2008). *Men, ageing and health: Achieving health across the life span (WHO/NMH/NPH 01.2).* WHO.

WHO. (2017). *Gender inequality in early adolescence must be addressed for health and well-being throughout life.* www.who.int/reproductivehealth/topics/adolescence/early-adolescence/en/

WHO. (n.d.). *Gender and ageing.* www.who.int/ageing/gender/en/

Wills, O. (2017). *Breaking the menstrual taboo: Why period stigma still holds women back, Ladies, we need to talk.* www.abc.net.au/news/health/2017-09-30/menstrual-cycle-taboo-holds-women-back/8996526

5
GENDER AND THE WORKPLACE

Chapter Highlights

Learning Objectives

After reading this chapter, the students would be able to

- Understand different models of career development and their gender analysis.
- Contemplate on different debates around career and family/social relational aspects.
- Identify the challenges one faces with respect to gender, career, and work.

Introduction

Since young adulthood, people of all genders aspire for various careers. It is not just skills and opportunities that make their aspirational dreams come true; they must also deal with gender-related hurdles to achieve their goals. Making choices about one's career as per one's interest is not a given as many of us imagine it to be. Family, peer and societal pressures, caste, class, gender, sexuality, gender stereotypes, and ideas of prestige, glamour, and fame are important influencers when young adults make career choices. Mainstream models look at this phenomenon in a linear fashion, while feminist models look at the subtler aspects of this process. Whether there is a real level playing field as far as higher education and transition to employment are concerned is a question that begs an answer. When men and women enter the workforce, women must wrestle with the complex issues of straddling their familial world along with their professional one. Have women's choices changed after more than 70 years of middle-class women's entering the workforce, or are they still plagued with the same dilemmas of marriage or work, family or

DOI: 10.4324/9781003453758-6

82 Gender and the Workplace

work, and how to balance family and work? When men climb the ladder of professional success, we are still resorting to the cliché that 'behind every successful man, there is a woman', while women are still expected to sacrifice or compromise careers, promotions, and professional challenges on the altar of marriage and family life. What are the familial and societal forces that have kept up this gender divide? This chapter will delve into this matter. There have been a few changes on the ground, where with D&I becoming a buzz phrase, some women must be included in the workplace to comply with D&I rules. Even with this tokenism being executed, the LGBTIQ community, the disabled, people from marginalized castes, and those with psychosocial disabilities continue to remain off the radar of a substantial number of workplaces. People of all genders are facing the challenges of sexual harassment at the workplace despite having laws in place. The ways to overcome such challenges are also addressed in this chapter. Work–life balance is also viewed as an employed woman's concern, and this point of view needs to be changed – this issue is duly examined. The erstwhile 'glass ceiling' has collapsed, but what new tightropes women, queer people, new employees, and those from marginalized castes must navigate in workplaces is also interrogated.

5.1 Models of Career Development and Their Gender Analysis

The models of career development from mainstream psychology (e.g., Holland's and Super's models) need to be analysed from a gender and intersection lens. In this section, there is an attempt to do so. Right from childhood up to young adulthood, career dreams and aspirations take wings. Ambitions are fuelled by many factors, such as but not limited to personal and family influences and expectations, information, and exposure to careers and aptitude testing (especially in urban areas). It is a well-established fact that many of the old-fashioned occupational tests and interest inventories are gender biased. They either push girls into gender-typed occupations, such as 'nursing' and 'teaching', or subtly tilt them away from 'manly occupations', such as 'medicine' and 'engineering'. They also carry racial and caste biases. Through active and engaged gender sensitization, affirmative action policies, the mechanism of hiring in workplaces has improved over the years. But it is still a matter of 'too little too late', and there is a lot of subjectivity in biases/or lack of them depending on how liberal senior management and experts involved in the process are. The system of fair, equal opportunities for all level playing field at the entry point in workplaces is still a distant dream.

Very often, boys' dreams are given 'wings' (familial readiness to put in money, encouraging them for glamorous, well-paid jobs), while girls must be content with 'roots' (stay at home, do not pursue more adventurous or risky jobs, do not take up jobs, and/or sign up for courses outside your hometown)! While growing up, boys and girls have played with different toys, read different sets of books, and have had gendered exposure and experiences. This impacts them while making career choices in numerous ways. For instance, '[a]t age 6, girls draw 70 percent of scientists as women, but this proportion flips around ages 10 to 11 and by 16, they draw around 75 percent of scientists as men' (Miller et al., 2018).

Key Insight

The first female physician and first female surgeon in the world were told they were better off as 'nurses' and had to fight for their right to make an entry in their respective fields. The first Indian female doctors, Dr Anandibai Joshi and Dr Kadambini Ganguly, had to contend with patriarchy, racism, and gender inequality to qualify and become doctors. In current times we cannot even imagine how damaging all this was for their self-esteem!

Now, let us understand how Holland's model explains career development. Holland classified people into six personality types and occupations into six ideal work environments as follows. Realistic personality-type persons are more suitable for the careers such as machine operator, pilot, draftsperson, and engineer. The investigative personality type is suited for such careers as marine biologist, computer programmer, clinical psychologist, architect, and dentist. Those with an artistic personality would find a career as a sculptor, actor, designer, musician, author, or editor a good match. Those with a social personality would match with the career of a counsellor, nurse, teacher, social worker, judge, minister, or sociologist. Persons with an enterprising personality should choose the career of a realtor, politician, attorney, salesperson, or manager. Lastly, those with a conventional personality are best suited to become bankers, accountants, timekeepers, financial counsellors, typists, and receptionists.

While this seems like a cohesive paradigm, how does it hold up when viewed through a gender lens? There is an assumption that while making these 'choices' there is an equal opportunity for exposure, exploration, and experimentation for all young adults, whereas the social reality is that economic, social, and gender-related factors impact these choices or take them away from many. For instance, let us consider a hypothetical situation where there are young adults from diverse backgrounds who attempt a battery of tests (personality, aptitude, interest) and discover that they have an 'investigative' personality. Would they be able to pursue careers indicated for that personality type? The cost, support, guidance, and social and cultural capital essential for both the entrance exams and these courses are out of the reach of most poor girls and boys, those from marginalized castes, tribes, or minority religions and the poor from the queer community. Hence, while this model is useful, it does not become accessible or meaningful for many young adults in India, as well as the rest of the world, who do not have the means and social, cultural, and economic capital for it.

84 Gender and the Workplace

According to Super's model (Zaccaria, 1970), people go through five stages and several sub-stages of occupational development during their lifespan. These include growth, exploration, establishment, maintenance, and decline. How are these stages gendered? In the growth stage (0–14 years, early childhood education, primary education), in India, a maximum number of girls, as well as some boys, from marginalized communities drop out of school due to poverty, schools being far away, or schools not having resources (material and human) in poorer villages and districts, as well as in poorer parts of urban spaces. In the exploration stage (15–24 years), if we take the example of STEMM in India, what I hear from my students from mofussil parts of India, as well as from rare urban cases (and see in my fieldwork and in documentaries and read in published research too), is that they rarely 'perform experiments'. Lack of infrastructure and poor material resources are the causes for this. Thus, the students either end up observing a teacher performing experiments or simply reproduce an experiment from an old journal as 'practical work'. Gender stereotypes abound, perpetuating notions such as 'girls are not good at maths' and 'it is not safe for them to work for long hours'. Discriminatory practices in schools, colleges, and homes compound the problems, and hence women, especially students from rural areas, find it very challenging to enter the domains of STEMM. Over the last two decades, professional education in India has become so expensive that most young adults from poor families find it out of their reach.

In the establishment stage (25–44 years), crucial choices about both career and marriage are made. Family, household tasks, and parenting are pitted against career entry, advancement, challenges, opportunities, and growth. Once again, women must work twice as hard as men to prove themselves – the glass ceiling is still there, albeit in a changed form; they also give up their jobs to take care of children, and LGBTIQ persons are restricted by gatekeeping (in education, as well as employment, with social and economic constraints working against them). With the multiple patriarchies that exist in India (as they do the world over), it is only those who are above others in social systems (caste, class, gender, sexuality, region) who get to 'establish themselves'. The institutional murders of both Rohith Vemula and Dr Payal Tadvi (among the many that have gone unrecorded) are cases in point with regard to the struggle that those from underprivileged backgrounds must face to establish themselves in professional careers (Natu, 2022).

The maintenance (45–64 years) and decline (65+ years) stages once again create problems of 'empty nest syndrome' (more for women), and physiological changes create challenges in the professional space as well (more for women). Very few women get to become 'complete career professionals' and achieve their full potential; they end up being employees who are dispensable, at worst, and at best, they get token promotions in order for the management to check the box of 'equal opportunity workplace' or bow to D&I checklists. This happens because becoming a career professional is a 24×7 job, and women have to face double burden/ double drudgery of the pressure of the workplace as well as catering to families and

Gender and the Workplace **85**

homes. This requires time, social and familial support, and multitasking which is not possible for many women. The personal and public sphere patriarchies are very challenging, and a lot of women cannot navigate them and do justice to the task of becoming a career professional and thriving.

In this way, when we look at these models of career development from a gender perspective, a nuanced understanding emerges. While they may be useful to a certain extent, they cannot be adopted in a linear fashion by several young adults who face economic, social, cultural, and gender-related hurdles while trying to achieve their career goals.

5.2 Maternal Employment and Gender

As early as the 1940s and 1950s, many studies attempted to determine the negative impact of their mothers' employment on children (Siegel, 1961). During those years, the benefits to the children of employed mothers were not studied (Jacklin & Mc-Bride-Chang, 1991). In psychology, human development, and family studies literature, as well as in society, up to the 1960s and 1970s, there was a constant discussion on the harmful impact of working mothers on their children! As a feminist psychologist, I prefer to use the term 'employed mothers' and not 'working' or 'non-working mothers', since all women work! Some of the work is unpaid (housework), and some of it is paid (employment). Let us understand how this discourse got built from the 1940s up to the 1990s in many countries in the world, including India.

The world over, the entry of middle-class women into the workforce (more in volume from the Second World War (1939) onwards) brought in a new era for women which shaped society's views about them. However, to dichotomize women's lives in terms of career versus marriage and motherhood has been problematic. It has not been marriage but motherhood and, specifically, women's responsibilities at the stage of family formation that have been germane to understanding women's entry into the labour force (Oerton, 1996). From the early days of research on gender and employment, there have been two conflicting views on whether the movement of women into paid work would drastically alter their lives.

'One' view has been that paid work changed little; women are exploited at home, and paid work is merely another form of enslavement. More women are spending more of their lives in paid employment outside the home, yet most women still see their main role as caring for the husband and children at the family home (Miranda, 1995). It has been suggested that women have acquired a dual role, or 'double burden', in which their paid employment is combined with their unpaid domestic labour for the family. This has also been called 'double drudgery'. It has been argued that this modification of gender-based division of labour, rather than its transformation, is the crux of the matter. In fact, the subordination of women in the family allowed for the specific exploitation of women at work.

86 Gender and the Workplace

The 'other' view has been that paid work changed women's lives a great deal; it gave them theoretical equality with men, financial independence, and broader horizons. Despite the low status of much of women's employment, a work identity, alongside the identity of being a wife and mother, has clearly been important to women. According to the second view, it is not surprising that women are reluctant to give up paid work, no matter how ill-paid or unrewarding such work may be. However, women's employment profiles or careers have not been systematically investigated from the point of view of women as self-reflexive, subjective agents, that is, what their aspirations as individuals are, if they have achieved their dreams, if they are satisfied with their professional success, and so on. This means that there has been more focus on determining how women negotiate their role as a wife and a mother and their professional lives, rather than on understanding their careers as individual persons. Their aspirational needs as persons/individuals have not been fully studied and understood.

This is obvious from the fact that in all sectors of work, women are asked questions about their marital status, the number of children, childcare, and so on, which are not asked to male candidates during a job interview! This is how the discrimination in workplaces starts, right at the entry point. This holds true for subtle preferences given to privileged castes and classes as well as heterosexual individuals, where oblique questions are asked to ascertain 'their background' and 'the vibe' they give are checked.

As we delve deeper into the debates around maternal employment, we come across some interesting facts. It is assumed that paid employment may provide exposure to non-traditional roles for women. Therefore, employed mothers are more supportive of beliefs and actions related to gender equality and have more flexible gender roles. It is possible that in child rearing they might show a more egalitarian approach (not discriminate between sons and daughters).

The most influential and persistent theoretical debate about maternal employment has been conducted largely within the psychology of child development, often referred to as 'working mothers' debate'. It is a consequence of the 'attachment theory' that said that the emotional development of a child depended to a large extent on the child's relationship with one person – the mother (Bowlby, 1951). The psychological studies on child rearing have focused almost exclusively on the importance of stable, full-time mothering (Bowlby, 1951). Shared child rearing has been discussed in the context of maladjustment – typically whether day care led to insecure attachment in children.

The approach has been to presume that the employment of the mother is disruptive for the family and damaging to the child (Broffenbrenner & Crounter, 1982). This discourse on motherhood highlighted the detrimental effects of 'maternal separation' or 'maternal deprivation' (Bowlby, 1951). It was reinforced by the media of that time: newspapers, magazines, television shows, and so on. In the West, magazines exhorted women to concentrate on mothering and not take up jobs or

Gender and the Workplace **87**

not go back to their jobs after childbirth. In India too, similar messaging was done through popular women's literature of those times.

Consequently, a lot of 'mother-blaming' studies took place in developmental psychology. To cite a few examples: mothers have been blamed for autism, which is now believed to be largely a disorder of the cerebellum; they have been blamed for schizophrenia, which is now believed to be largely genetic and related to neural transmitters (Meltzer, 1987 as reported in Miranda, 1995); and they have been blamed for psychosomatic diseases, emotionally maladjusted children (Miranda, 1995), homosexuality, stuttering, and a large variety of negatively marked phenomena (Miranda, 1995).

While mainstream psychology was flooded with such research, many studies by Hoffman (1989, p. 89) highlighted that 'maternal employment' per se does not adversely affect children; the argument continues to be framed in terms of whether and to what extent children suffer from the lack of full-time mothering, rather than the extent to which children and mothers thrive when the care of children is shared with others. A typical solution offered is for the mothers to balance work and childcare through working part-time (Hoffman, 1989; Hoffman & Nye, 1974).

Feminist psychologists pointed out that it was not 'maternal deprivation or separation' but merely 'maternal absence' for some hours that happens in case of employed mothers. This led to only grudging acceptance of maternal employment and not positive approval. There are conditions attached to this acceptance. The major responsibility of the children remains with the mothers. Maternal employment is acceptable only if the mothers continue to discharge this responsibility. It is only since the late 1990s that 'absent fathers' and lack of sharing of the parental role and responsibilities have been discussed and debated!

There is a belief that childcare is a totally private responsibility to be managed within the household, without any external support. However, in France and in countries of Scandinavia, some degree of social responsibility for childcare is accepted. In Denmark, it is accepted that the parents and society would jointly share this responsibility. In Sweden too, the society ensures that the children obtain good-quality childcare. Economically, this has been a pipe dream for most underdeveloped countries, as well as developing countries, like India, where social responsibility for childcare and availability of the affordable and good-quality childcare facilities that an employed couple need are still scarce.

Some ground has been gained with the following aspects being brought to the fore: the employed mother brings financial gains to the family; she becomes a role model for both daughters and sons; and her sense of self-fulfilment, as well as enjoyment of the maternal role, is beneficial to the children and family. Whether this could help in smoothing out the family dynamics depends on her own validation of her role as a professional and the validation from significant others (spouse, family, offspring; Natu, 2002).

88 Gender and the Workplace

In India, too, the theoretical underpinnings of maternal employment have followed an identical path, as suggested by the preoccupation with role conflict and the problems of working women. The assumption has been that the role of a homemaker and nurturer is natural and a source of gratification for a woman. When she ventures into employment, it is her role at the workplace (by virtue of not being natural) that becomes stressful, while the home is thought to be a stress-free refuge and protective shelter (Sudhakar & Rao, 1988). Also, role conflict among employed mothers/women is a relatively middle-class and post-independence phenomenon in India, and lately of upper-middle-class women, illustrative of only a small segment of Indian women (Sudhakar & Rao, 1988).

For boys, maternal employment might influence their concept of the female role, but its effects on their attitudes towards the father and themselves depend on the circumstances surrounding the maternal employment. The effects of maternal employment are much less clear for sons, perhaps because the modelling theory is less direct for them and depends on how maternal employment affects the father's role (Hoffman & Nye, 1974). Natu (2002) also found that the mother's self-image and the father's egalitarian approach or lack of it contributed in a major way towards the son's attitude towards employed mothers and employed women in general.

In the last 25 years, there has been more acceptance of maternal employment but also the expectation that employed women will be 'super women': efficient at their workplace; house-proud; diligent at parenting; homemakers; hospitable to guests; taking care of the sick, ailing, old, so on and so forth. This is a tall order! Some men as fathers are trying to share the tasks at home, but such examples are still few and far between. Hence, all in all, middle- and upper-middle-class women are still faced with the dilemma of career versus marriage and motherhood.

The recent resignation of Jacinda Arden, PM of New Zealand, from office saying that 'she had next to nothing left in the tank' after five-and-a-half arduous years in office needs to be discussed and debated as an academic- and policy-level exercise. She wanted to get married to her long-time partner and spend time with her young daughter. The focal point about women in politics being supported by public institutions and men helping to raise children being supported in families is raised here.

Also, 'give women education and employment and their status in society will go up' has proved to be a myth – significant others, social conformity, pressure, and control, are formidable roadblocks to women living their dream of personal and professional excellence. The impact of maternal employment on sons and daughters and their mutual relationships and how the latter perceive employed women has shown mixed results. Some sons and daughters admire their mothers for all the work they do, both professionally and at home. They also help and assist their mothers. However, there are also those who feel that they have to become independent at a young age, fend for themselves, and come back from school to locked houses and miss having a homemaker mother (Natu, 2002).

Gender and the Workplace **89**

> **Key Insight**
>
> *Mothering a Muslim* by Nazia Erum throws up important questions about hatred in classrooms, prejudices that start with names, and dealing with the experience of 'othering'. This is motherhood that needed to be articulated in the Indian context. It is also important to understand the exclusion of minority motherhood from psychology and gender and the way in which this book shines a light on it.

5.3 Career Versus Marriage and Domestic-Labour Debates

> **Key Insight**
>
> PepsiCo's India-born CEO Indra Nooyi, counted among the world's most powerful women, acknowledged that it is difficult to maintain a work–life balance and that women cannot 'have it all'. She said she doubts that her daughters think she was a good mother. 'I don't think women can have it all. I just do not think so. We pretend we have it all. We pretend we can have it all'. She expressed that while the biological clock was ticking, one has the career clock ticking too! She was full of guilt that she could not be present for her daughters' activities. The entire family needs you, and you cannot cater to them. Even when she became president of PepsiCo, once she got home, her mother expected her to don the hats of wife, mother, homemaker, and daughter-in-law!

Without personalizing this vignette, if we analyse it from a psychology and gender lens, some moot questions arise.

Why is work-life balance perceived almost always as a 'woman's problem'? Men go through corresponding life stages and decision-making – on career choice, marriage, becoming a householder, fatherhood, taking care of old parents, extended family, and so on – while climbing up their occupational ladder. How is it that they rarely go through guilt pangs and do not have to negotiate between important meetings at the workplace and challenges at home? This is because employed women are expected to take up the double burden of workplace and home responsibilities. They are reared and conditioned to feel guilty about 'abandoning their home and children'; 'mother blaming' still works! Families, as well as workplaces, are patriarchal, and it is women who are thought to be transgressing if they do not prioritize the domestic sphere over professional responsibilities and opportunities. The label of 'being a bad mother' baits many employed women, and they go through a lot of stress in order to avoid it. This social trap is a big hindrance. On the other hand, it

90 Gender and the Workplace

is rare for men to take up or share responsibilities of the household. Hence, they are free to focus almost entirely on their career and enjoy their breadwinner status!

The other aspect that needs to be dealt with is that if the CEO of a multinational giant, with house staff and personal staff at the workplace, as well as support from family, could think that she was a 'bad mother' and not performing her domestic duties at par, then women with few or absolutely no resources and very little or no familial and social support have no fighting chance of 'having it all'! I have used this vignette to flag all the issues around the choices between marriage and career and between career and motherhood which women must make. It is tragic that even after years of women's education all over the world (at least for middle-class, upper-middle-class, and upper-class women), it is not smooth sailing for them, and they have to choose one over the other!

Let us understand all the aspects around these dilemmas and choices. Working-class women have no choice but 'to earn' and support their families. Hence, they have always been earning wages as farmers, agricultural labour, domestic labour, or factory workers, all in the unorganized sector, with hardly any safeguards and assurances or social security. Therefore, these dilemmas and conflicts are faced by middle-class and upper-middle-class women – employment becomes a 'choice', since economic needs are not imperative. Also, patriarchal structures restrict women from pursuing paid employment as their right. The irony is that in matrimonial ads, young men are asking for 'employed girls' so that the latter's earnings would contribute to the upkeep of the family and support consumerist lifestyles!

The other interesting aspect is about housework or domestic labour and how it has always been devalued. In all cultures across the world, it is a given that the women of the house will perform all the domestic chores. The word 'housewife' has given way to the misleading 'homemaker'. The homemaker too is as devalued as the housewife was earlier. How many of these homemakers are co-owners of property? They are merely responsible for the domestic chores that never cease while the houseowner is the man of the house!

Feminist sociologist Ann Oakley (1974) wrote about the 'I am just a housewife' syndrome, wherein housework is thought to be not work or labour but just an extension of a woman's role. It remains invisible, uncounted, discounted, and unacknowledged. Women who perform myriad tasks as housewives feel dissatisfied, suffer from low self-esteem, and say, 'I do not work. I am just a housewife.' Even now, for a lot of young women, there is still a choice between remaining homemakers alone and trying to straddle the two worlds of housework and professional work. Even after they start working, many of them feel compelled to take a break after childbirth and do not return to their professional spheres. It is a tussle between full-time motherhood (for a short time or for good) and their job/career/profession. Flexi-time work, work from home, and part-time work have emerged as alternatives, but only in some sectors and in urban spaces. Even after making such compromises, women continue to feel the pressure, both at work and at home!

Mid-chapter Exercise

A woman who qualified in the UPSC exam in India found that her eligibility in the marriage market went down several notches, since she was immediately branded as 'ambitious', 'aggressive', 'too career-minded', and so on. She was told that she would have to 'compromise' if she wanted to hear wedding bells ringing!

Can you recount coming across such instances in your vicinity? What was your immediate reaction to such assumptions? Do you agree with these thoughts? Yes/No and state your reasons.

This vignette is representative of young female achievers who also want marriage and a family (not just women in civil services but also almost all female professionals). The word 'compromise' is always bandied around and is directed at women. There is a subliminal message that if you are a professional achiever, marriage, which means compromise, may be out of bounds for you. There has been a sociocultural message that the man must be older, more educated, and earning more than the woman, and endogamy (marriage within the same caste) and intra-religious marriages are always the norm. Couples who are brave enough to attempt inter-caste and inter-religious marriage must pay a heavy price for the transgression. The Marathi movie *Sairat* produced in 2016 portrays this in a realistic fashion.

It is interesting to note that while many young men engage in professional-life management (making career choices, acquiring essential skills and qualifications, searching for the right job, and so on), very rarely do they pay attention to personal-life management. (Will they choose their own life partner? What does marriage mean to them? Would they want their partner to be employed? How would domestic tasks be shared? And so on.) In my research I found that while many young men did want to choose their life partner, they confessed that they would succumb to family pressure and give in to their family's choice. They wanted a life partner who was employed, but they had not given much thought to her career, sharing of domestic tasks, childcare when both partners would work, her identity, and so on (Natu, 2002). While young girls are aiming for the sky – achievement of professional aspirations, an equal marriage, shared domestic tasks, a loving partner, and so on – the problem is, how would young men respond to this dream? It is unfortunate that not much has changed in the last 25 years in terms of the gap between the expectations of the two genders, arranged marriages still being the norm (getting costlier and more opulent for those who can afford it and having a trickle-down effect!) and matrimonial websites that are as casteist as matchmakers and family networks thriving.

In most societies and cultures across South Asia, including India, a woman has a derived identity – she is somebody's daughter, mother, sister, wife – rather than

92 Gender and the Workplace

the autonomous identity of an individual in her own right, a person, a professional. Very rarely do women have the agency to straddle the two worlds of the public and the private and derive satisfaction from both. Their role is presumed to be synonymous with the domestic sphere, and as they move towards being part of the workforce, the double burden of home and occupational space has been a huge challenge for most middle-class and upper-middle-class women.

The bone of contention is who will perform the million domestic chores, and the traditional answer has been 'the woman'. Germane to this was the shift from an agricultural society to an industrial one, whereby women were pushed into domesticity while males became breadwinners. The women who moved out to perform occupational roles outside the home, whether due to economic exigencies, to contribute to the family income, or since they had an education and a desire to prove themselves in the professional world, were given that opportunity, provided they did not 'neglect' their familial responsibilities!

This scenario has changed only marginally in the last 50 years. Housework and childcare are still considered feminine chores, and most men either do not participate or only help and support while the main responsibilities continue to be shouldered by women! There are many reasons for this: Foremost, the traditional gender stereotypes about the male- and female-gender roles still prevail to a large extent – that women are better equipped to cook, clean, and do other housework and men are better at doing outdoor tasks and being breadwinners continues to be the popular perception. Since the woman gives birth, she is naturally more nurturing and caring, and hence she should be the primary caregiver (and often the only caregiver!). Research has proved that the only gender difference is in giving birth and breastfeeding; all the other tasks of nurture can be done equally well by both men and women.

Men want to or succeed in escaping from the domestic chores and childcare under the patriarchal garb of being 'inept' or 'ill suited'. The idea of mothers being more nurturing is essentializing their gender role and does not hold water. Both fathers and mothers can learn parenting and childcare (mothers are not intrinsically endowed with compassion and nurturance; it is socially constructed!). What is essential is a shift from 'mothering' (and the glorification of motherhood) to 'parenting', where both parents share, enjoy, and learn childcare. Many studies show that shared parenting is beneficial for children in many ways: The children learn that gender-based division of labour is not the norm (both parents are seen performing all the tasks, and there are no stereotypical men's and women's tasks), and since both parents are participating in child rearing, the children can imbibe the skills, interests, and worldviews of both parents. Men can overcome their typical masculine role and become compassionate, kind, and sensitive and reduce their aggression when they are around young children, which is beneficial to their mental health.

Much data from various sectors from India and abroad show that male employees take leaves for health reasons, whereas a majority of female employees take leave to take care of sick children or attend to ailing relatives, for domestic exigencies,

Gender and the Workplace **93**

and for personal reasons. This difference shows up because men do not have the sole responsibility (like most employed women do and which they very rarely share) of nurturing, taking care of sick relatives, or dealing with domestic crises!

The psychological guilt that employed mothers go through, often expressed as 'abandoning their children', 'being a bad mother', 'giving up their primary role of a stay-at-home mom', has to be witnessed to believe. Societal pressure is tremendous, and a lot of women succumb to it. Some mothers genuinely believe that childcare, at least for the first 2–5 years, is their sole responsibility and are willing to give up their jobs and careers. Returning to work after that period proves professionally and psychologically difficult for many of them. The only solution is for men to realize and women to believe that parenting should be a shared responsibility and for them to discuss and plan for this; such belief in egalitarian parenting would trigger a tremendous shift in the gendering of childcare.

Depictions that are given in the following Key Insight box hold true even now.

Key Insight

Media portrayals are now trying to hijack feminist agendas, like gender-sensitive roles, through applauding men in nurturing roles. Pioneers are the films like *Three Men and a Baby* and *Mrs. Doubtfire*. Can Indian versions be far behind? The remarkable *Chachi 420* and the forgettable *Aunty No. 1* are two examples. It is a curious fact that a host of comedies have been made redeeming and celebrating fatherhood. These films are interesting manifestations of the concerns for father's rights and the controversy over surrogate motherhood in the West.

Three Men and a Baby glorifies collective male fatherhood (where the father is doing the mother's work of nurture and childcare) and makes room for the mother at the very end of the film. The film speaks of the legitimate desire on the part of women for men to assume greater responsibility for childcare. It shows that it is possible for men to respond to this feminist demand in such a way as to make women more marginal than ever. It gives men more options than they already have in patriarchy – of being real fathers, imaginary fathers, godfathers, and surrogate mothers.

In *Mrs. Doubtfire* and similar Indian films, the absentee, absconding father returns in his new avatar disguised as a woman. Then he performs his caring, nurturing role, as if suggesting that a man must look like a woman, dress like a woman, and in fact 'become a woman' to do women's work (so-called feminine tasks).

The film underlines the mother's role as the surrogate, while the father (when he is discovered) is the 'real thing'. The mother is excluded from this charmed circle, and children accept the parent's separation as final only when they know that they can bask in the warm cocoon of his love via his television programme (Natu, 1998).

94 Gender and the Workplace

Lack of adequate and good-quality day care services in India is also a factor that directly impacts women's employment after childbirth. Though some corporate and government set-ups are offering this service, it has not become accessible to all, neither has it become an institutionalized practice. Also, besides day care, there is a need for participation of the father and the rest of the family in childcare and child rearing. This important point remains unaddressed and is largely dismissed as a non-issue.

While the domestic-labour debate is a hoary chestnut, there are many 'outliers': house husbands, straight couples who share parenting tasks and manage professional careers, and single parents who manage homes and careers and raise children, as well as queer parents and adoptive parents who do the same. What is it that they do differently from typical couples and families where stereotypical gender roles in parenting are followed?

The 'house husband or stay-at-home dad' has emerged as a choice for some men in Western countries, sometimes due to unemployment, disability, lower qualifications than wives who earn more, and social benefits. However, there is a small population for which this is an informed choice and where there is acceptance of undertaking of household tasks and fathering by men for the short or long term. While feminists do not want role reversal but want to share domestic labour and childcare, this turning of stereotypes on their head by choice, even if less frequent, does help in diminishing patriarchy to some extent. In India, 'what will people say' plagues most men, but there are examples of those who have been house husbands and done parenting chores for short or long terms. It has really helped them build strong bonds with their children, follow their hobbies, and take care of domestic chores – tasks normally done by women.

The most 'egalitarian model' is of course where both parents happily and with prior planning share domestic chores and childcare, including adjustments according to work demands and 'me time' for both. Though this too is a rare occurrence, in the West as well as in India, the tribe is growing slowly but steadily. What makes this work (partners in a love marriage or those who have chosen each other mutually without parental and family interference are likely to do more sharing of roles) is having a rational discussion about division of labour, planning parenthood, experiencing the joy of parenthood, and willingly sharing the tasks. The parents also need to have mutual respect for each other's education, careers, and life together and believe that since it is everybody's home, everyone needs to chip in. The man has to discard the privileges of patriarchy, and the woman too has to shed her internalized patriarchal practices, and both have to adopt egalitarian attitudes and beliefs (women are better parents, a father's task is discipline, and a mother's task is nurture, and so on).

Mid-chapter Exercise

Let me share an anecdote. A father once took his infant son for vaccination. The infant was not wearing a diaper, and the father cleaned his shit when

> he pooped. All the people around applauded him and also asked where the mother was, what she was doing, and why no female relative was accompanying him! Reflect on this scenario and react to it.

The third category of outliers is 'single parents': either a mother or a father trying to do all the work in both the domestic sphere and the professional sphere and child rearing, alone. Though this is an uphill task, many single parents are managing very well. Those in cities do have paid help, while those in rural areas get help from the extended family. Single parents defy and break the mould and stereotype of male- and female-gender parental roles: Men and women alike undertake the responsibilities of nurture, care, discipline, and socialization (training in behavioural skills, values). If this can be done when circumstances of divorce, death, or estrangement compel one to do so, the moot question is: Why cannot these sharing and mutuality be followed by cohabiting marital partners as parents?

The other unique categories are 'adoptive parents' and 'queer couples as parents'. Most adoptive parents are careful about child rearing and take their responsibilities very seriously. In most countries, they attend training on parenting. They have an opportunity to follow egalitarian patterns, since their decision is premeditated and well thought out. Queer parents also defy gender norms and break the gender binary of mothers and fathers as prescribed by society. In the case of a gay couple, the child has two fathers, and in that of a lesbian couple, two mothers. Such couples face social stigma, distancing, and alienation, but sometimes this serves to strengthen the bonds between their children and them.

Thus, this section has attempted to highlight that issues of shared parenting, role of the father in childcare and child rearing, and changing patriarchal attitudes towards women's employment have been left unresolved for a long time all over the world. This has proved detrimental to both the genders and society at large. There are also some outliers whose lived experiences need to be understood and emulated by others.

5.4 Career Development, Gender, and Intersectionality

We have discussed the various problems that women face with reference to careers and the household and family. It is also important to understand how LGBTIQ, disabled, and marginalized persons experience access to education and employment. For these groups, access to education and higher education and then opportunities for employment are slim. With D&I becoming a catchphrase in the corporate sector, some lip service is being paid to the values of D&I in principle, but employment often stops at women and does not extend to other diverse groups.

96 Gender and the Workplace

In Western countries, there are some efforts at addressing the needs of these marginalized groups, and hence there is some representation for them in education and higher education, as well as some openings in the corporate sector and in not-for-profit companies. This is because all these groups are mobilized, and they have lobbied and fought for their rights and are still negotiating with governments and corporations to secure better opportunities.

There is also an attempt being made to scrutinize the queer sensitivity of workplaces. McKinsey & Company's (Ellsworth et al., 2020) report states that there is underrepresentation and isolation of LGBTIQA+ persons in the corporate sector overall. Some of its observations are that queer persons are subjected to the following practices: being pressured to play along with sexist discussions, humour, and actions; being made targets of sexist jokes; and being made targets of sexual harassment. They face barriers, and hence there are long-term effects on their career progression, and they are unable to bring out their full self at work. Looking ahead, the report suggests creating structural support for trans employees, stamping out inappropriate behaviour, removing tokenism and widening the hiring pool from the outset, promoting inclusivity in remote working environments, and improving sponsorship to support career progression.

In India, however, the picture is far from satisfactory. That the Rights of Persons with Disabilities Act (2016) has absolved the state of performing its duties is the criticism that has been levelled against it by several disability rights groups. Calling the disabled *divyang* (celestial beings!), instead of *viklang*, which means disabled, has added insult to injury! A negligible number of schools, colleges, universities, and workplaces have basic facilities for the disabled (such as ramps, lifts, and other utilities and services for them). In such circumstances, without state and social support, higher education and employment remain outside the reach of several disabled persons, especially the rural and poor.

The Transgender Persons (Protection of Rights) Act, 2019, has miffed the community since it does not differentiate clearly between intersex and transgender persons. The act also does not acknowledge several persons who do not conform to the gender binary of male/female (we have discussed the terms 'gender-fluid' and 'pansexual' earlier). This act is supposed to give them a range of entitlements, such as provisions specifically for them in the health and education sectors, skill development, employment opportunities, and protection from abuse and torture. However, the community feels that unless the nuances of the categories are understood and representation is given to them, they would not have the full rights of a citizen, like civil rights, including the rights to marriage, partnership, divorce, and adoption. All this is a long way ahead!

In 2018, the Supreme Court of India read down Section 377 of the IPC, and many companies have been hiring LGBTIQA+ persons, with some of the fears and uncertainties getting out of the way, but this remains largely at the level of tokenism and 'pinkwashing'. Parmesh Shahani, with his book *Queeristan*, hopes that companies will understand the dos and don'ts while hiring queer people after reading his book, which reads like a manual. New efforts, like RISE (Reimagining Inclusion for Social Equity), India's first LGBTQ+ job fair held in July 2019 and February 2020, and the Indian LGBT Workplace Climate Survey of 2016, are steps in the right direction, in terms of both taking stock of the situation and taking steps in the right direction. Some companies are offering jobs, as well as facilities ranging from insurance, medical cover for gender reassignment surgeries, maternal leave benefits, and leaves for adoption to sensitization programmes for co-workers, ensuring that there is no microaggression so that queer employees feel truly included. However, such companies that are gender-fair and gender-agnostic (non-discriminating, where sexual orientation is not used to keep people away) in hiring practices are few and far between.

The nub of the problem is that engaging in window dressing for international clients and trying to prove best practices in D&I instead of making real inclusions are prevalent. Queer employees' not being able to rise to leadership positions or not taking up such positions to avoid conflicts (as is the case with many cis women) is the norm. Also, only those who are qualified candidates from among the LGBTIQA+ community can make inroads into the corporate space, while the less-educated, especially trans persons, who have other skills and experience in the social sector do not stand a chance. This gap needs to be addressed.

Key Insight

These are the names of some famous and successful professionals from the LGBTIQA+ community in India (these are the exceptions and not the rule!): Vasu Primlani (stand-up comedian); Dutee Chand (international athlete); Vikram Seth (poet, author); Onir (film director); Sridhar Rangayan (film director); Menaka Guruswamy and Arundhati Katju (lawyers); Manabi Bandyopadhyay (college principal); Ashok Row Kavi and Bindumadhav Khire (who run NGOs for the community); Laxmi Narayan Tripathi, Gauri Sawant, Sonali Dalvi, and Disha Pinky Shaikh (activists).

5.5 Challenges in Career and Work and Gender

There are several challenges that women and queer persons face at the workplace. Some of them have already been dealt with in the previous sections. In this section, some more pressing issues are discussed. One of them is career advancement for women and LGBTIQA+ persons. For instance, although women have made important entries into science and the life science industry over the years, both fields still face large gender differences when it comes to the career advancement of men and women (Hidalgo, 2017). In the case of application patterns of women and men in scientific fields, the results are not clear-cut – some studies show that women apply for posts and promotions to a lesser extent than men, while other studies do not verify this difference.

The results also point in different directions regarding the question of whether there is discrimination against women in the employment process. Some studies indicate differences in the way women's and men's qualifications are evaluated, while other studies indicate that, in fact, a higher proportion of women are offered employment. Thus, the glass ceiling that existed earlier has been made opaque, and there is a lot of tokenisms when it comes to promotion and opportunities for growth, as well as representation at the highest echelons of office and leadership. Discrimination in hiring continues, and lack of day care systems and absence of support from both family and partner continue to haunt women in challenging positions and stop them from achieving their full professional potential.

'Work from home' has acquired a new meaning in the 2020 Covid-19 scenario. Especially, with both partners working from home, children attending school from home, taking care of the elderly, a whole lot of psychosocial issues have arisen. Initially, domestic workers were stopped from coming to work as a precautionary measure, which added the entire housework to the domestic chores of middle-class and upper-middle-class employed women. The latter have gone through a lot of distress, since, once again, the man's work has been prioritized over their work, and their double burden has increased considerably during this pandemic. Many women have lost their jobs, and many live with the dread that they would be pushed into full-time domesticity! The double standards on work–life balance for employed men and women have been redefined! Transgender men and women have also lost their sources of livelihood during this crisis.

There is another interesting layer to this challenge; while privileged employed women have been vocal about their entitlements – being paid during the pandemic, trying to negotiate with bosses, as well as spouses, for dignity and space – they have haggled to grudgingly pay their domestic workers (who are from the unorganized sector and hence have no social security or rights) their full wages during the lockdown! This exposes the terrible hypocrisy of the middle, upper middle, and upper classes in Indian society about the rights of poor labouring women.

Let us look at some examples that illustrate the various contentious issues at stake in the sphere of women and work. The dogged issue of 33 per cent reservation for women in the Indian parliament has been on the back burner since 1993. In 1993, the 73rd Amendment to the Constitution granted 33 per cent reservation for women in gram panchayats, panchayat *samitis*, and corporations, allowing female representatives to take up pertinent local and grassroots-level issues and bring them to the fore. However, the Women's Reservation Bill has remained pending since 2010. The opposition is manifold: It comes from the many patriarchies of political parties, as well as male politicians. The current Lok Sabha (elected members in 2019) has 14 per cent female members, and the current Rajya Sabha (nominated members) has 10.24 per cent female members. This is dismal representation indeed!

Even after India made it mandatory for all companies to have at least one woman on their board of directors, the representation of women on boards as per various reports is a mere 15.2 per cent (also, the spirit of the law is marred through the tokenism of appointing female relatives of those who have power and authority in the company). India has had nine powerful female bankers who have led banks and major financial institutions. Their names are

Arundhati Bhattacharya – State Bank of India
Chandra Kochhar – ICICI Bank
Shikha Sharma – Axis Bank
Usha Ananthasubramanian – Allahabad Bank
Naina Lal Kidwai – HSBC Bank, FICCI (Federation of Indian Chambers of Commerce and Industry)
Archana Bhargava – United Bank of India
Vijayalakshmi Iyer – Bank of India
Kalpana Morparia – JP Morgan India
Kaku Nakhate – Bank of America Merrill Lynch, India

This is indeed heartening, but the irony is that the oldest bank in the country, the 217-year-old State Bank of India, appointed Arundhati Bhattacharya as its first-ever female chairperson only very recently, which means that the glass ceiling has morphed such that in almost all sectors, women are present at junior and middle-management levels, and only very, very few get a fair opportunity (or tokenism rules) to reach top positions.

Another concern all over the world and in India too has been access of women to various professional careers and sectors: 20.4 per cent women work in the organized sector as employees (NSSO survey conducted in 2010), and 26.97 per cent according to a World Bank report published in 2018. The psychosocial concern is that this number is nowhere close to 50 per cent, and out of this small percentage, only a miniscule number get to become professionals (engage in professional work 24×7, skill up, get growth and career advancement opportunities, or put in efforts to achieve professional goals). The rest remain just cogs in the wheel!

Similarly, access of women to STEMM careers and their getting back to science post marriage and motherhood have also been big challenges all over the world, including in India. There is a huge amount of gender disparity in STEM fields in the West and in India too. The causes of this disparity are perceptions and stereotypes that girls cannot do well in these subjects, overt and covert discrimination at all stages (education, entry into careers, promotion, career advancement and so on), lack of mentorship and support, harassment, lack of role models, and lack of confidence. Several strategies have been put in place worldwide to get women into STEMM fields, retain them, and get them back after marriage and motherhood, such as childcare and day care amenities, special allowances, fellowships and scholarships, psychosocial support, training and mentoring, and self-affirmation exercises. More

100 Gender and the Workplace

needs to be done to sensitize male colleagues, as well as male partners and families. In India, two of the efforts to get women back into science are the Women Scientist Scheme for women to return to the mainstream after a career break through research projects and the mobility scheme to address the relocation of female scientists working in government organizations (both schemes come under the Department of Science and Technology, Government of India). The Task Force for Women in Science was constituted under the Department of Science and Technology in 2005.

There is a plan to honour these female scientists from the past with chairs in their names in institutions of national importance. There is also a glimmer of hope with current female scientists who are trailblazers, have braved the storms, ranging from facing microaggression to being side lined; and made their mark despite all odds to become role models for young female science students and budding female scientists. Brief biographical illustrations of some female scientists are given in the following box, though this list is certainly not exhaustive or comprehensive.

Key Insights

- **Gagandeep Kang**: Executive Director, Translational Health Science and Technology Institute, and first female Indian Fellow of the Royal Society
- **Sunita Sarawagi**: Institute Chair Professor, Computer Science and Engineering, Indian Institute of Technology (IIT), Bombay
- **Vidita Vaidya**: Professor, Tata Institute of Fundamental Research (TIFR), and neuroscientist
- **Farah Ishtiaq**: Senior scientist, evolutionary ecologist, Tata Institute for Genetics and Society
- **Devapriya Chattopadhyay**: Associate professor, paleo-ecologist, Department of Earth Sciences, Indian Institute of Science Education and Research (IISER)
- **Kalika Bali**: Principal researcher, human language technology, artificial intelligence, Microsoft research
- **Aditi Sen De**: Professor, quantum computation, information, cryptography, Harish Chandra Research Institute
- **Muthayya Vanitha** and **Ritu Karidhal:** Senior scientists at Indian Space Research Organisation (ISRO). Vanitha was project director and Karidhal was mission director of Chandrayaan-2
- **Tessy Thomas**: Director General, Aeronautical Systems, Defence Research and Development Organisation
- **Rohini Godbole**: Professor, Centre for High Energy Physics, Indian Institute of Science (IISc), Bangalore
- **Aditi Pant**: Oceanographer
- **Sujatha Ramdorai**: Mathematician, TIFR, IISER, Pune

Source: Compiled from various sources

During the Covid-19 crisis of 2020, women in STEMM, as well as female researchers across all fields and at all levels – senior and junior scientists, doctoral and postdoctoral students – have been facing challenges in data collection and analysis, as well as in publishing, due to the lockdown, and since they also must attend to domestic chores. *Lilavati's Daughters*, an anthology of biographical essays brought out by the Indian Academy of Sciences, Bangalore, in 2008, gives a bird's-eye view of the trials, tribulations, and triumphs of female scientists in India. Similarly, *Nature Cell Biology*, Volume 20, September 2018, describes similar experiences of female scientists from various countries in the West.

Both these readings underscore the fact that attitudinal change at the societal level which is brought about through social activism, a movement on the ground – sensitization of and creation of awareness for all stakeholders – remains imperative to create truly equal opportunities for women in all worlds of work, including STEMM. Policy-level initiatives such as Indian Women Scientists Association which is at the forefront of trying to close the gender gap in the participation of women scientists in policymaking in Indian National Science Association (INSA) are an important breakthrough; more needs to be done. The International Science Council has also taken a few initiatives on Women in Science such as holding a world forum for Women in Science in 2022, but such efforts need to be consistent.

Disciplines that are positivist and empirical, like psychology and economics, have also created a glass ceiling for female researchers. In the beginning, the latter's efforts were made invisible, and they were not acknowledged. While the forefathers were celebrated, these foremothers were relegated to the shadows. It was only after the humungous efforts put in by organizations dedicated to getting equal opportunities for women within these disciplines and with the women's movement at the international level gaining momentum that women could gain a toehold in these patriarchal disciplines! The battles are by no means over!

Key Insight

When it comes to women in academia in India at higher posts, there is no parity, and when it comes to tribal women, chances are even remoter! But in May 2020, Sonajharia Minz, professor at Delhi's Jawaharlal Nehru University (JNU), was appointed vice chancellor of Sido Kanhu Murmu University in Dumka, Jharkhand. She is an exception and not the rule, drawing our attention to the fact that at the intersections of caste, tribe, region, religion, and gender, a lot of women are still at the fringes in education and employment.

Last, but by no means least, is the Pandora's box of sexual harassment at the workplace. It deserves independent space and enquiry, but nevertheless, let me flag the salient points of this issue in the context of career, work, and gender. This issue has legal, social, psychological, organizational, and micro and macro implications.

102 Gender and the Workplace

Let us begin with the global context and then move on to the local and try to understand both. 'Me too' is a phrase that was used by Tarana Burke, a sexual harassment survivor and activist, for the first time in 2006 on social media in the United States. Soon after the Harvey Weinstein (Hollywood producer) incident in 2017, it became a viral hashtag on Twitter. After that, a Pandora's box opened, and allegations and proofs came out against people from almost all walks of life: those in advertising and media, entertainment industry, STEMM, corporate sector, academics and politics, Nobel prize awardees, and so on. The movement also spread across all countries. This does not mean, however, that this was the first time that perpetrators were called out. The history of the women's movement in the West has been witness to many brave women who have spoken out.

Archives can give one details of the famous/infamous Anita Hill/Clarence Thomas case of 1991. In fact, the term 'sexual harassment' was coined in 1976 by a group of women working at Cornell University, United States. What the 'Me Too' movement did was spark conversations and signal the need for immediate action and intervention with the snowballing effect of social media. African American women and those from several ethnic and sexual minorities have been facing abuse and sexual harassment at the workplace for a long time; they too could give voice to the injustices meted out to them.

Contrary to popular belief, in India, this issue has a long history of struggle, and it only got more visibility due to the 'Me Too' movement. Issues of rape, assault, and abuse of women have been taken up by the women's movement in India since 1975. It was thanks to the struggle on the ground that several laws were implemented and revised, and with appeals, petitions, protests and lobbying, new laws that were pro-women, including the Protection of Women from Domestic Violence Act (2005), came into existence.

Now let us understand the background that led to a law being framed to prevent sexual harassment at the workplace: the iconic fight of Bhanwari Devi in the year 1992, a *sathin* (grassroots social worker) working to prevent child marriage in villages in Rajasthan. Bhanwari Devi's work led to the displeasure of powerful upper-caste men in the village, who gang-raped her. The state machinery – police station, primary health centre, district court – did not help her, and the upper-caste men were acquitted, and she did not get justice. It was the women's organizations from Jaipur, and later several from across India, that rallied around her. It was Kavita Srivastava, a lawyer and activist who guided her, and Bhanwari's own grit and determination to fight that won the day. This was a journey of five years, and in 1997, a public interest litigation (PIL) was filed in the Supreme Court of India, which led to the institution of the Vishaka Guidelines (Vishaka was one of the main NGOs) that were to be followed at workplaces to prevent and provide redressal for sexual harassment at the workplace. It was only in 2013 that the current law (Sexual Harassment of Women at Workplace [Prevention, Prohibition and Redressal] Act) came in place. That it was a semi-literate woman's struggle, with solidarity and help from the women's movement and individual activists, that yielded this victory is a lesson for all of us who benefit from it.

There are several and far-reaching psychological effects of sexual harassment, as well as its threat perception. These range from severe distress, panic, anxiety, and depression to post-traumatic stress disorder (PTSD) in clinical terms. In psychosocial terms, the victims experience low self-esteem, all their relationships at the workplace are impacted, they face victim blaming when they complain (though the procedure is confidential, hunches and gossip abound), and their families often compel them to leave their jobs. Women end up paying a lot of collateral damage, despite the law being pro-women, and hence, since 2013, the number of complainants has not increased as exponentially as was feared by a lot of men.

Though the law is pro-women and aimed at their protection and redressal of wrongs done to them, many workplaces have put in place policies that are 'gender-neutral'; that is, men too can access the Prevention of Sexual Harassment (POSH) Committee for interventions. Though having a law in place puts the onus on organizations, several undercurrents (like caste, patriarchy, power, and suppression of lower-caste women, as in Bhanwari Devi's case) and intersections operate. These have a traumatic impact on women: fear of antagonizing superiors (if they are the perpetrators), fear of retaliation or revenge (there are several serial offenders, as data from many sectors prove), and fear of upsetting the apple cart.

The grey area is where the line between consensual intimacy and harassment is blurred. Employees must negotiate their way through these behavioural minefields. Men must be sensitive and understanding about the nuances of communication and behaviour and not indulge in patriarchal overreaching (e.g. though office parties are semi-formal, a presumption that female colleagues who are free-spirited and open-minded are 'available' and can be inflicted with overtures is unjust and erroneous). Women must avoid sending out mixed signals and be clear about how to negotiate friendships, collegiality, and intimacy. All these possibilities have also had an impact on cordiality and collegiality between the genders at the workplace. However, the primary principle always remains the woman's consent, at all stages (including a woman's withdrawal from a once-consensual relationship with an office colleague).

This issue is very knotty and multilayered psychosocially and has thrown up several challenges, especially around behavioural norms at the workplace. All the cases from India (as from the rest of the world) in the limelight point to abuse of power, position, and patriarchy by men at high places to use sexual harassment as a tool (just like rape) to exploit female employees, mostly juniors and newbies (from rural areas, marginalized castes, minority religions) that are powerless and voiceless and less likely to protest or fight for their rights. The sexual harassment law applies to the organized sector, and most women who work in the unorganized or informal sector must take recourse to the local committee.

104 Gender and the Workplace

Though having an internal committee (POSH Committee) is mandatory for all workplaces in the organized sector, there are several lacunae: These committees are non-existent or non-functional or have no teeth (since they are a recommendation-making quasi-judicial body and the management has to take action based on their recommendations). Very few women would attempt to approach the police and take the legal course of filing a criminal case. The best of workplaces that believe in gender justice are adhering to the rules and creating gender harmony at the workplace, organizing sensitization and awareness workshops, and being proactive. It is considered a best practice in transparency and good governance, and hence compliance to it is mandatory for the credibility of organizations; this too has compelled some organizations to take the matter seriously.

LGBTIQ employees, new employees, those from marginalized communities, and the disabled are more vulnerable to facing sexual harassment at the workplace, and this needs a nuanced understanding. They are confronted by unwelcome sexual advances, unwanted touching, rape, and sexual assault at the workplace. The fear of being 'outed' is used to exploit LGBTIQ employees sexually. The incidence of such attacks is shockingly high. What they need is to feel supported and accepted for who they are at the workplace. It is not enough for companies to just support gay pride marches; for them to be truly inclusive, it is necessary to offer more jobs to queer persons and help make them employable, which is a step that is desperately needed. Otherwise, it ends up being just 'pink washing' and tokenism.

Review Questions

1 Explain the models of career development and their gender analysis.
2 Comment on the research done on maternal employment.
3 Describe the domestic-labour debate.
4 Explain the psychological impacts of sexual harassment at the workplace.

Critical Thinking Questions

1 Discuss the misconceptions about women performing well in STEM areas.
2 Describe the challenges that queer employees face at the hiring stage, as well as the areas of exploitation.
3 Has the 'glass ceiling' disappeared? Why is there tokenism vis-à-vis female leaders?

Bibliography

Bowlby, J. (1951). The nature of the child's tie to his mother. *International Journal of Psychoanalysis, 39*, 350–373.

Broffenbrenner, U., & Crounter, A. (1982). Work and family through time and space. In S. B. Kammerman & C. D. Hayes (Eds.), *Families that work: Children in a changing world* (pp. 39–83). National Academies Press.

Diwan, N. (1995). *Derived identity, need for social approval and sex role identity: Some aspects of sex role socialization and their relationship* [Unpublished PhD thesis, Mumbai University].

Ellsworth, D., Mendy, A., & Sullivan, G. (2020, June). *How the LGBTQ+ community fares in the workplace* (*McKinsey report*). McKinsey & Company.

Hidalgo, A. (2017). *Gender differences in career choices*. NORDIC. http://nordiclifescience. org/a-girl-or-a-boy-thing-gender-differences-in-career-choices/

Hoffman, L. W. (1989). Effects of maternal employment in two-parent families. *American Psychologist, 44*(2), 283–292.

Hoffman, L. W., & Nye, F. I. (1974). *Working mothers*. Jossey-Bass Publishers.

Holland, J. L. (1985). *Making occupational choices: A theory of occupational personalities and work environments* (2nd ed.). Prentice Hall.

Jacklin, C. N., & McBride-Chang, C. (1991). The effects of feminist scholarship on developmental psychology. *Psychology of Women Quarterly, 15*(4), 549–556.

Kauhanen, A., & Napari, S. (2011). *Gender differences in careers*. ETLA. www.etla.fi/wp-content/uploads/2012/09/dp1241.pdf

Meltzer, H. V. (1987). Biological studies in schizophrenia. *Schizophrenia Bulletin, 13*, 93–127.

Miller, D. I., Nolla, K. M., Eagly, A. H., & Uttal, D. H. (2018). The development of children's gender science stereotypes: Meta analysis of 5 decades US draw a scientist studies. *Child Development, 89*(6), 1943–1955. https://doi.org/10.1111/cdev.13039

Miranda, J. (1995). *Feminism in psychology: Accelerating paradigmatic shifts*. SNDT University.

Natu, S. (1998). *Women and work: A feminist critique of the resistance by mainstream psychology* [Paper presentation]. Paper presented at National Conference of Indian Association of Women's Studies, Pune.

Natu, S. (2002). *A psycho-social enquiry into the gender roles and other related factors of young males with special reference to maternal employment* [Unpublished thesis, Pune University].

Natu, S. (2022). Enabling spaces for and with marginalized young people: The case of the Disha peer support and speak out group. In J. Batsleer, H. Rowley, & D. Lüküslü (Eds.), *Young people, radical democracy and community development*. Policy Press.

Oakley, A. (1974). *Housewife*. Allen Lane.

Oerton, S. (1996). *Gender change and society. Beyond hierarchy: Gender, sexuality, and the social economy*. Taylor & Francis.

Pekkarinen, T., & Vartiainen, J. (2006). Gender differences in promotion on a job ladder: Evidence from Finnish metalworkers. *Industrial & Labor Relations Review, 59*, 285–301.

Siegel, A. E. (1961). *Research issues related to the effects of maternal employment on children*. University Microtilme.

Sudhakar, U. V., & Rao, K. V. (1988). Women's dimension in psychological research: A critique. *Economic & Political Weekly, 23*(WS), 20–22.

Zaccaria, J. (1970). *Theories of occupational choice and vocational development*. Houghton Mifflin.

6

EXPLORING GENDER AND SEXUALITIES

Chapter Highlights

Learning Objectives

After reading this chapter, the students would be able to

- Understand the differences between sexuality, sexual orientation, gender, and various gender identities.
- Gain clarity on the relationship between psychology and sexuality.
- Gauge the impacts and effects of homophobia, transphobia, and social marginalization.
- Know about movements for same-sex marriage, constitutional provisions, and so on.

Introduction

In the first chapter on basic concepts, we have already familiarized ourselves with the terms that connect sexualities and gender. It would be important to go back to them before reading this chapter. In this chapter, there is an attempt to understand the nuances of 'sexuality', since the concepts of 'sex', 'sexuality', and 'gender' are often confused with each other (though they are interlinked, they are distinct in their own ways). We will also try to understand how sexuality plays out differently in a person's everyday life depending on gender, culture, and society, and what its psychological impact is. While mainstream psychology has treated queer persons as 'deviant', 'diagnosed' them as abnormal, and treated them with aversive therapies, feminist psychology, LGBT psychology, and other critical fields in psychology have addressed queer persons as fellow human beings. Understanding

DOI: 10.4324/9781003453758-7

the tensions between sexualities, sexual orientation, and gender is also essential to understand how difficult it is to move from a biomedical and pathological viewpoint to a more humane and rights-based approach.

Trying to get a bird's-eye view of the lived reality, familial and other interpersonal relationships of LGBTIQA+ persons, the challenges they have faced, and their psychological implications would also be illuminating for the readers. The psychosocial aspects of coming out or not, dealing with prejudices, harassment, violence, homophobia, transphobia, and heteronormativity are other areas that are ignored in mainstream psychology and its texts – this is an attempt to shine a light on them. Obtaining the rights to become equal citizens, in India and in the rest of the world, for LGBTIQA+ persons has been a momentous and Herculean task. Some battles have been won, but the war to live fully functioning, productive, and loving lives with equal choices of marriage/cohabitation, ownership of property, job security and adoption, and the psychological trauma and emotional labour for being treated with dignity remains. Queer persons also carry the markers of caste, religion, region, and nation. An intersectional approach of understanding their multiple identities would be helpful to learn about their multiple psychological vulnerabilities.

The struggles of these sexual minorities have also challenged the bulwark of various existing paradigms, including mainstream psychotherapy and practice. A brief discussion on that will be undertaken since more details will follow in the next two chapters too. The work of organizations that have helped queer persons in their struggle for rights, as well as in overcoming physical and psychological distress and gaining education and employment, will be highlighted. The intersectional aspects of queer lives will also be underscored: Queer persons also hold and carry markers of caste, class, region, religion, and nation, and this makes understanding their psychology intriguing, challenging, and insightful. It is also important learning for straight individuals, since their lives are not as completely alienated from queer lives as they think they are. It would also contribute towards refashioning an equal diverse society.

6.1 Meaning of Sexuality and the Relationship Between Sexuality, Sexual Orientation, Gender and Concepts of Identity, and Multiple Identities

Sexuality is part of ourselves, as well as all our relationships. Human beings are essentially sexual beings, and according to Dr Sigmund Freud, sexuality begins right from infancy. Even if Freudian theory hypersexualizes human lives and refers only to heterosexuality, to give it its due, sexual instincts are especially important, though not singularly central, to our lives. However, sexuality extends beyond sex drive to our interpersonal relationships with the opposite sex: those with the opposite-sex parent and siblings and, later, intimate relationships. It is rarely acknowledged within families that relationships with parents of the opposite and

108 Exploring Gender and Sexualities

same sex and those with siblings of the opposite and same sex have an impact on an individual's relationships outside the family. Psychoanalytical literature points out that those who are deprived of warm and lasting relationships in the family are in search of 'father and mother figures', and unresolved Oedipus and Electra complex can lead to attraction towards the actual 'mother and father' or towards one's 'mother and father figures outside the family', respectively. Sexuality also encompasses our choice of clothes, fashions, and aesthetics, since sexuality, sensuality, and gender role are also intricately linked.

Here too stereotypes prevail, right from the long-standing 'pink for girls and blue for boys' to 'soft fabrics for feminine women and tougher fabrics for macho males'. Those who fall between these stools or make out-of-the-box choices are ridiculed as 'pansies', 'effeminate men', and 'tomboy girls'. Of course, the gender benders are pansexual and gender-fluid persons who break all these rules and binaries, as we shall discuss shortly.

The confusions between sex (sexual intercourse), sexuality, and gender continue unabated. Many times, when people talk about sex, they limit it to the act of intercourse. While it is important to understand the linkages between biological sex and the social and cultural connotation of genders, it is also important to emphasize the broader concept of sexuality, which is growing up male, female, lesbian, gay, bisexual, transgender, intersex or asexual, and one's interpersonal and sexual relationships across genders. Adolescents need 'sexuality and gender education' and not 'sex education' that focuses on biology (that too often badly) and gives psychology, sociology, culture, and gender a miss! Sexuality also encompasses desire, pleasure, pain, and violence, an entire spectrum of physiological and psychological experiences, once again across genders! It is essential to have conversations and dialogues around the crushes and infatuations that pre-teens and adolescents experience, whether it is heterosexual or queer in nature, and to accept both kinds as 'normal' and 'everyday'.

Whether 'sex education' should become part of the syllabus for children, adolescents, and young adults has been debated ad nauseam by educationists, psychologists, parents, and policymakers. Formally, and sometimes informally, it has been introduced: the workshops range from the cursory and entirely biomedical to the exceptionally creative and fun. The debates have been around the why (It would morally corrupt the children! They would misuse the information! This is a Western concept!), the how, and the who (which experts should do this – doctors, teachers in general, psychologists, or counsellors, or should we leave it to the parents). This way of going about an interaction on such a sensitive and complex subject is outrageous. The ideal way is to engage in transparent, creative interactions on sexuality with children.

NGOs are conducting such well –thought-out and age-appropriate, marvellously curated workshops. These organizations include RAHI Foundation (which focuses on CSA [child sexual abuse]), Talking About Reproductive and Sexual

Exploring Gender and Sexualities **109**

Health Issues (TARSHI), Agents of Ishq, MAVA, and Akshara Centre, to name a few. Instead of sermonizing and holding moralistic diatribes, such workshops allow children to ask questions and address their valid and legitimate curiosity on the taboo subject of sexuality.

Besides, all sorts of research from across the world on sexuality education have demonstrated that 'information is power', that it enables children, adolescents, and young adults to understand 'sexuality' as a core concern and need rather than looking at it as 'undesirable' and allows them to make informed choices and to practise safe sex rather than experimenting without thinking of consequences. Sexuality awareness and education sessions at all stages and ages help people look at the 'pleasure to pain/violence/exploitation' panorama of sexuality, and with a multidisciplinary approach – including psychology, biology, gender studies, sexology, sexuality studies, and communication studies – it proves to be really effective. By bypassing this, we allow children/adolescents and young adults to seek answers to their doubts from and quench their curiosity through (yellow journalism, earlier) Google *chacha*, Quora, porn sites, and peers! The information they get can be unscientific, exaggerated, sexist, damaging, mythical, full of misconceptions, exaggerated, and/or plain rubbish. This goes a long way and has a huge impact on impressionable young minds. Hence, it is particularly important that formal structures in education – schools, colleges, universities – engage in sexuality and gender sensitization education that imparts knowledge and the right perspective and that the informal structures (NGOs, parents) are equal participants in this process.

In Maharashtra, there has been a tradition of experts using different forms for mainstreaming sexuality awareness and education which is truly inspiring and has made a positive impact: Dr Vitthal Prabhu, through his popular book titled *Niramay Kamajeevan*; Dr Anant and Dr Shanta Sathe, through workshops undertaken under the auspices of the Family Planning Association of India; Dr Jeevan and Dr Leena Mohadikar, through their Q&A (question-and-answer) columns in newspapers and articles in popular press; and Dr Prakash Kothari through articles in Marathi and English. All of them (barring Dr Shanta Sathe) were practising sexologists too.

Key Insight

Dr Mahinder Watsa, who passed away in December 2020, wrote a popular column, 'Ask the Sexpert', for *Mumbai Mirror* and *Pune Mirror*, where he responded to questions about sexual health in an empathetic, witty, humane, and liberal fashion. A reading of these archived columns will offer us a bird's-eye view on not only what ails the sexual health of people in India but also a way ahead by sifting through all the threads to make meaning, using Dr Watsa's responses.

110 Exploring Gender and Sexualities

TABLE 6.1 Some Major References on Human Sexuality

Alfred Kinsey	Kinsey Reports
Masters and Johnson	*Human Sexual Response* and other works
Havelock Ellis	*Studies in the Psychology of Sex* (1897–1928; six volumes)
Sigmund Freud	*Sexuality and the Psychology of Love*
Michel Foucault	*The History of Sexuality* (1976–2021; four volumes)
Albert Ellis	*Sex without Guilt in the 21st Century*
Judith Butler	*Bodies that Matter: On the Discursive Limits of Sex*

Source: Internet and the author's archives

Some of the earlier works and studies on sexuality dotted with seminal work are listed in Table 6.1 (do note that it is not a comprehensive list).

The other important aspects are that there are huge double standards in overt expression of sexuality and sexual permissiveness: while a man who flaunts his libido is celebrated and envied as a Casanova and can boast of his sexual exploits in an exaggerated manner, a woman who does so is labelled 'loose' and promiscuous and called a whore or slut! Sex is also posited as premarital (taboo) and extramarital (transgression), and live-in relationships and sex within them are also stigmatized; hence, only sex within marriage gets social sanction! Objectification and commodification of women as sexual objects in everyday life, in media, and on the internet continue to flourish in a consumerist, neoliberal society.

Reproductive sexuality is viewed through the binary of fertility and infertility, and infertility is only the woman's problem! Pornography is looked at as a social ill, whereas it proliferates across all ages and genders. It creates an exaggerated, obnoxious image of human sexuality which is lapped up by all, and its illicit nature adds to its allure. X-rated movies and porn sites are the staple of young adults (in fact of all ages – mostly men and some women too) and have a distinct impact on attitudes towards sexuality. In India, particularly, while on the one hand popular media is inundated with depictions of sex and violence, mature and upfront discussions and conversations on sex and sexuality are still missing!

To complicate matters further, both in practice and in media depictions, we see tropes of 'one-night stands', as it was called in the late 1980s and 1990s, and what is lately being called 'hooking up'. The response to this has largely been moralistic and derogatory from mainstream society. Psychologists, however, have studied the linkages of both phenomena involving aversion to commitment, movement from temporary to long-term sexual and emotional relationships, and exploration of sexuality. It is important that as students of psychology and gender we do not stigmatize one-night stands and hook-ups but instead try and tease out a nuanced understanding of a sexually repressed society and youngsters trying to navigate their way around exploring their sexualities. The advent of the apps like Tinder and Grindr has enabled youngsters to do so (Natu, 2021).

> **Mid-chapter Exercise**
>
> **Vulnerability:** Many cases of gay men being robbed, beaten up, and black-mailed on dates fixed through dating apps have been reported in various cities recently.
>
> Thus, on the one hand, while technology allows them some choice, the dangers that they face due to taboos and possibilities of being targets of exploitation continue to loom large.
>
> • Discuss the complexities of such scenarios, using news items as resources.
> • Discuss some possible solutions.

Polyamory, the practice of consensual, intimate relationships with more than one partner, has also emerged as an option for a lot of people. Some people are comfortable with an 'open marriage' or 'open live-in relationship' where monogamy is not a given. All these patterns of intimate, sexual relationships for heterosexual and queer persons must be understood in their cultural and historical context.

Sexual orientation is a very problematic term, since it seeks to define identity, attraction, and behaviour through pre-existing heteronormative and biomedical norms. In Chapter 1 and other chapters, we have discussed how sexuality and gender do not always match neatly. For example, a lesbian who cross-dresses may or may not identify as a trans man, a bisexual person (who is defined as attracted to both male and female genders) may prefer identifying as gender-fluid rather than being boxed into the category of bisexual, and so on.

For instance, Harnaam Kaur, famous as the 'bearded lady', is a real gender bender. She has had a beard right since adolescence, as a side effect of polycystic ovary syndrome (PCOS), and continues to maintain the beard. She realized that she was pansexual and accepted it. She maintains that for her, 'pansexual means loving people regardless of who they are'. Her work has contributed to defying gender stereotypes that only 'men and beards' belong together and given a lot of hope to girls who suffer from PCOS and could develop this condition, as well as trans men. Her example also helps cis men and cis women accept their sexuality, with its highs and lows, more openly. Cis persons are also traumatized when women start sprouting more facial hair and men have more rounded chests (man boobs) and feel less 'feminine' and 'masculine', respectively. Kaur's acceptance of her condition and celebration of its vantage point could help persons of all genders and sexualities look afresh at how they get defined by heteronormative cultures but rarely question them.

Another person in point is Durga Gawde, who is a sculptor, artist, and 'drag king' who prefers to use the pronoun 'they' for themself. They speak about 'riding

112 Exploring Gender and Sexualities

the cusp between male and female' and identify as gender-fluid. They have overcome economic and psychological odds to become the 'person' they want to be, with mind, body, and soul aligned to their identity. This courageous person who dares to lead the life that they identify with as a survivor fills many young minds with hope – that those who are grappling with these twilight zones between sexes and genders and are non-binary have hope only if they persist in defying the shackles of restricting gender identities.

It is also important to understand that LGBTIQA+ persons are not devoid of other identities such as caste, class, religion, and region. Thus, when people say, 'How can you be Hindu/Muslim/Christian and gay/lesbian/bisexual/transgender', they are unaware of the fact that intersectionality extends to queer lives too just as it does to cis lives. Multiple identities of sexuality, caste, religion, region, and nationality allow people to inhabit many worlds at the same time and put them into extremely challenging situations too. A young woman from rural Maharashtra got the insight that she was a lesbian when she came to a city and started working in an NGO working on health issues. Until then, she was confused about her sexual identity and knew that she was not like the rest of the girls and did not feel attracted to boys. However, the language and experience of her sexuality and its acceptance were not part of her rural background. This is not to say that 'queerness' is an urban concept; rather, its articulation and acceptance are possible easier in urban spaces. Language itself constricts acceptance of all sexualities, since even now we must resort to English for LGBTIQA+ vocabulary (the words in most Indian languages have not gone beyond the inadequate *samalingi*). A young trans woman coming from a rural area faced a great dilemma in deciding between cross-dressing and going for a gender reassignment surgery and the psychological costs of either. Awareness and social support are much less in rural places than in an urban milieu, as far as acceptance of queerness is concerned.

Acceptance of sexuality as an integral part of life, in general, and queer sexuality, specifically, has been a real challenge. Depending on the culture, location, space, and one's privilege, the variance of experience and expression is huge. In my gender and sexuality workshops with diverse groups of young adults, the interactions, role-plays, articulations and expressions through dialogues, art, and performances are fascinating and enlightening. They range from treating sexuality as a taboo and having confusions and questions about sexual practices to engaging in very direct discussions about experiences, contraception, and use of dating apps like Tinder and Grindr. Open discussions about sexualities and genders and how caste, religion, and rural and urban settings influence both attitudes and behaviours with respect to sexuality help them speak out and engage not just with the facilitator but also with each other and learn from peers and diversity. Media depictions and social media play a significant role in building, breaking, and constructing stereotypes about sexuality, especially post globalization.

The complex phenomena like sexual violence and sexual violation need to be understood through unpacking the social determinants of caste, religion, and region and their linkage with sexualities and genders. In the Indian context, the Nirbhaya, Unnao, and Khairlanji cases have to be understood not simply as 'rape cases' but with the nuances of urban–rural divide (region), religion, caste, gender, and sexuality.

6.2 LGBTIQA+ Relationships and Psychology

Until the 1970s, all over the world, LGBTIQA+ lives were examined largely through the prism of pathology in psychology, instead of intimate relationships different from those that most heterosexuals have. Many myths abound, such as that LGBTIQ individuals are unhappy, their behaviour is deviant, and their relationships are transient and dysfunctional. Later research in the 1980s proved that some of the queer relationships are long-lasting (just as only 'some' heterosexual relationships are long-lasting!).

If queer people were unhappy people and with low self-esteem, it was only due to the discrimination, stigma, and taboos about their being queer and the lack of social acceptance. There has also been a strong distrust of psychology as a discipline and psychologists and practitioners, and rightly so. This was against the backdrop of homosexuality (and all other forms of alternative sexuality) being viewed and diagnosed as abnormal (sociopathic personality disorder) till DSM-II (Diagnostic and Statistical Manual), and it was only with DSM-III and DSM-III-Revised that it was removed from the category of abnormality. APA and the American Psychiatric Association made the necessary changes. However, at the ground level, we still find several mental health professionals who continue to believe that queer people need treatment and need to be made 'normal', read 'heterosexual'. A great deal of sensitization is essential even now. (There will be more discussion about this in Chapters 7 and 8.)

The removal of homosexuality as a category of abnormality was due to the pressure from the queer movement, which has been lobbying for equal rights for queer persons all over the world. APA and the Association of Psychological Sciences were also compelled to become inclusive, and the divisions such as Society for the Psychology of Sexual Orientation (and its journal) and Gender Diversity (APA) and the research focus on LGBTIQ issues in APS were some by-products.

Historically, it was the HIV/AIDS challenge that brought queer persons and their lives (in the 1980s, particularly gay lives) into public focus. It also started conversations around sex education for people of all sexualities. It is perhaps this history of pathologizing sexualities which does not allow us to accept and understand all sexual lives as normal, diverse, beautiful, and indeed a rainbow of lived experiences! It is also unfortunate that the sexuality discourse, at least in the mainstream, remains firmly embedded in the biomedical model.

Now let us understand some of the terms of endearment and intimacy which are used in the LGBTIQA+ vocabulary. 'Queer' is moved from a pejorative to an umbrella term; nancy, dyke, butch, femme, pansy, drag queen, fag/faggot, homo,

114 Exploring Gender and Sexualities

asexual/aromantic/agender, bottom/top M to F, F to M, binding, cruising, trans-feminism, closeted/out, and so on are some of the terms used by queer persons for self-description, and some terms are those put out by society and which have stuck. It is an entire world not just of vocabularies but also of lives!

If we are to become allies and support LGBTIQA+ persons, then we cannot stop with just turning up at pride marches; we also have to speak out on their behalf and respect them and their relationships as 'equal'. Mainstream psychology has thought of queer persons as those who give primacy to their sexuality, which is not true. They too emphasize love, ambition, and warmth and strive for the same goals that straight persons strive for. This is conveyed very poignantly by Manoj Bajpayee's character in the Hindi film *Aligarh* (based on the real-life Dr Siras of Aligarh Muslim University), who says, '[H]ow can you encompass my entire life, dreams, hopes, desires in just one word "gay"?'

In 1984, Rock Hudson (Hollywood film star) was one of the first celebrities to disclose that he was gay (and that he had HIV/AIDS). We have come a long way since then. In the last few years in India and abroad, several celebrities and people in public life have 'come out', and more have done so after Section 377 got decrim-inalized. This is something that psychologists need to take note of and understand – that homophobia and transphobia among mental health professionals is not simply wrong and unethical but is also inhuman and does not behove the profession.

LGBTIQA+ persons and queer groups are suspicious of psychologists, and some of them abhor psychology due to the queer-insensitive practices of psy-chodiagnostics, psychotherapy, prescription practice, and medication employed by mainstream psychology and psychiatry. This tension between queer persons and psychology disciplines is recurrent, despite some tangible changes in policies due to the strong element of obsession with heteronormative practices among all kinds of mental health practitioners.

6.3 LGBTIQA+ Individuals and Their Experiences with Parents and in Relationships Across Their Lifespan, in Brief

For a lot of parents across the board, acceptance and understanding of their chil-dren's sexuality are a real challenge. Hence, the relationships between queer per-sons and their parents range from complete disownment to total acceptance. What is essential is awareness and handholding. An important step in this direction has been taken by Humsafar Trust, one of India's oldest queer community network-ing and advocacy organizations, and Sweekar: The Rainbow Parents, a 70-strong support group for parents of queer adults in Mumbai. The first of its kind in India, the Prabal programme of Humsafar Trust, began in November 2018. It has been designed to provide parents of LGBT children information on all things queer – sexual orientation, gender terminologies, sexual health, and the legalities associ-ated with it. Intended for open-minded parents who can, in turn, educate other parents and become valuable queer allies, the programme fosters understanding of alternate sexualities. It also enables and equips them with the vocabulary to explain their son/daughter's sexuality to others (Chakraborty, 2019).

Parents of queer persons also need a support network that can help them adjust to and accept the realities of their children's lives so that they can support them and become their allies. As one of the queer persons associated with a support group says, 'when queer persons come out of the closet, their parents go into the closet, and they need help to either not do that or come out too!' There is hope that along with showing acceptance, armed with correct information, parents could work as change agents and help create more acceptance for alternative sexuality in the larger society.

Despite decriminalization of homosexuality in India, the social stigma remains, and it deters many parents from openly accepting their children's sexuality or extending support to them with the fear of social ostracism and being thrown out of social networks looming large in front of them. This lack of support from home and alienation makes LGBTIQA+ persons more vulnerable to mental health issues. Many parents persist with finding treatment (trying aversive therapy or faith healing, going to quacks), trying to cure them and make them 'normal' and forcing them into unwilling marriages due to lack of knowledge and being bound by tradition.

In March 2022, chief election commissioner, government of Maharashtra, started a drive of helping queer persons to enrol as voters across the state. This campaign culminated in a 2-day state seminar in September 2022 with discussions with experts on the rights of the LGBTIQA+ community as citizens. I was invited to anchor a panel discussion with parents and family members who had accepted and supported their queer wards. The discussion was really poignant. Many insights were gained from this discussion. The first one was that due to enormous social pressure families faced a lot of constraints in accepting that their child was different. Hence supporting them is not just a familial responsibility, the onus lies on entire society. Secondly, acknowledging their children's sexuality in a houseful auditorium was an overwhelming and validating experience for them. Many of them were really proud of the resilience and achievements of their children, and this bond could be a model for other parents and also civil society.

A 2012 Humsafar Trust survey of men who have sex with men in Mumbai found that 45 per cent reported having suicidal thoughts, while 29 per cent were severely depressed and 24 per cent suffered from anxiety-related disorders. According to a 2018 study of 2.5 million adolescents published in *Pediatrics*, a journal published by the American Medical Association, young people who identified as homosexual had a significantly higher suicide risk than their heterosexual peers (Chakraborty, 2019).

A course like Prabal does help parents bridge the gap between resistance (due to lack of awareness) and the total acceptance that their children want. Indian tradition and culture, which rarely allows an open dialogue about sexuality in homes, and the respect that children are supposed to give parents make it extremely difficult for queer persons to confide in their parents and actively seek their help. Parents

116 Exploring Gender and Sexualities

are also worried about sexual health problems of their children, their future, their multiple sexual partners, and the different way of life they may lead.

Much research in India with lesbian and gay persons has described the family as a significant site of violence and a force that pushes heteronormative rules in the life of these individuals. Families have been identified as the place where psychological, physical, and sexual violence against lesbian, bisexual, and transgender individuals take place. A study on lesbian women in India drew forth cases of beating, imprisonment, and the forcible use of 'remedial' treatments, like shock therapy, by family members. Studies have emphasized the heightened stress faced by gay men and lesbian women in India because of the family pressure on marriage, which sometimes even results in forced marriages (Ranade et al., 2016).

Other research studies have documented examples where lesbian/gay individuals continued to receive economic support from the family but with the marked absence of any acceptance, love, or care from their family members. All these data indicate how imperative it is for LGBTIQA+ individuals to be accepted and supported by society, starting with their families. A recent study (LABIA, 2013) highlights the extent and impact of familial violence on queer persons assigned the female gender at birth (PAFGB). Out of the 50 respondents in this study, as many as 13 recounted stories of attempted suicide while still living with their natal families. The study further underlines that rigid controls and policing, violence from parents and siblings, forced separation from partners and/or increased marriage pressure on one or both young people in a relationship led many to flee their homes, either alone or with their partner.

There are very few family members who are supportive of their children's sexuality and willing to participate in research on familial responses. Family members who have a high degree of homonegativity, prejudice, and stigma are unlikely to be willing participants in research on homosexuality. Also, for the several reasons mentioned earlier such as the compulsory nature of marriage, familial/kinship control over individuals' sexuality, and its expression and violence from family members towards non-normative genders and sexualities, fewer lesbian and gay individuals may choose to 'come out' to their families in India.

In the American and European contexts, however, a broad review of literature suggests that 'coming out' to the family is a required task in the formation of LGBTIQA+ identity. However, in general, 'coming out' to the family is not easy, since there is a considerable amount of antagonism, negativity, and even disapproval towards same-sex relationships from parents. Hostility or denial from parents/in-laws may persist even years after the initial disclosure, which tends to have an adverse impact on the same-sex relationships. One of the common initial responses after discovering the child's sexual orientation has been that of 'not knowing one's child anymore'.

In the Indian context, some parents identified structural factors, such as socio-economic and caste privilege leading to an English education, exposure to Western materials on LGBT issues, exposure to societies with pro-LGBT laws, and

Exploring Gender and Sexualities **117**

exposure to societies in which LGBT issues are discussed openly, which helped with their acceptance of homosexuality.

How the child responds to the parent in this situation helps the parent come to terms with their child's 'difference' as well. Some mothers interviewed in a study stated that it was their lesbian daughters who stood by them in their times of difficulty, while they were dealing with violent relationships with their husbands and in-laws, the stigma of divorce, and the lack of support systems, alongside poverty and deprivation.

Some studies have shown that parents who understand the social stigma and ostracism that their children are going to face support them regardless of their views about queer lives, since they empathize with their trauma. Another finding from a study was that it was the inevitability of their children's sexuality which made acceptance a forced choice! A few reconciliatory steps are taken, like meeting the child's same-sex partner's parents and giving them practical support, but many parents do not go the extra mile to share the truth about their child's sexuality with extended family or relatives.

Parents' concerns are about whether these queer relationships will last, their child's possible loneliness, fear of HIV/AIDS in the case of gay offspring, financial security, acceptance that they might not become grandparents, and coming to terms with a narrative that is completely different from heterosexual life scripts.

Recognizing the need for creating more allies in the form of parents, friends, social activists, wider community, and civil society and getting them involved in different forms of the struggle for queer equality, many organizations have taken several initiatives, such as inviting them for pride marches and awareness sessions for allies and getting them to write. In one such initiative, Samapathik Trust, Pune, has produced the following edited books: *Manachiye Gunti* (Marathi)/*Beautiful People* (English), a compilation of stories of parents of LGBT people which could be eye-opening for readers who wish to understand the travails of the individuals, as well as their families; *Saptaranga* (Marathi), a compilation of stories of third-gender and transgender people; and *Antaranga* (Marathi), an anthology of auto-biographies in Marathi by gay and lesbian people from Maharashtra. More such initiatives in various Indian languages are needed. For students of psychology and gender, close reading of such books and engagement with organizations is essential to be able to work with queer persons.

Mid-chapter Exercise

While sexist jokes (jokes targeting cis women) continue unabated in the real world and on social media, those targeting queer persons, disabled persons, and people from the Northeast (or other regions) in India also abound. All such jokes are objectionable. The origin and spread of such jokes are embedded in multiple hegemonies loaded against various minorities: sexual and religious minorities, the disabled, those from under-represented regions, and so on.

Discuss all the complex aspects and avoid, protest, and shun such jokes!

6.4 Coming Out, Prejudice, Homophobia and Transphobia, Social Marginalization, and Psychological Vulnerability

The act and phenomenon of 'coming out' (disclosing one's sexual identity to others) or indeed remaining 'in the closet' is both a process and a negotiation for many queer persons. Literature from the West tells us that this process is much more acceptable and seamless in that context, since sexual taboos are not as overarching as in South Asia, but of course with individual differences within families and sub-cultures. In India, this process is also impacted and controlled by caste, class, and region (urban/rural), as well as acceptance of sexualities and genders and prevailing attitudes towards them.

For instance, tribal cultures are more accepting; since there is more openness towards different sexualities and cross-dressing, identifying with another gender is not treated as a taboo. On the other hand, in urban cultures, people may know early that who they are is different from what is seen as normative and ideal. Sharing this self-knowledge might not bring them any great rewards. In fact, it might bring them serious consequences. Telling someone about your sexual orientation is a negotiated activity, not necessarily intra-psychic or inside your own head. If one has not come out to ten significant people in their life, that does not imply that one is a closeted, depressed, unhappy homosexual person. People might be living full, thriving lives and yet decide not to tell their parents, which is termed as 'situated complexities' by Ranade (2019).

In the Indian context, there are a lot of things at stake: family honour (so-called), weddings of siblings, the guilt and shame of non-conformity, and the impact on larger kinship networks as 'bad relatives who are to be excommunicated'! In two recent Hindi films, *Shubh Mangal Zyada Saavdhan* and *Ek Ladki Ko Dekha Toh Aisa Laga*, the respective male and female protagonists are gay and lesbian, respectively, and 'come out' in front of their entire families; the films address the issues of forced marriages and presumptions of heterosexuality in a playful manner while also attempting to bring the matters of desire, choice, and normality of being gay to the centre stage. This signals a welcome change in depictions of LGTIQ characters in films and the film's narrative where very often the queer persons were caricatured (with some honourable exceptions) or else the film had to be dedicated to HIV/AIDS and was not about intimate relationships among persons who are just different from straight people.

Of course, there are parents who come to terms with the 'coming out' and embrace the idea of 'coming out' themselves as parents of a queer person, but this number has to increase. In the West, there is not sufficient data of such parents of colour or those from other ethnic minorities, just as in India we do not know enough about parents of queer persons from rural and marginalized communities. Many siblings from different strata are more accepting and supportive of queer persons since there is no age barrier. They are also eager to help and feel left out when not asked or if their sibling takes too long to come out to them!

A study shows that after disclosure, some parents chose to talk to counsellors, psychiatrists, or even their family doctor after 'finding out' about their child. For some, the motivation was to merely ask an expert to help them make sense of this new challenge in their lives, whereas for others seeking help from a doctor was an attempt to determine if the child's sexuality could be changed, reversed, and made 'normal'. Apart from seeking information from multiple sources, respondents described using interpersonal resources, that is, conversations with their child/sibling, as well as their partner/s, to develop further clarity. Some of the respondents stated that the comfort and acceptance around homosexuality emerged primarily from the meaningful and engaging conversations they had with their child/sibling. Listening to their family member's journeys towards knowing about themselves and accepting themselves, as well as getting to know their current lives, which included information on partners, friends, social life, parties, and support systems, helped them move towards accepting their child/sibling.

Research indicates that the quality of family relationships prior to the disclosure of sexual orientation influences the relationship post disclosure. In the absence of cohesion and communication among family members, chances of disclosure itself may be low, and so may be those of acceptance. Respondents in a study too emphasized the primary importance of the quality of the relationship they generally shared with the gay/lesbian individual. This closeness also led parents to have concerns for their child's future, stability, loneliness, growing old alone, and so on. Knowing that their child was in a relationship and engaging with the child's partner helped parents deal with some of these concerns and better accept homosexuality. One of the main concerns post disclosures for parents was intimate relationships. They would want to know if their child was in a 'steady' or committed relationship, the nature of such a relationship, and its future. Family members were therefore looking for stability, dependability, and commitment in the intimate relationships of their lesbian or gay child, to feel assured about the future of their child, which, in turn, aided acceptance. Some parents/siblings expressed that their own experiences of non-conformity or breaking of norms in some form in their lives made it easier for them to empathize with their child/sibling. Examples of norm breaking include having an inter-caste/-community marriage, standing up against a violent relationship in one's life and seeking divorce, being part of a social movement, such as a feminist group, or knowing about other gay people in one's family (Peplau & Beals, 2004).

Prejudice and discrimination against queer persons, homophobia, and transphobia are rampant, and there is an urgent need for myth busting and engaging with the community to understand their lived experiences, struggles, and politics better. Their psychological vulnerabilities are immense and involve family dynamics and conflicts, discrimination in educational spaces, dilemmas related to 'coming out', taking care of their psychosocial health and sexual health, negotiations with partners and at the workplace, dealing with police, harassment, violence, and the stigma in society. As we discussed earlier, their parents too need hand-holding and

120 Exploring Gender and Sexualities

support. Straight persons need to understand these challenges faced by both queer persons and their parents to become useful allies and supporters. As students of psychology, we need to engage with the struggle of queer individuals, with the queer movement and its complexities, especially in terms of region, caste, and religion, if we want to work in organizations working with queer persons or use queer-affirmative therapies and since they are our fellow human beings – different but equal. It is important to understand that 'sexual identity' is not the only identity of a queer person. Like straight persons, careers, interpersonal relationships, socio-cultural aspirations, universal fears, dreams, enjoyment, and entertainment are all sought out by queer persons too.

6.5 Battles Across the World for Same-Sex Marriage, Decriminalizing Homosexuality in India and Its Psychological Impact

The world over, various LGBTIQA+ groups have different opinions about 'same-sex, queer marriages', and the battles both within and with the legal community are far from over. While some groups feel that as equal citizens marriage is one of their rights, some others advocate a critique and disavowal of the institution of marriage. However, for those who want to get married, the process of having to run away and/or live in another country, since the laws of their state or country or both stop them from leading a life of love (married) with their partner, comes at a huge psychological price: distress, trauma, and a sense of constant insecurity.

In India, in criminalizing homosexual acts, Section 377 meant that those practising them had to remain at the margins of society, keeping their sexual preferences and activities secret from families, communities, and the authorities, for fear of blackmail or prosecution. As the following examples show, even in the absence of successful prosecutions, the law has facilitated widespread, institutionally tolerated discrimination against those whose sexual preferences are different from those of the majority.

Several incidents have highlighted the vulnerability of gay, lesbian, and transgender Indians because of Section 377. Homosexually inclined men who meet at parks and other public places are often trapped and blackmailed by the police, who use the threat of penalty under Section 377 against them. It was in response to this type of harassment and arrest of men in Central Park, Connaught Place, New Delhi, that the non-governmental group AIDS Bhedbhav Virodhi Andolan (ABVA) organized the first-ever protest demonstration that openly demanded 'gay rights', in August 1994, outside the Delhi police headquarters.

This demonstration followed the 1991 release of 'Less than Gay', the first document to publicly demand gay rights in India. Many NGOs working with individuals marginalized because of their sexuality have also been harassed. Section 377 was likely to have had an adverse impact on the fight against HIV and AIDS in India. Social stigma, backed up by the threat of 10 years' imprisonment for homosexuality, helps drive the epidemic underground and heightens the risk of transmission, as gay men may be less likely to present for testing, prevention services, and treatment, lest they be found out (Misra, 2009).

In 2018, after Section 377 was scrapped, the battle was won, but the war continues. Some of the concerns remain since legal sanction does not put a stop to discrimination and violence against queer persons. Hence, the state should provide safe houses for those subjected to attacks, as well as counselling and health services. To prevent repeats of harassment, more stringent punishments for offenders should be combined with efforts to educate officials about the changes to the law and about the need to treat all individuals equally and fairly. These efforts are needed among police forces, health facilities, including sexual health facilities, legal professionals, and courts. Provision of services should also be stepped up. At present, many LGBT individuals do not have access to sexual health facilities, and many are reluctant to attend general health facilities because of the risk of discrimination. The same is true of legal services.

Many organizations in India have a long-standing commitment to bettering the lives of LGBTIQ persons, such as Humsafar Trust, Mumbai, one of the foremost ones; Naz Foundation, which led the fight for scrapping of Section 377; Udaan Trust; Sangama; Sangini; Sappho; LABIA; Samapathik Trust; Adhikaar; Bharosa Trust; and Orinam, to name a few. Several magazines, portals, and websites dedicated to the issues faced by LGBTIQ individuals have come up in the last several years. Mainstream therapists, as well as queer communities and organizations working with them, are offering queer-affirmative therapies. Queer film festivals take place across India, and pride marches are held in a lot of cities. However, rural and mofussil areas and smaller towns have not yet become more open about alternative sexualities, and even within cities, not everyone has become more accepting. The intersectional aspects of multiple identities of queer persons – aspects of caste, religion, and region – remain unaddressed, such that privileged queer persons have a few more options than a rural, Muslim, gay person, or an urban, poor, Dalit, trans person has to be acknowledged and worked with.

Hence, despite the work done by many pioneering organizations, a lot remains to be done. Many steps need to be taken for the country's hitherto marginalized LGBTIQ individuals to gain broad acceptance and equality within the wider society. For sexual minorities to become full citizens in the true sense and for their psychosocial health and psychosocial justice, they need to get all the rights that straight persons have easy access to: the rights to ownership of property, education, equal opportunities in employment, marriage (amendments to the existing Special Marriage Act or a new law, as is the demand of many LGBTIQ support organizations), adoption, health, and mental health services.

The psychological impact of criminalizing queer, intimate relationships has been huge and is yet to be documented fully, in both research and intervention work in psychology and gender. Much work has been done by activists, sympathizers, and supporters of the queer movement and queer individuals. Feminist psychologists

122 Exploring Gender and Sexualities

need to understand the intricacies, impact, pain, and trauma faced by queer persons in leading stigmatized lives and being under the lens of the family, police, and the larger society. Although Section 377 has been scrapped, the scars of previous times remain, and the taboos against coming out to families, colleagues, and the larger society also continue for many. This leaves them open to blackmail and exploitation and leaves them with no agency in their intimacy.

Same-sex marriages all over the world have an uneven trajectory; some states/countries have allowed it after legislative battles led by queer groups, whereas others still prohibit them. This means that queer persons who believe in the institution of marriage (some find the idea and institution 'heteronormative' and do not subscribe to marriage), togetherness, and companionship that heterosexual couples enjoy as their right face psychological distress, loneliness, and low self-esteem, since they do not enjoy these rights as citizens.

Hence, there is a long way to go!

Review Questions

1 How can we understand the differences between sexuality, sex, sexual orientation, and gender?
2 What are the misconceptions held about queer relationships and queer individuals?
3 What are the problems faced by the parents of queer individuals?

Critical Thinking Questions

1 What are the major issues before queer persons and the queer movement in India post scrapping of Section 377?
2 As students of psychology, how will you engage with the lived realities of queer persons? Identify films, serials, books, magazines, and online portals for the same.

Bibliography

Chakraborty, R. (2019). Indian LGBT workshop helps queer people bring parents 'out of the closet' on sexuality and gender. *South China Morning Post*. www.scmp.com/lifestyle/family-relationships/article/3024706/indian-lgbt-workshop-helps-queer-people-bring

LABIA. (2013). *Breaking the binary report*. Labia Collective.

Misra, G. (2009). Decriminalizing homosexuality in India. *Reproductive Health Matters*, *17*(34), 20–28. https://dx.org/10.1016/S0968-8080(09)34478-X

Natu, S. (2021). *Interview on FM channel Ahmednagar, Maharashtra on 'hook up culture'*.

Peplau, L. A., & Beals, K. P. (2004). The family lives of lesbians and gay men. In A. Vangelisti (Ed.), *Handbook of family communication* (pp. 233–248). Routledge.

Ranade, K. (2019). *Growing up gay in Urban India: A critical psychosocial perspective*. Springer.

Ranade, K., Shah, C., & Chatterji, S. (2016). Making sense: Familial journeys towards self-acceptance of gay and lesbian family members in India. *The Indian Journal of Social Work*, *77*, 437–458.

7
UNDERSTANDING FEMINIST PSYCHOTHERAPIES

Chapter Highlights

Learning Objectives

After reading this chapter, the students would be able to

- Understand what feminist psychotherapies entail.
- Realize how feminist practices are incorporated into psychotherapy techniques.
- Identify how feminism and psychoanalysis relate.
- Recognize how gender-sensitive family therapy helps.

Introduction

Mainstream psychotherapies have a long history full of highs and lows. In the process of engendering psychology, as well as psychotherapy, several feminist psychotherapeutic practices have emerged. Female clients called out the sexual, emotional, and mental harassment by male psychotherapists, and there were violations related to racial, ethnic, and alternative-sexuality discrimination and harassment in therapy. These events and processes called for redressal, changes, and the emergence of new practices. As a result, in the late 1970s, many feminist psychotherapies that were women-centred and race- and ethnicity-inclusive emerged and are now established practices. Over the last few years, queer-affirmative therapies and narrative therapies best suited to various communities have flourished all over the world. All these therapies challenge hierarchies, the biomedical model, discrimination, and prejudices. Mainstream psychology has not recognized feminist therapies and does not unequivocally value them, and hence these therapies are not learnt or understood all over India or all over the world uniformly. However,

DOI: 10.4324/9781003453758-8

124 Understanding Feminist Psychotherapies

feminist therapies respond to the complexities of race, gender, ethnicity, caste, region, and nation and are relevant as a tool and a practice in today's world full of persistent inequalities. They have evolved from the women's movement the world over and are tied to people's lived realities and complexities of multiple identities, much more and much better than several mainstream psychotherapies that follow a top-down, therapist-led paradigm. Feminist therapies are also interrelated to queer-affirmative and narrative therapy practices organically and hence allow for extension and value addition.

7.1 Feminist Psychotherapies: Engendering the Theory and Practice of Psychotherapy

Psychology has always embraced a biomedical approach to be connected to natural sciences. Psychotherapies have also had a biomedical perspective embedded in them. Despite the shift to a bio-psychosocial approach, oftentimes this is merely to pay lip service to the psychosocial and not really unpack the social determinants of both the self and health and mental health. Besides, despite some humanistic psychotherapies that are sensitive to clients, far more than generic psychotherapies, there has always been a 'male bias and patriarchal slant' in all psychotherapies. In the Indian context (also South Asian), there is a dire need for decolonizing psychology, psychotherapy, and psychiatry. Against this backdrop, it would be important to understand how feminist psychotherapies came to be practised as a clarion call to engender the theories and practices of psychotherapies.

The history of feminist psychotherapy goes back to feminist criticism and activism in the West; though these interventions were uneven, they were a strong moral and intellectual force that questioned therapeutic practices, which had gone unquestioned until then. Broverman et al. (1972) and her colleagues demonstrated that many therapists based their knowledge on stereotypes and biases just like ordinary citizens and not on scientific sources. These biases and stereotypes about women (as also African Americans, ethnic minorities, queer persons) permeated diagnosis and treatment and affected the prognosis too. For instance, the classification of premenstrual syndrome (PMS) and premenstrual dysphoric disorder (PMDD), also called late luteal phase dysphoric disorder, as a diagnostic category was challenged by feminists, since PMS and PMDD entail just a bunch of symptoms and are catch-all terms for what women go through during their menstrual cycle, and there is 'nothing abnormal about it'! Eventually, it was discarded as a diagnostic category, but the myths about it continue to prevail.

It was observed that misdiagnosis, underdiagnosis, and overdiagnosis prevailed, since what was considered 'normal' behaviour for women (children, queer persons, ethnic minorities, black people, and so on) was all socially constructed and socially controlled. These norms were applied to all these categories of persons, including women, which amounted to labelling and discrediting them, and were highly discriminatory, as well as oppressive. A classic diagnosis was 'hysteria' (which

Understanding Feminist Psychotherapies **125**

has an interesting origin in the Greek word for uterus, *hystera*, also thought of as a 'wandering uterus'), which was shorthand for a hyperemotional state of mind.

This diagnosis was almost exclusively reserved for women (though several men too displayed the same classic symptoms) due to the strong gender bias that women exhibit hysterical behaviour! This diagnosis was also strongly contested, and eventually it was removed from DSM as a diagnostic category. The political meaning of diagnosis, in terms of who is diagnosed, who gets to diagnose, how social control works in terms of what is acceptable and unacceptable behaviour, the persistent inequalities and how they lead to psychological distress, and the fact that mental health is also deeply political, was something that feminisms foregrounded.

The second realm that was deeply problematic was psychiatric medication and treatment. Whether in the West or in India, the field of psychiatry has been male-dominated and -populated for long. (A 2010 article says that the number of female psychiatrists in India is 14.64 per cent of that of male psychiatrists!) There was a history of overmedication and diagnoses that pandered to what new miracle drugs pharma companies had to offer. This meant that a multitude of women ended up taking antidepressants that they did not need and enduring their side effects for a long time. This too was challenged by feminists. The horrific practice of sexual harassment by some psychotherapists earned them the dubious distinction of becoming the anagram of therapist (the rapist), and with feminist activists and lobbyists at the forefront of raising an alarm about this, APA had to take strict action. APA incorporated ethical guidelines for therapists, and the latter's breaking these rules meant getting their licenses revoked.

Also, such issues as violence against women, trauma, sexuality, race in the West, caste in South Asia, and HIV/AIDS brought to the fore the narrowness and inadequacies of mainstream psychotherapies. The issues of rape and shelters for battered women all over the world were proof that systemic violence and various patriarchies colluded to create violence against women, and a different kind of understanding outside mainstream approaches was essential to engage with these problems and offer real succour to women.

Feminist psychologists who questioned the inadequacies and ills of mainstream psychotherapies were frontrunners of feminist psychotherapies. Broadly, various forms of feminist psychotherapy are heterogeneous and come from feminist philosophies and practices, such as consciousness raising (CR), speak-out groups, assertiveness training, support groups, and self-help groups. CR groups were part of feminist collectives in the 1960s and 1970s. The pattern was leaderless and egalitarian, embedded in validating that the 'personal is political' – at the root of a lot of subjective problems, there are systemic issues. Societal conditions, pressures, and control were acknowledged as causes of several interpersonal conflicts, dynamics, and strife.

The solidarity and sisterhood among members (mostly women, and sometimes groups of men and women) facilitated the speaking out, handholding, care, and healing. CR groups also engaged in a 'collective questioning of patriarchy which

126 Understanding Feminist Psychotherapies

TABLE 7.1 Some Initiatives of Feminist Therapy

West	*India*
Women's Therapy Centre (1976–2019), London, Susie Orbach and Luise Eichenbaum	Women's Centre, Mumbai, Speak Out Group (the 1970s)
Women's Therapy Centre Institute, New York, United States	Nari Samata Manch, Pune Boltya Vha Speak Out Group (the 1970s)

Source: Internet and the author's archives

helped in catharsis'. Speak-out groups were a corollary to the CR groups. The women's movement recognized that repression and lack of voice led to several psychosocial issues. Hence, facilitators helped women speak out and vent, and the latter were given support. A list of some (not exhaustive) such pioneering efforts is presented in Table 7.1.

While mainstream psychotherapies are related to the status and power of the therapist, and the terminology depicts the therapist's worldview (problem, intervention, goals), they also distort women's experience – oppression, negotiation in the clinic, reinforcement of gender stereotypes. These therapies push women back to the same milieu that has created problems for them by telling them to 'adjust'. Feminist psychotherapies, on the other hand, are about women's viewpoint; they are non-hierarchical; involve no victim blaming; use narrative analysis; use sensitive (non-intrusive, non-invasive) techniques; and mainly question power relations within families, organizations, and systems of all kinds. There are several studies from the West which foreground the principles and importance of feminist psychotherapies.

For instance, McClellan (1999) in her study pointed out that historically, psychotherapy has largely failed women and other marginalized people. Created by the mainstream to serve the mainstream, traditional therapy focuses on the individual and works to bring all individuals in line with the status quo. In contrast, feminist therapy (as one of the radical alternative therapies) emphasizes the need for psychotherapy to be based on a socio-political philosophy that names oppression as the cause of most of the emotional and psychological distress experienced by individuals. Major emphasis is on change rather than on adjustment. Traditional therapy is charged with (a) reinforcing society's mystifications/lies/deceit and (b) allowing itself to be used and degraded in service of the mainstream. The role of demystification, honesty, and the pursuit of justice as therapeutic endeavours are important in feminist psychotherapy.

In an Indian study, Joshi (2015) highlights the following as the markers of a gender-sensitive approach to counselling by a counsellor: (a) building an egalitarian relationship with the client; (b) situating individual realities in the larger social context; (c) empowering the client; (d) taking a stance against gender injustice;

and (e) identifying one's personal biases and internalized gender messages. The term 'gender-sensitive counselling', rooted in feminist ideology, is concerned with psychological distress experienced by both women and men while being aware of the power differentials that exist between them. This is also what separates it from non-sexist counselling. Feminist therapy questioned sexist assumptions that existed within traditional forms of psychotherapy and feared that these biases could lead to pathologizing of a client's gender-atypical behaviours. Given the close link between gender and mental health, it is important that psychologists and other mental health professionals actively engage with issues of gender.

Gender-sensitive counselling links the personal to the political by situating individual realities and distress in the socio-political–cultural context in which they occur, thus intersecting gender with other powerful determinants such as caste, class, sexuality, religion, and ethnicity. Gender is a critical determinant of mental health, and distress is often intricately linked to an individual's gender roles and corresponding societal expectations. Initial theories attributed the high prevalence of common mental disorders in women to biological and reproductive health causes; however, recent research points towards psychosocial origins.

7.2 Feminist Practice in Therapy

There are many frameworks used by a variety of feminists to summarize their principles of practising feminist therapy. Some of them are outlined here. Susie Orbach and Luise Eichenbaum said that what started as pioneering efforts in feminist therapy in the 1970s (at the Women's Therapy Centre, London) would today be called a 'social enterprise start-up'; then, there was a need to bring what they had been learning from feminism (socialist feminism) and psychotherapy and psychoanalysis together (a) to create a place for women of whatever background to come to therapy and be listened to and to be understood in the context of what it had meant psychologically to grow up as a girl – what psychological costs were associated with that, whatever their class or ethnic or geographical location; (b) to build a new theory on gender; (c) to build new practice; (d) to transform mental health policy and the often reactionary state of psychotherapy; (e) to destigmatize therapy; (f) to create a work environment where women could learn together and also disseminate what they were learning; (g) to create a practice in which women were aware of their identifications with the people they were seeing – not that they shared those in sessions – but they were not distant; they were the same as they tried to theorize new ways of working, which included an understanding of therapists as well.

Sommers-Flanagan and Sommers-Flanagan (2018) describe feminist practice in psychology as one derived from the realities that lie outside, beneath, and at variance from the visions of the dominant patriarchal mainstream. It is an integrative and competency-based paradigm that perceives human beings as responsive to the problems of their lives, capable of solving those problems and desirous of change.

128 Understanding Feminist Psychotherapies

It is also a politically informed model that observes human experience within the framework of societal and cultural realities and through the dynamics of power informing those realities. Feminist theory and therapy are a historical effort to bring awareness about inequities based on gender and sex and to resolve them using egalitarian solutions. Feminist theory places great importance in multicultural feminist scholarship, CR, subversion, intersectionality, and social transformation; it is not linked to any specific technique. Feminist therapists' techniques are not defined by strategies; instead, feminist therapists are driven by feminist theory.

Feminist therapy is about connections, and it involves egalitarian interconnection; mutual empathy; and empowerment of the oppressed, neglected, and marginalized. Feminist therapists provide an open and safe space for discussing relationships, sexuality, and intimacy, as well as for self-disclosure. There are three primary feminist principles that guide feminist therapy in practice: (a) sex and gender powerfully affect identity; (b) deviance comes from a dysfunctional culture; and (c) CR is part of healing and change. Therefore, becoming a feminist-therapy practitioner is more about embracing ideologies of social change and less about just tools and techniques!

Various feminist philosophies have given rise to some of the core principles of feminist therapeutic practice: the personal being political; commitment to social change; women's voices being heard; ways of knowing and experience being valued; egalitarian relationship in counselling; reframing of the problem and psychological distress; all forms of oppression being recognized; individual and social change being aimed at; gaining of understanding that socio-political context and individual lives are intertwined; recognition of marginalization, subordination, and stereotyping as being harmful; understanding of external factors leading to internal distress; transformation of individuals and society, freeing of men and women; aim of making women understand and accept that their own needs, relationships, and social self are balanced; equality and mutuality with the clients; recognition that clients are experts on their own lives; living and coping rather than pathology; belief in client's strengths and abilities; rejection of the biomedical model; recognition that women, queer, and disabled are all 'othered'; diversity and complexity being valued and respected; lived reality being respected; the external and internal being connected; and avoidance of jargon. These feminist practices in 'therapy' make feminist psychotherapy unique.

Feminist therapy was intended originally for women and focused mainly on women's issues; however, men can certainly benefit from the feminist perspective, as they too can feel limited by the social expectations and gender stereotypes. Other core values of feminist therapy are the ideas of empowerment and de-pathologizing. This means that the emphasis is on the individual's strengths and capabilities, rather than on the weaknesses or remediation of symptoms. For instance, feminists made enormous contribution to trauma theory and practices, especially around the trauma of sexual abuse. Trauma was 'normalized', 'symptoms' were reframed as 'coping skills', and 'victims' were reframed as 'survivors' (Burstow, 1992).

One of the greatest gifts of the feminist approach is that it paved the way for a different style of therapeutic relationship. Being sensitive to how power differences may impact people, feminist therapists strive to create egalitarian relationships with clients, demystify the therapy process, and encourage clients to be equal participants in the assessment and treatment process (Corey, 2009; Matlin, 2008). A journey towards empowerment begins with handing back power and control to clients within the therapeutic setting. The therapist brings the psychological knowledge, but clients are the real experts of themselves. The role of the therapist is not to stay aloof and detached behind the 'expert' role but to be a real and authentic human being, to be present in such a way that people are truly empowered to find their unique voices and expand the range of possibilities in their lives. This is the hallmark of feminist therapy in practice!

The empowerment model put forth by Worrell and Remer (1992) elaborates the process of becoming a feminist therapist. They list out 'trust, protection, egalitarianism, respect, flexibility, self-disclosure and affirmation' as important principles. The model uses the principles such as the personal being political, egalitarian relationships and valuing of the female perspective. They also describe techniques of gender role analysis, power analysis, assertiveness training, use of CR groups, and reframing and demystification of therapy. Feminist psychotherapy aims to identify gender biases in mainstream therapies and make them compatible with feminist goals. Therapists are encouraged to be change agents and use theories of feminisms in practice. Case history taking and assessment should be done using a feminist perspective, bringing in the sociocultural, individual, interpersonal, and gender role socialization factors. Worrell and Remer suggest that therapists blend self-examination, self-evaluation, and self-awareness and analyse their own blind spots and biases all the time and rectify them. This is something that is completely missing in mainstream therapy with therapists and psychiatrists playing God!

While the initial practitioners of feminist psychotherapy (mostly being activists too) were white, educated, upper-class women who were privileged, it has now become broad-based to include all kinds of women and men too, both as therapists and as clients. Understanding the need to be inclusive and intersectional, since women and men differ based on class, caste, race, ethnicity, and other stratifications, feminist psychotherapy the world over has become much more multidimensional in philosophy and practice. It is a real need of the hour in the current times too, since the 2020 Covid-19 pandemic has resulted in a mental health pandemic and a humanitarian crisis of humungous proportions, and mainstream therapies and the biomedical model will be totally ineffective in dealing with it.

Feminist practice in therapy or feminist psychotherapy is hinged as much on egalitarian philosophies and ideologies as it is on tools, techniques, and theories. My own feminist psychotherapy practice draws a lot from intersectional feminism and subversion of some of the principles of mainstream therapies to better suit the class, caste, gender, sexuality, region, and location of the individual client. I am also mindful of the community locations (caste, region – urban/rural). For example, the

130 Understanding Feminist Psychotherapies

social space available to an urban client is rarely available to a rural one, whereas the community spirit lends more support to rural and semi-urban clients (cannot be generalized but has to be tested and can be used as a thumb rule). Avoiding 'homogenizing' individuals (a practice that mainstream psychotherapy adopts) is the hallmark of feminist psychotherapy. The lived experiences of the individual are extremely important, and phenomenologically, a feminist psychotherapist not just has to put herself in the shoes of 'a client' but also faces a much taller order: think like a first-generation learner, understanding the nuances of identity of a person who lives at the fringes of rural and urban spaces, who is impacted by both cultures and must make choices. This cannot be achieved unless one is able to observe subaltern lives, empathize with people who are not at all like you, understand the intersections of caste, class, gender, and region, and unravel all these strands. Being a feminist psychotherapist is exhausting, challenging, and rewarding.

In my practice as a feminist psychotherapist, I have also encountered a few female clients who have come for marital therapy and expect me to 'take their side and validate solely their experiences as women'. I am not surprised by this misreading of feminism in general and feminist psychotherapy in particular as 'for women by women and anti-men'! I have patiently explained to them that both men and women face patriarchal pressures in family and society albeit differently. Feminist psychotherapy is about deconstructing these experiences from all the locations of caste, class, genders, sexualities, and the power dynamics therein to arrive at some solutions.

7.3 Feminism and Psychoanalysis

There was an interesting relationship between psychoanalysis and feminism. Personally, I have a love–hate relationship with Freud! He was ahead of his time in terms of bringing the master motives of 'sex and aggression' to the forefront of human engagement (something that we have still not done sufficiently in social sciences even in the 21st century). However, the reductionist tenets of psychanalysis that he put forth, such as anatomy/biology is destiny, penis envy, castration complex, the Oedipus complex, and the Electra (female Oedipus) complex, to name a few, were deeply problematic and misogynist.

Therefore, the feminist critique of Freud targeted his biological determinism (women are natural nurturers, their fulfilment lies in motherhood, and so on). There was also a strong criticism to the fact that Freudian psychoanalysis had overlooked external sociocultural factors and their complexity completely in a bid to universalize the inner world, the unconscious, and other tenets and principles. Freud's model pathologized psychological problems using biomedical norms, and the unkindest cut of all was that his theory and practice of psychoanalysis used 'male = norm; female = deficient = abnormal' as a template! These hallmarks of Freudian theory and therapy of psychoanalysis prompted a response from several women within psychology and from feminists, and psychoanalysis became a much-contested

Understanding Feminist Psychotherapies **131**

arena! As a woman, you are damned anyway; if you are normal, you are mad by implication, and if you are abnormal, you are mad by definition. My favourite quotation from Sylvia Plath, best sums up how the social construction of gender and pathologizing psychological distress intersect in the arena of psychoanalysis (as well as other mainstream psychotherapies, as discussed earlier). Various female psychologists who learnt from and followed Freud, and therefore called neo-Freudians, also disagreed with Freud on many counts and made departures from Freudian principles while borrowing some of his relevant and meaningful concepts. Notable among them were Freida Fromm-Reichmann, Helene Deutsch, Marie Bonaparte, and of course Anna Freud. They disagreed with Freud on several counts: ideas about psychosexual stages of development and the importance of the unconscious, as well as the explicit and implicit misogyny in all aspects of the theory and practice of psychoanalysis.

Freud's major critics from within psychology were fellow psychoanalysts Karen Horney, Clara Thompson, and Melanie Klein. Karen Horney critiqued the centrality of penis envy. She coined a term 'womb envy', the Neo-Freudian feminist equivalent of 'penis envy', to mean men's fear and jealousy of women's power to give birth and nurture life, leading them to take up other pursuits of powers, such as physical or political. She also connected women's overvaluation of love to socio-economic dependence on men and marriage.

Clara Thompson examined cultural pressures on women, their economic dependence, and derogation of their sexuality as against the established complexes and cathexes of Freudian psychoanalysis. Melanie Klein thought that Freud's timing (age of the child) of the Oedipus complex was incorrect, and contradictory to Freud, she maintained that the superego (the morality principle) was present since birth. She and Anna Freud were also considered rivals, battling for the mantle of Sigmund Freud's true successor! They were precursors to the feminist critique of Freud by Simone de Beauvoir, Betty Freidan, Shulamith Firestone, Kate Millet, and others.

Simone de Beauvoir, in her classic, *The Second Sex*, counters various premises of Freudian psychoanalysis by shifting attention to women as secondary, second-class citizens in a patriarchal world, calling them the 'other' and the second sex in comparison to males (the self and first sex!). Betty Freidan, in her classic texts *The Feminine Mystique* and *The Second Stage*, deconstructed womanhood and what ails women in completely different ways from Freudian interpretations of feminine psyche in an empathetic and sensitive manner. Shulamith Firestone, a radical feminist, argued that 'Freudianism wiped out the radical force of feminism and tried to contain women into familial roles' in her classic, *The Dialectic of Sex*. Kate Millet, in *Sexual Politics*, highlighted the neglected political aspect of sex and concluded that Freud and several others looked at sex in a patriarchal and sexist way.

Germaine Greer's irreverence towards Freudian tenets in *The Female Eunuch* was inspired by Simone de Beauvoir's work. She highlighted the unacceptable facts about female sexuality, which was brave during those times and in the times

132 Understanding Feminist Psychotherapies

to come (readers should read the original texts mentioned earlier and some primary texts written by Freud, as well as some of the vast amount of studies based on comparing the work of Freud and some of the feminists mentioned previously, for gaining an insight). We should of course note that Freudian psychoanalysis could be loved or hated but never ignored by feminists and that his tenets triggered a lot of reflection, critique, reformulation, and new formulations around several concepts, especially sex and sexuality.

Other feminist psychologists such as Carol Gilligan (*In a Different Voice*), Jean Baker Miller (*Toward a New Psychology of Women*), Rhoda Unger and Mary Crawford (*Women and Gender: A Feminist Psychology*) and Sandra Bem (gender schema theory and androgyny), all responded to Freudian and Neo-Freudian psychoanalysis in myriad ways in their several studies, theories, and books.

Thus far, we have discussed criticism from female psychologists of Freudian psychoanalysis and departures made by female Neo-Freudians who trained under Freud, as well as feminist critiques of Freud's work by notable feminists. We have also understood that much work of feminist psychologists was answering some of the questions posed by psychanalytic tenets that followed the 'women as deficient/deviant' model.

Against this backdrop, let us understand psychoanalytic feminism, which is an offshoot of all the things mentioned earlier. This school of feminism engaged in reinterpretation of the Oedipal complex and searched for non-patriarchal meanings in Freudian tenets. Psychoanalytic feminists examined Freudian thought for its true liberating and enslaving potential. They explained women's oppression as rooted within psychic structures and reinforced by the continual repetition or reiteration of relational dynamics formed at infancy and in childhood. Because of these deeply engrained patterns, psychoanalytic feminists wanted to alter the experiences of early childhood and family relations, as well as linguistic patterns, which produce and reinforce masculinity and femininity. Critical of Freudian and Neo-Freudian notions of women as biologically, psychically, and morally inferior to men, psychoanalytic feminists addressed political and social factors affecting the development of male and female subjects. Like radical feminists, they saw as key issues sexual difference and women's otherness in relation to men. The two major schools of psychoanalytic feminism are Freudian and Lacanian. Freudian feminists, mostly Anglo-American, are more concerned with the production of male dominance and the development of gendered subjects in societies where women are responsible for mothering, whereas Lacanian feminists, mostly French, analyse links between gendered identity and language.

Early feminist appropriations of Freud in the works of Alfred Adler, Karen Horney, and Clara Thompson emphasized the uniqueness of each human being over rigidly gendered developmental tracks and explained women's psychic pathologies as generated and sustained by their inferior social status within patriarchy, rather than by a biologically determined lack. These theorists reinterpreted some women's neuroses as creative attempts to address ongoing social subordination. Later feminist appropriations of Freud critique the traditional family structure in which primarily women mother and assume other caretaking responsibilities.

In *The Reproduction of Mothering*, Nancy Chodorow, for instance, argues that differential experiences in infancy orient girls and boys towards different developmental paths, with boys definitively separating from their mothers to identify with the father's social power and girls developing a more symbiotic/continuous sense of self in relation to the mother. These relational dynamics that emphasize autonomy and separation for boys render men emotionally stunted and less capable of intimate personal relationships but better prepared for public life and the world of work. Girls, who in contrast develop as subjects in closer relation with their mother, have more fluid psychic boundaries that facilitate a greater capacity for intimacy but leave them less prepared to negotiate the public sphere. Chodorow and other object relations theorists advocated dual parenting as one way to eliminate the characterological imbalances generated by gendered extremes, as children would be able to view both parents as individuals-in-relation, experience men and women as both self- and other-oriented, and view both sexes as inhabiting private and public domains.

Putting into practice Chodorow's theoretical restructuring of the family would, of course, require considering some substantial changes in current policies and practices: reasonable parental leave, adequate compensation for part-time work, quality childcare staffed with both male and female caretakers, and early/elementary education with both male and female teachers. Psychoanalytic feminists in the Lacanian mode privileged the analysis of self-construction through discourse over the biological and psychosocial implications of parenting, arguing that to alter gender relations, we need to change language. In Lacanian psychoanalysis, the phallus is symbolic of the child's entry into language and culture under 'the law of the father', and Lacanian feminists wanted to interrogate and resist oppressive constructions of gender and sexuality encoded in language.

One group of French Lacanian feminists, including Luce Irigaray, Hélène Cixous, and Catherine Clement, are known for their project of *écriture féminine*, an attempt to write from or to discursively embody the position of woman in order to challenge women's positioning in phallogocentric culture. These writers argued that women needed to forego the neutral, scientific, and masculine language and embrace a rebellious creativity based in subjective experience of the body and the feminine. For this, they attempted to realize a female/feminine sex/subject outside of patriarchal definitions of 'woman'. For Irigaray and Cixous, this involved celebrating women's diffused and autoerotic sensuality, in contrast to the linear, focused dynamic of phallic sex, as well as critiquing the symbolic order through parody.

Some classic psychoanalytic feminists and their texts are listed in Table 7.2.

Jacques Lacan, called the French Freud, is also viewed as a controversial psychoanalyst by feminists. Many of his principles and tenets have been challenged by feminists. His work is seen as elitist, male-dominated, and phallocentric. Winnicott,

134 Understanding Feminist Psychotherapies

TABLE 7.2 Classic Psychoanalytic Feminists and Their Field-Defining Texts

Judith Butler	Gender Trouble
Nancy Chodorow	*The Reproduction of Mothering*
Hélène Cixous	The Laugh of the Medusa
Teresa de Lauretis	*Alice Doesn't* and *The Practice of Love*
Dorothy Dinnerstein	*The Mermaid and the Minotaur*
Elizabeth Grosz	*Volatile Bodies*
Luce Irigaray	*This Sex Which Is Not One*
Julia Kristeva	*Desire in Language* and *Tales of Love*
Juliet Mitchell	*Woman's Estate* and *Psychoanalysis and Feminism*
Juliet Mitchell and Jacqueline Rose	*Feminine Sexuality*

Source: Internet and author's archives

a British psychoanalyst, has been both criticized and commended by feminists. He was attacked for normalizing women's traditional role but praised for conceptualizing relationships that are free of the I–other oppositions. His followers view him as a participant who values the transformative qualities of social interaction and public deliberation. Gerson (2004) argues that while Winnicott does hold participation up as an ideal, he relegates other pursuits to subsidiary roles that are distanced from participation and so divides the world into two realms that complement and exclude each other. His work is therefore at odds with feminism's project of overcoming the division between the private and public spheres.

That both psychoanalysis and psychoanalytical feminism still hold sway is ably demonstrated by the fact that recent feminist and psychoanalytic accounts of mothering have been profoundly shaped by the work of Melanie Klein, D. W. Winnicott, Nancy Chodorow, and Julia Kristeva. Although their work spans many decades, these writers share the goal of understanding object relations, that is, the child's relation to internalized 'objects' – most often the mother, as the child's first caretaker. Doane and Hodges (1992) chart the development of 'mother-centred' psychoanalysis and its influence on feminist thought in a number of fields and show how the effort to elevate the importance of the mother has become implicated in the current effort to restrict possibilities for women to 'opportunities' associated with hearth and home.

The authors argue that discussions of the maternal role always exist within an ideological framework in which they are purveyed to groups at times. In our own historical time, ideas of maternal propriety have been vigorously argued, as in custody battles, where experts debate whether individual women are 'good enough' mothers. The review traces the ways in which object relations accounts of mothering have worked to encourage the view that 'good enough' mothers find 'their whole self' at home. What does this view of mothering mean for working women? How does it help promote arguments that 'foetal rights' are more important than a mother's own desires? By recovering the historical context of object relations

Understanding Feminist Psychotherapies **135**

theory and closely attending to the language of important theorists, Doane and Hodges (1992) make visible the extraordinary influence of object relations on the discourses in many fields and demonstrate the power of psychological theory to shape both popular and academic discussions of maternal propriety.

7.4 Gender-Sensitive Family Therapy

Awareness of gender issues and understanding of the impact gender has upon relationships within families are vital for family counsellors in providing effective services. Gender practices and roles can form a continuum from abusive, sexist behaviours, through traditional gender values with some power imbalance in gender issues, to egalitarian family practices striving for gender neutrality. Family therapy or family systems therapy is an important therapeutic practice that needs to be engendered. In this section, let us understand how family therapy/counselling has fared as far as gender sensitivity is concerned.

Forrest and Steigerwald (2004) believe that counsellor empathy, acceptance, genuineness, trust, and professional competence are essential to effective family counselling. Counsellors need to become aware of the many gender concerns, such as how differences in the gender of the counsellor affect the therapeutic process, the ways in which societal gender norms are supported by the counsellor, how the therapeutic interventions created may differ when working with heterosexual couples compared to gay or lesbian couples, the responsibility that counsellors have in working with couples that have functioning and satisfactory non-egalitarian relationships and the emphasis on the inequities inherent in such dyadic structures, and the impact that culture and development have on the way that men and women communicate with each other. This attempt towards gender-sensitive family therapy is to help families restructure themselves such that both partners can grow and achieve their full potential as individuals as well as a couple.

Parents draw on prevalent gender beliefs to develop a narrative about their children, and this in turn shapes the interactional patterns that develop between them. Gender was constructed as a dualistic category and was thought to be opposite and polarized; that is, female cannot be male, and masculine is that which is not feminine. Now, these gender polarizations are being questioned as feminists argue that moving away from gender stereotypes would be beneficial for women's mental health because so many female characteristics have been devalued by society. Burck and Daniel (1995) observe that '[g]ender characteristics be interactional and relational, not belonging to individual women and men, but to the relationships between them as they develop over time'.

Family therapy/counselling, as well as couples counselling/marital therapy, is a space where spouses, as well as family members, of either gender come into the therapeutic space. Hence, gender sensitization of therapists of either gender is essential. If they do not pay attention to the inequalities in families and the hierarchies in society, their family therapy would push people into the same stereotypical

136 Understanding Feminist Psychotherapies

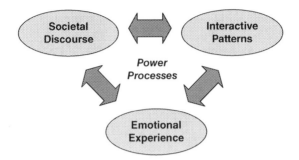

FIGURE 7.1 Power Processes
Source: Knudson-Martin and Wells (2014)

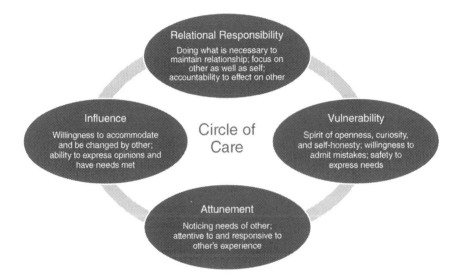

FIGURE 7.2 Circle of Care
Source: Knudson-Martin and Wells (2014)

gender roles that are causing the problems in the first place (marital conflicts, domestic violence, discrimination among children, and so on).

Societal discourse (narratives in society and social sciences), emotion, interaction, and power are key factors that help maintain the gender systems status quo. They reflect how sociocultural forces and power disparities are involved in family interactions and often impact the problems that bring persons to couple and family therapy (Knudson-Martin, 2017). To create a gender-sensitive paradigm in family and couple therapy, therapists need to undergo training and adopt an egalitarian perspective.

The harmful effects of the societal gender systems on couple and family power dynamics can be offset by focusing on four key relational processes designated as forming the circle of care in the socio-emotional relationship therapy (SERT), namely mutual vulnerability, shared attunement, mutual influence, and shared relational responsibility. It means that the therapist needs to focus on mutuality in relationships (relationships are two way, and hence communication needs to be two way, and accountability needs to be shared by both/all). He or she needs to address the hierarchy in relationships, deconstruct 'influence', and see that the needs of both/all are met. Both/all need to accept and address each other's vulnerabilities (this is a complex arena). Finally, attunement means paying complete attention to the needs of the other/others and respecting their experience. Such a process of gender-sensitive family/couples therapy can not only bring about a sea change in the dynamics within the relationship but also gear families/couples towards complete acceptance and positivity.

These couples and families come from different racial, ethnic, socio-economic, and cultural (caste, regional, and religious, in the Indian context) backgrounds. Gender and power affect them in vastly different ways in all the choices they make careers, love/marriage, child rearing, domestic labour, professions, interactions within families, dealing with conflicts and violence, and so on. Hence, intersectionality and gender have to be considered together in the therapeutic space for healing to happen. The tensions between race/caste and gender also need to be addressed in family and couple therapy in the case of cis men and women, as well as LGBTIQ couples and their families. It is these nuances of feminism which are missing in mainstream family and couples therapy, which needs to be set right. Many feminist psychologists are using a Gendergram to create peace among warring couples and families. It involves some questions used to elicit information from and then work on with clients.

Gendergram

- In what ways have these people had a lasting influence on how you view yourself as a woman or man?
- How did changes in your physical appearance, whether due to maturation, accidents, or illness, influence how you felt about yourself as a man or woman?
- What did you learn about your sexuality during this time? How did you learn it?
- In what ways did what you learn impact your definition of yourself as a woman or man?
- What spiritual/religious influences were important to you at this time, and how have they informed your feelings about yourself as a man or woman?

138 Understanding Feminist Psychotherapies

- Describe the emotional climate of your home during this time.
- How was affection expressed between women, between men, between women and men, and between parents/adults and children?
- How was conflict handled?
- Did men and women express the same emotions differently?
- How secure did you feel when you were at home?
- How was conformity to your family's gender norms rewarded? How was nonconformity punished?
- What did men/women in your family do currently in the family, at work, in the community, for recreation, as disciplinarians, and in general?

Source: *Psychology Today* (1996)

Gendergrams are used for assessing the dynamics among couples and families. The information is useful in charting out the course of gender-sensitive interventions, as well as outcomes. It is a handy tool that when meshed with an egalitarian philosophy yields really good results.

7.5 Queer-Affirmative Therapies, Narrative Therapies

The world over, mainstream psychotherapy has been criticized and critiqued by feminists, and this has resulted in the emergence of highly creative and politically vibrant forms of feminist psychotherapy (we discussed this earlier in the chapter). Similarly, LGBTIQ groups were extremely dissatisfied with procedures and processes (especially aversive therapy and coercive efforts in therapy to 'make them straight'!). This led to the emergence of affirmative therapies and gay-/queer-affirmative therapies.

Affirmative therapy considers the needs of marginalized persons and takes an intersectional approach. Affirmative psychotherapy, despite having the institutional support of major professional bodies, including the APA, unfortunately has not been fully integrated within the psychological and social work professions. Therapists working with trans and gender-non-confirming communities are often viewed by the latter as gatekeepers who need to be convinced about their transgender status. There is resistance due to fear that the therapist has the power to diagnose them or due to anger that they require a therapist's diagnosis to receive medical care (Lev, 2019).

Nodding and silence may convey respect and to some extent non-judgemental practice, but they border dangerously on erasure if these actions are done in isolation without later circling back to what has been spoken about. This is the crux of the difference between neutral/friendly practice and affirmative practice. Only by doing this is a safe space established, where lived experience is acknowledged and made visible deliberately. Hence, queer-affirmative therapy has yet to gain ground and take roots, both in the West and in India, but it is surely doing so.

Queer-affirmative practice, as described by Ranade and Chakravarty, is an approach to counselling that encompasses counsellor self-work, attitudes, knowledge, ethics, and process skills, where the fundamental principles include 'understanding and combating heterosexism, recognizing heterosexual privilege where it exists, and understanding and combating homophobia in clients as well as in self'. The authors outlined eight major themes that emerged from their interviews with affirmative therapists – inclusive language and terminology, queer-friendly counselling set-ups, knowledge about diversity and queer resources, emphasis on confidentiality, counsellors' self-awareness of their biases, avoidance of assumptions about clients, addressal of misinformation and misconceptions of clients, and working on internalized homophobia and self-acceptance.

Initially centred on cisgender homosexual individuals, this approach was later modified to include gender minorities and currently encompasses all 'non-normative' sexual and gender identities. An affirmative approach is one that validates rather than pathologizes queer identities; it is rooted in awareness of societal structures and their impact on mental health. At the same time, it honours queer individuals' strengths and resilience. Such an approach can help interrupt the negative impact of minority stress (Wandrekar & Nigudkar, 2019).

Banerjee and Siobhan (2020) have also given some thumb rules for identifying queer-affirmative therapy and therapists: For instance, the latter are certified to practise queer-affirmative therapy, are from the community themselves, answer questions about the parameters of their practice honestly, take help from identified queer persons in referral, take help from queer groups on social media platforms for referral, and check with the therapist whether they are open to the queer identity. They also differentiate between queer-friendly practice and a queer-affirmative practice. In the former, while there is acceptance of a queer client, there may not necessarily have the resources for, and the therapist may not be trained in, queer-affirmative therapy, but the latter is a practice where the therapist is engaged in self-work that helps them identify homophobic and transphobic elements, understand the therapeutic space deeply, and work on it.

Another therapeutic practice that speaks to both feminist therapy and queer-affirmative therapy is narrative therapy. Here is a brief overview of this therapy.

Narrative therapy is a form of therapy that aims to separate the individual from the problem, allowing the individual to externalize their issues rather than internalize them. It relies on the individual's own skills and sense of purpose to guide them through difficult times. This form of therapy was developed in the 1980s by Michael White and David Epston. They believed that separating a person from their problematic or destructive behaviour was a vital part of treatment (White, 2015). For example, when treating someone who had run afoul of the law, they would encourage the individual to see themselves as a person who made mistakes

140 Understanding Feminist Psychotherapies

rather than as an inherently 'bad' felon. White and Epston grounded this new therapeutic model in three main ideas.

7.5.1 Narrative Therapy Is Respectful

This therapy respects the agency and dignity of every client. It requires each client to be treated as an individual who is not deficient, defective, or not 'enough' in any way.

7.5.2 Narrative Therapy Is Non-blaming

In this form of therapy, clients are never blamed for their problems, and they are encouraged not to blame others as well. Problems emerge in the lives of many people due to a variety of factors; in narrative therapy, there is no point in assigning fault to anyone or anything.

7.5.3 Narrative Therapy Views the Client as the Expert

In narrative therapy, the therapist does not occupy a higher social or academic space than the client. It is understood that the client is the expert in their own life, and both parties are expected to go forth with this understanding. Making the distinction between 'an individual with problems' and a 'problematic individual' is vital in narrative therapy. White and Epston theorized that subscribing to a harmful or adverse self-identity could have profound negative impacts on a person's functionality and quality of life.

There are a few main themes or principles of narrative therapy:

1. Reality is socially constructed, which means that our interactions and dialogue with others impact the way we experience reality.
2. Reality is influenced by and communicated through language, which suggests that people who speak different languages may have radically different interpretations of the same experiences.
3. Having a narrative that can be understood helps us organize and maintain our reality. In other words, stories and narratives help us make sense of our experiences.
4. There is no 'objective reality' or absolute truth; what is true for us may not be the same for another person or even for ourselves at another point in time (Standish, 2013).

These principles tie into the postmodernist school of thought, which views reality as a shifting, changing, and deeply personal concept. In postmodernism, there is no objective truth – the truth is what each one of us makes it, influenced by social norms and ideas. Thus, the main premise behind narrative therapy is understanding individuals within this postmodern context. If there is no universal truth, then people need to create truths that help them construct a reality that serves themselves and others. Narrative therapy offers those story-shaping skills. It is amazing how much easier solving or negating a problem can be when you stop seeing the problem as an integral part of who you are and instead as simply a problem.

The following five techniques are the most common tools used in narrative therapy.

7.5.3.1 Telling One's Story (Putting Together a Narrative)

As a therapist or other mental health professional, your job in narrative therapy is to help your client and their voice and tell their story in their own words. According to the philosophy behind narrative therapy, storytelling is how we make meaning and purpose in our own experience (Standish, 2013). Helping your client develop their story gives them an opportunity to discover meaning, and healing, and establish or re-establish an identity, all integral factors for success in therapy.

This technique is also known as 're-authoring' or 're-storying', as clients explore their experiences of and make alterations to their story or make a whole new one. The same event can tell a hundred different stories, since we all interpret experiences differently and with different senses of meaning (Dulwich Centre).

7.5.3.2 Externalization Technique

The externalization technique leads your client towards viewing their problems or behaviours as external, instead of as an unchangeable part of themselves. This is a technique that is easier to describe than to embrace, but it can have huge positive impacts on self-identity and confidence. The general idea of this technique is that it is easier to change a behaviour you do than to change a core personality characteristic. For example, if you are quick to anger or you consider yourself an angry person, then you must fundamentally change something about yourself to address the problem; however, if you are a person who acts aggressively and angers easily, then you need to alter the situations and behaviours surrounding the problem. It may be challenging for the client to absorb this strange idea at first. One first step is to encourage your client not to place too much importance on their diagnosis or self-assigned labels. Let them know how empowering it can be to separate themselves from their problems and allow themselves a greater degree of control in their identity (Bishop, 2011).

7.5.3.3 Deconstruction Technique

This 'deconstruction' refers to reducing the problems a client is experiencing, thus making it easier to understand the 'whole picture'. Our problems can feel overwhelming, confusing, or unsolvable, but they are never truly unsolvable (Bishop, 2011). Deconstructing makes the issue more specific and reduces overgeneralizing;

142 Understanding Feminist Psychotherapies

it also clarifies what the core issue or issues are. As an example of the deconstruction technique, imagine two people in a long-term relationship who are having trouble. One partner is feeling frustrated with the other partner who never shares her feelings, thoughts, or ideas with him. On the basis of this short description, there is no clear idea of what the problem is, let alone what the solution might be.

A therapist might deconstruct the problem with this client by asking them to be more specific about what is bothering them, rather than accepting a statement such as 'my spouse doesn't get me anymore'. Deconstructing the problem helps people understand the root of problems (in this case, someone is feeling lonely and vulnerable) and what this means to them (in this case, their partner does not want them anymore or is not willing to commit to the relationship like they are). This technique is an excellent way to help the client dig into the problem and understand the foundation of the stressful event or pattern in their life.

7.5.3.4 Unique-Outcomes Technique

This technique is complex but vital for the storytelling aspect of narrative therapy.

The unique-outcomes technique involves changing one's own storyline. In narrative therapy, the client aims to construct a storyline to their experiences, which offers meaning or gives them a positive and functional identity. This is not as misguided as 'thinking positive' but rather a specific technique for clients to develop life-affirming stories.

We are not limited to just one storyline, though. There are many potential storylines we can subscribe to, some more helpful than others. Like a book that switches viewpoints from one character to another, our life has multiple threads of narrative, with different perspectives, areas of focus, and points of interest. The unique-outcomes technique focuses on a different storyline or storylines other than the one holding the source of one's problems. Using this technique might sound like avoiding the problem, but it is just reimagining the problem. What seems like a problem or issue from one perspective can be nothing but an unassuming or insignificant detail in another (Bishop, 2011). As a therapist, you can introduce this technique by encouraging client(s) to pursue new storylines.

7.5.3.5 Existentialism

You might have a particular association with the term 'existentialism' which makes its presence here seem odd, but there is likely more to existentialism than you think.

Existentialism is not a bleak and hopeless view on a world without meaning. In general, existentialists believe in a world with no inherent meaning; if there is no given meaning, then people can create their own meaning. In this way, existentialism and narrative therapy go hand in hand.

Narrative therapy in India is still in its nascent stage. Narrative Therapy India is a social media platform that came up in 2014. It is dedicated to documenting how narrative ideas and practices are used in India in supervision, training, and practice and encourages its translation into Indian languages. Children with special needs, families, women, and various diverse populations can benefit from it. Narrative therapy also speaks beautifully to our diverse Indian culture. Various helping professionals, parents, and activists can use this therapy after undergoing some formal training and gaining a people-centred perspective. Feminist psychotherapies, queer-affirmative therapy, and narrative therapy are the need of the hour for diverse people in India and everywhere in the world.

Review Questions

1 Describe the problems with mainstream psychotherapies.
2 What are the principles of feminist psychotherapies?
3 Why do family therapy and couple therapy need to be gender-sensitive?

Critical Thinking Questions

1 What are the strong points and weaknesses of Freudian psychoanalysis which were adopted and critiqued by feminist psychologists?
2 Queer-affirmative therapies need to pay attention to intersectionality. Why?
3 Narrative therapies use creative forms. Comment.

Bibliography

Banerjee, & Siobhan. (2020). www.shethepeople.tv

Bishop, W. H. (2011, May 16). *Narrative therapy summary. Thoughts from a Therapist.* www.thoughtsfromatherapist.com/2011/05/16/narrative-therapy-summary/

Broverman, I. K., Vogel, S. R., Broverman, D. M., Clarkson, F. E., & Rosenkrantz, P. S. (1972). Sex role stereotypes: A current appraisal. *Journal of Social Issues, 28*, 58–78.

Burck, C., & Daniel, G. (1995). *Gender and family therapy.* Routledge. https://doi.org/10.4324/9780429475252

Burstow, B. (1992). *Radical feminist therapy: Working in the context of violence.* SAGE Publications.

Corey, G. (2009). *Theory and practice of counseling and psychotherapy.* Brooks/Cole.

Doane, J., & Hodges, D. (1992). *From Klein to Kristeva: Psychoanalytic feminism and the search for the 'Good enough' mother.* The University of Michigan Press.

Dulwich Centre. *What is narrative therapy?* Dulwich Centre. http://dulwichcentre.com.au/what-is-narrative-therapy/

Forrest, A., & Steigerwald, F. (2004). An examination of gender and ethics in family counseling: A case study approach – Part 1. *The Family Journal, 12*(2), 174–176. https://doi.org/10.1177/1066480703261978

Gerson, G. (2004, November 1). Winnicott, participation and gender. *Feminism and Psychology.* https://doi.org/10.1177/0959353504046872

Joshi, A. (2015). Need for gender sensitive counselling interventions in India. *Psychological Studies, 60*(3), 346–355. https://dx.doi.org/10.1007/s12646-015-0317-7

144 Understanding Feminist Psychotherapies

Knudson-Martin, C., & Wells, M. (2014). Gender in couple and family therapy. In J. Lebow, A. Chambers, & D. Breunlin (Eds.), *Encyclopedia of couple and family therapy*. Springer. https://doi.org/10.1007/978-3-319-15877-8_532-1

Lev, A. I. (2019). *Queer affirmative theory. Headcase: LGBTQ writers and artists on mental health and wellness*. Oxford University Press.

Matlin, M. W. (2008). *The psychology of women* (6th ed.). Thomson Wadsworth.

McClellan, B. (1999). The prostitution of psychotherapy: A feminist critique. *British Journal of Guidance and Counselling, 27*(3), 325–337.

Sommers-Flanagan, J., & Sommers-Flanagan, R. (2018). *Counseling and psychotherapy theories in context and practice: Skills, strategies, and techniques*. Wiley Publishers.

Standish, K. (2013, November 28). *Introduction to narrative therapy*. www.slideshare.net/kevins299/lecture-8-narrative-therapy

Wandrekar, J., & Nigudkar, A. (2019). Learnings from SAAHAS – a queer affirmative CBT-based group therapy intervention for LGBTQIA+ individuals in Mumbai, India. *Journal of Psychosexual Health, 1*(2), 164–173.

White, M. (2015, July 24). *Good therapy*. www.goodtherapy.org/famous-psychologists/michael-white.html

Worrell, J., & Remer, P. (1992). *Feminist perspectives in therapy: An empowerment model for women*. Wiley and Sons.

8

GENDER AND MENTAL HEALTH CHALLENGES

Chapter Highlights

Learning Objectives

After reading this chapter, the students would be able to

- Understand the implications of gender bias and sexism in psychology.
- Conceptualize about rethinking DSM classifications from gender and queer perspectives.
- Differentiate between aspects of men's and women's mental health.
- Identify the need for gender, caste, and queer sensitization of mental health professionals and disciplines.

Introduction

In the previous chapters, the underpinnings of the need to engender psychology have been pointed out. This chapter spells out exactly how sexism in psychology began and continues to be perpetuated. The classification and diagnosis of disorders using the manuals like DSM have been challenged by various groups such as feminists, the LGBT community, and Black and other ethnic minorities in the United States, as well as in Europe. It has compelled them to rethink but not entirely stopped misdiagnosis, discrimination, and biases in mental health practice across the world. The earlier understanding about men's and women's mental health merely revolved around gender differences; in the last 25 years, it has shifted towards approaches that include intersectional understanding. The narratives and discourse around gender and mental health in a post-globalization world have been shaped and reshaped by neoliberal policies, popular culture, and socio-political

DOI: 10.4324/9781003453758-9

146 Gender and Mental Health Challenges

mechanisms, as well as the lived realities of users and diagnosed persons. A sub-topic in this chapter will map out the large terrain briefly.

The last section is devoted to establishing the felt need for gender, caste, race, and queer sensitization of mental health professionals all over the world. While there is an impetus right from global policies (UN sustainable development goals (SDGs)) to local challenges to tease out the structural stratifications and social inequalities that lead to psychosocial ill health and lack of well-being, mental health practice, as well as practitioners, by and large remains enslaved by the biomedical model. As discussed in the previous chapter, feminist psychotherapy, narrative therapy, and queer-affirmative therapy have offered succour and an equal engagement to persons confronting psychosocial distress. Even so, most mainstream mental health practitioners need to be gender-, caste-, and queer-sensitized. This is discussed and contextualized in this chapter.

8.1 Gender Bias and Sexism in the Organization of Psychology

Most of the social and biological sciences have been sexist and gender-biased. The history of psychology in the West tells us that since the earliest psychologists came from the fields such as biology, medical science, neurology, physiology, physics, and chemistry, mainstream psychology was influenced deeply by the practices of physical sciences. However, even after 140 years, it continues to remain an empirical, biomedical, and positivist science. The sexism in psychology has manifested in many ways: Women were missing as subjects, women in the field were invisible, and research and practice showed sexism in language and interventions (discussion in the previous chapter). While the forefathers and pioneering men in psychology have been immortalized, the foremothers of psychology have mostly been forgotten, at least in mainstream psychology. Hence, engendering psychology has been a process of making women in psychology visible and initiating a 'psychology of women' agenda (with the Society for the Psychology of Women in the APA, as well as panels on psychology of women across associations in several countries) and later that of 'feminist psychology', which has broadened the horizons of doing psychology by bringing in all the diversities of race, class, nation, region, gender, and sexuality.

Against this backdrop, in this section, there is an attempt to unpack the gender bias and the sexism and discrimination in the various applications of psychology. If we examine the history of clinical psychology since ancient times, this is what emerges: Aristotle held that 'a woman was a deformed or mutilated male'! Hippocrates wrote, 'I will not give to a woman, a pessary to cause abortion.' Aristotle said, '[W]omen are weak, men are strong.' Socrates asserted, '[W]omen should have the same activities and pursuits as men, but in all of them they are inferior to men.' Health, mental health, and clinical psychology trace their roots to these philosophers, and they were biased against women.

The period of demonology and witch-hunt that followed in the West was a phase of anti-women practices in the early period of clinical psychology. Even in the days of the mental health movement and in contemporary 20th century, women were ignored and given a secondary status in mental health. Other marginalized communities were also invisible in this discourse. In India, in the early days, clinical psychology was caught between traditional and modern influences. Within tradition, since women had a secondary status, stereotypes about them prevailed. The modern in 1915 was what came in from the West and was deeply problematic too.

In the 1970s, there was a crisis in clinical psychology brought in by the disenchantment with existing models and methods. The narrative was framed and dictated by white, Caucasian, able-bodied, heterosexual males! This led to a rethinking of psychology all over the world, and social movements, such as the women's movement, LGBTQ movement, and Black movement, challenged these canons in academia, research, and practice. This led to the creation of the fields such as feminist psychology, Black psychology, and LGBTQ psychology, which continue to offer counterpoints to, critique, and challenge mainstream clinical psychology.

The history of research in psychology can be described as missing women, extrapolation of findings about men to women, and 'women as deficient/deviant' models! There were many biases in the attitudes of the predominantly male researchers, as well as the methodologies, which were androcentric. The pervasiveness of gender bias at all stages of research – question formulation, research design, data analysis and interpretation, and conclusion formulation – is evident from many reviews of research. Feminist psychologists and researchers have frequently criticized the practice of treating 'so-called subjects as objects of the study' and objectifying women in the research studies. Hence, the terms such as 'participants' and 'respondents' are used now. The findings from such androcentric, patriarchal research are also biased again women and ethnic and sexual minorities.

Teaching of psychology as a social and behavioural science was a field that was occupied by white, upper-class males and females. In India too, it has been the domain and preserve of upper-class, upper-middle-class (replacing the erstwhile middle class) and upper-caste teachers. Hence, it has always been a discipline populated by the urban elite. It carries caste-, race-, and sexuality-related biases in India, as well as in the West. It homogenizes the individual into a middle-/upper-middle-/upper-class person and excludes all others. Hence, it is imperative to decolonize psychology and engage with the concepts and phenomena in a bottom-up fashion.

Therapeutic interventions (discussed in detail in previous chapter) have shown gender bias and sexism in terms of misdiagnosis, over-prescription, and overmedication for women, as well as other marginalized persons. Based on the lived experiences of clients, associations and professional bodies have been compelled to issue guidelines to make some fundamental changes in the way therapists work.

148 Gender and Mental Health Challenges

Key Insight

The APA issued a fresh set of guidelines to help therapists who treat girls and women, noting that changes to 'education, work, reproductive and caregiving roles, and personal relationships' in the last several decades have led to greater equality but have also changed the ways in which women encounter adversity in the United States and around the world.

The guidelines include the following:

- Recognizing women's resilience and using affirmative approaches.
- Understanding multiple layers of identity and oppression (race, disability, sexuality, economic background, and so on).
- Being aware of contradictory messaging around what it means to be female.
- Confronting one's own personal and institutional biases.
- Offering diagnosis only when necessary and using unbiased assessment tools.
- Knowing about alternative forms of healing, including indigenous methods and community resources.
- 'Therapists are sexist and racist, too.'
- Therapists are human, and no human is impervious to cultural attitudes about gender or race. The guidelines encourage practitioners to think about how their own experiences and beliefs may impact their treatment.
- The guidelines note that psychotherapy often includes biases, such as over-valuing autonomy while undervaluing relationships or basing definitions of positive mental health on behaviours that are most consistent with masculine stereotypes or life experiences.
- In addition to self-awareness, the guidelines encourage diversity and gender sensitivity training and therapists to 'build their knowledge about racial, sexual orientation, elitist, ablest, ageist, and other types of microaggressions and how these intersect with their beliefs and attitudes about girls and women'.

Source: Dasatagir, A. (2019, May 13). *USA Today*

8.2 Rethinking Diagnostic and Scientific Manual Classifications from Gender and Queer Perspectives

For many years since the first edition of the DSM was published in 1952, both feminists and queer rights activists have been battling with many objectionable, unjust, and irrational diagnostic categories outlined in it. Psychodiagnostics, psychopathology and clinical practices were called 'objective', but their underpinnings were (and continue to be) by and large androcentric. The two quotations

Gender and Mental Health Challenges **149**

below echo these sentiments. 'Objectivity has been little more than male subjectivity' (Adrienne Rich); 'What passed off as scientific knowledge was the ideology of a masculinist society dressed up as objective truth'.

There were many categories in DSM that feminists objected to, such as masochistic personality disorder, PMDD, sexual sadism disorder, and sexual hypoactive desire disorder, to name the prominent ones (DSM-III, DSM-III-R, DSM-IV). The objections that were made were that such diagnoses came from the lack of understanding of female sexuality and an attempt to enforce prevailing moralities regarding gender norms and order that were highly discriminatory. They draw attention to the fact that though women all over the world continue to remain one of the highest consumers of mental healthcare and psychoactive drugs, they are not identified as 'vulnerable' in DSM-5 (Marecek & Gavey, 2013). The excessive use of biomedicine and the lack of attention to the alternative work in narrative therapy, ethnomethodology, ethnographies, post-structural practices, and discursive psychology show that scant care has been paid to what sufferers and users go through and including it in the understanding of mental health.

Feminist engagement is very reflexive about feminist knowledge as well. In response to DSM-5, Swartz et al. (in Marecek & Gavey, 2013) turn a reflective eye on feminist knowledge practices. Drawing on their experiences in the clinic and the community, as well as on the historical record, they sound some cautionary notes. What is at stake, Swartz asks, in calls for clinical practitioners to jettison psychiatric diagnoses, in effect to 'Just say no' to the DSM? What is being omitted, Lester worries, when academic analyses of borderline personality disorder (BPD) seem to regard BPD as nothing but a pejorative label? Hornstein warns against critical analyses that appear to 'theorize away' sufferers' accounts when those accounts do not coincide with feminist formulations.

They remind us of the necessity for disciplinary reflexivity not only as regards mainstream psychology but also regarding feminist knowledge practices (Wilkinson, 1988). By documenting tensions among feminist thinkers, there is an attempt to make one aware of important fault lines in feminist theory. It is hoped that new knowledge – and better feminist therapeutic practices – may emerge from respectful dialogue and debate while examining DSM-5 and mainstream psychotherapy and psychiatry as practices impacted by DSM-5.

Similarly, the queer analysis and critique of DSM-5 throw up many challenges, the foremost being the tension between gender identity as biological versus gender identity as cultural (activists and theorists point out that this debate is not new, but DSM-5 has made them revisit it). The other issue is that changing the name of the diagnostic category from gender identity disorder (GID) to gender dysphoria (GD) has not resolved the problem of stigma or healthcare. The third major problem the queer lobby is highlighting is why trans identity is still a diagnostic category (Bento, 2018).

Davy (2015) argues that the criteria proposed by the DSM-5 are derived from stereotypes applied in the gender identity clinics serving trans people, rather than

150 Gender and Mental Health Challenges

being empirically developed from biological standpoints. Many inconsistent theories illustrate that the debate surrounding biological causation is far from settled, and it weakens any possibility of arguing that there is something inherent in masculine and feminine behaviours. Atypical gender expressions in children are still depicted in the DSM-5 as a manifestation of inverted masculinity or femininity and, consequently, gender. Research has also suggested that adult trans people often think that if they do not express stereotypical masculinities and femininities and anatomic dysphoria, it may obstruct their access to transitioning healthcare pathways.

Davy has demonstrated that trans people tend to tailor their clinical narratives because they realize that psychiatrists have the power to stop their transitioning (gender reassignment, earlier called sex change) process. The criteria used to diagnose GD help psychiatrists determine whether someone is experiencing distress about incongruence with their experienced gender through a gender-normative frame, but this does not necessarily have anything to do with experienced gender identity. This then leads to the situation where trans people must express 'dysphoria' about their natural body and incongruent behaviour and demonstrate to the psychiatrist that they prefer activities that are traditionally gendered and opposite to the gender norms applied to their assigned sex at birth.

The notion that intersex people inherently belong to one gender or the other and are compelled to transition because of an underlying biogenetic position is too simplistic, and research illustrates that there is more variability to gender identity outcomes than was previously assumed. Another problem psychiatrists may have to face is that of attempting to determine whether their patients' distress is due to GD or some other reasons. For trans people who suggest they want to self-determine their gender identity but have no dysphoria, utilizing the diagnosis of GD inevitably places them at odds with the DSM-5 criteria. The majority of trans activists reject the pathologizing of gender variance, some advocate complete de-medicalization, and others, diagnostic reform, and the advocacy for each position is influenced by the perceived costs of access to medical procedures versus the benefits of diagnosis. The Gender Identity Disorder Reform Advocates website also says that trans people should not be diagnosed with a psychiatric condition because 'difference is not disease, nonconformity is not pathology, and uniqueness is not illness'.

Daley and Mulé (2014) outline a community-based collaboration in Toronto, Canada, which led to an official response to the APA's call for comments and suggestions regarding diagnostic criteria revisions for the DSM-5 with a focus on disorders that have or may have an impact on the lives of LGBTQ people. Two diagnostic categories were identified: GD and paraphilias. Importantly, while LGBTQ people may be affected by a range of diagnoses, including those seemingly unrelated to gender and sexuality, GD and paraphilias exclusively focus on gender and sexuality. GID diagnoses have been critiqued for their dependence on rigid, binary, and uniform categories of gender and associated gender role expressions and behaviours and lack of reliability and validity of the diagnostic criteria.

Moser and Kleinplatz (2005) argued that these clinical evaluations are subjective, as there is no consensus regarding the same in scientific literature. They argued that the paraphilia section should ultimately be removed from the DSM, as the criteria for unusual sexual interests as pathological were found to be based on unproven and untested assumptions and leading to misuse. What is lacking is objective data that would support the classification of paraphilias as mental disorders, as well as the fact that healthy sexuality is not defined in the DSM. Their analysis is also premised on the belief that the requirement of a formal mental disorder diagnosis for access to health insurance coverage for expensive and scarce medical interventions for the trans community constitutes a social process of 'gatekeeping' that exposes systemic abuses of power that can influence personal identity.

Critical queer analysis that was conducted gave rise to three primary thematic concerns in relation to the 'disorders' included in their position statement, which included problems with diagnostic criteria, reliability, and validity of the diagnoses and whether or not they actually constituted mental disorders. The removal of gender dysphoria in children (GDC) from DSM-5 was supported by the work group, given its potential to contribute to the surveillance and pathologizing of children's diverse developmental exploration, creativity, and expression related to gender; the APA recommendation that a GD diagnosis be given on the basis of the 'A' criterion alone and that distress and/or impairment be evaluated separately and independently was also supported. However, the inclusion of sexual orientation as one of six dimensional informational questions was not supported. The gender- and sexuality-related disorders included in their analysis were determined based on an unjust and inequitable gendered, racialized, classed, and sexualized social order.

It was specifically highlighted that the socio-political environment appeared to have more of an influence on the APA and DSM, suggesting a lack of reliability and validity for the sexual and gender identity diagnoses included in this analysis. In addition, there has been little scientific evidence to support the reliability and validity of the criteria, as they relate to GDs and the paraphilias. The conflation of attractions and internal arousing with behaviour in relation to the diagnosis of paraphilias by the APA represents significant risk to LGBTQ people who express diverse sexual expressions by way of a dangerous level of control over people's thoughts and feelings, regardless of whether they are acted upon or not.

The DSM has also been critiqued for its inability to distinguish between gender nonconformity and GD. Efforts to establish reliability and validity are problematic from a critical queer perspective, as they tend to simplify and reduce the shifting complexity of human thoughts, expressions, and behaviours into restrictive categories. This process constitutes a normalizing project that inevitably results in the

152 Gender and Mental Health Challenges

individualizing and pathologizing of diversity and difference, as well as distress, associated with the social processes of discrimination and stigma. The DSM has a global impact that can extend to child custody decisions, self-esteem, whether individuals are hired or fired, security clearances, and curtailment of other rights or privileges. Political agendas have been served, and crime sentencing can also be affected based on diagnoses. Thus, this is not only a scientific issue but also a human rights issue (Moser & Kleinplatz, 2005).

These studies ably demonstrate that there is an urgent need to rethink DSM from a gender-sensitive and queer-sensitive perspective.

8.3 Men's Mental Health and Women's Mental Health

Bringing women's mental health to the centre stage in the West and in India has been a challenge. It did not receive attention from the health movement, feminist movement, and mainstream psychology till the early 1980s. The reasons were many. Even for the health movement, mental health, and specifically women's mental health, was a 'grey and complex area'. The feminist movement was wary of 'abnormality and pushing women into the medicalization of their problems' and of aligning with inner worlds and interiority! Women's experience with psychiatry in India was generally unhappy and at best hazy. Mental illnesses were thought to be better addressed by friends, family, and religious and cult groups (Shatrughna, in Davar, 1999). The women's movement in India, like its Western counterpart, does use CR in its campaigns, albeit without explicitly calling it so, to awaken awareness about the oppressive situation in women's lives. However, unlike in the West, where CR involved sharing and discussion of experiences of restricted and stereotyped expectations for how women should conduct their lives and was therapeutic for many, the women's movement in India did not really make this connection. The central focus was and continues to be predominantly on societal restraints and practices and not so much on attention to the personal self and individual distress (Vindhya et al., 2001).

The initial rejection of mainstream psychology slowly led to a recognition that the women's movement had helped in averting many breakdowns and that, in fact, feminist scrutiny of women's mental health treatment and the mainstream practice of psychotherapy were essential. Davar (1999) argues that feminism 'must be interested in the psycho-politics of creating men's and women's mental health in Indian culture'.

Historically, in the West and in India, the research and intervention on men's and women's mental health moved from studying gender differences in ageing, socio-economic status, marital status, and prevalence of mental illness to understanding and accepting through feminist psychology the structural inequalities that led to psychosocial distress. (The previous chapters in the book also echo this.) Violence against women became a milestone in creating a shift in the approach of feminists towards women's mental health. Recognition of structural violence and the various patriarchies (caste patriarchy, class patriarchy) that were the leading causative agents of the various forms of violence against women – rape, assault, sexual harassment, domestic violence, sexual harassment at the workplace – and their linkages with distress, anxiety, and depression helped build a case for feminist psychology and feminist psychotherapy.

There is a lot of research literature available now which points out that the socialization patterns of boys need to be scrutinized. Stereotypical and traditional male-gender roles are responsible for encouraging toxic masculinity, the belief that emotional expression is a sign of weakness and so on. Hence, men rarely express sorrow, helplessness, frustration, and failure. Help-seeking behaviour when in psychological distress is less in men than in women. Conflicts, challenges, and trauma push women towards clinical depression and men towards substance abuse.

Throughout life, there are differences in the psychological disorders that men and women are likely to go through, and the causes are not biological but mainly psychosocial. Betty Freidan mentioned 'a problem that has no name' in her book *The Feminine Mystique*, which typified middle-class women in the 1960s. To some extent, it persists, since women take a long time to seek help for physical and mental distress and tend to either trivialize their problems or wait till, they becomes severe.

While both men and women are prone to various common and severe mental disorders, there are some contested psychological and psychosomatic disorders that are gender specific. For instance, post-partum/post-natal depression (PP/PND) among women is one such contested disorder that mainstream psychology, biology, and medical science regard as fairly common among new mothers. Feminist psychologists, however, do not pathologize or place this distress in the clinical domain. They analyse it as lack of social support to the mother (from the natal and or marital family, the husband), and especially if she is an employed woman who wants to go back to work, this distress is created by uncooperative families who place the entire responsibility of childcare on her. Son preference, unwanted childbirth, and other complex psychosocial factors also increase the challenges for a new mother. Treating this distress as a biological and psychological disorder takes the gaze away from the family and husband who should be partners in the process of childcare and who lead to this distress that the woman ends up facing! This feminist deconstruction of PP/PND needs urgent attention.

The emotional labour – when you are constantly required to express emotions for the fulfilment of other people – is talked about more in professional settings and intimate relationships. However, in India, where families play a huge role in upbringing, it takes a higher toll on women's mental health, and research has always been supportive of this effect. An existing illness often becomes a reason for a woman to become a victim of domestic violence too – either from the

154 Gender and Mental Health Challenges

partner or from family members. Learned helplessness is a mental state that was first assigned to animals, as observed during experiments by the infamous Martin Seligman in the 1960s. The specimens were continuously subjected to an aversive stimulus to the extent that they stopped thinking about escaping it. This made the animals display helplessness and compliance to whatever they were put against. Researchers assimilated this finding to women who could not escape abusive interpersonal relationships (Sharma, 2017).

While workplace sexual harassment continues to correlate itself with major mental health issues in victims, female employees already struggling with a mental illness go through a double battle as soon as they step into office. Body dysmorphic disorder, found equally in both men and women, makes one obsess over a flaw in their appearance that may or may not be visible to others, creating extreme distress. Despite no gender differences in occurrence, cultural norms do have an impact on women suffering from it. Not only is access to non-judgemental healthcare challenging for women, but therapists' bigoted nature has also made it difficult for them to push their willingness to seek it in the first place.

A range of studies contributed by Dr Thara R. of Schizophrenia Research Foundation (SCARF), Chennai, stress upon the psychosocial rehabilitation of women, which is only possible through promoting gender-sensitive mental healthcare services in India.

When women narrate their experiences about what happened with them, the first thing that is important for any therapist to do is to validate them and to convey that they know where they are coming from. The techniques like CBT and rational emotive behavioural therapy (REBT) focus on replacing thoughts that are irrational in nature and somehow harm the person's well-being; a feminist modification is suggested: Discussions on patriarchy and sexism should be incorporated during group therapy sessions. There is a demand for a feminist approach to therapy because the awareness is increasing too.

Gay-affirmative therapy is principled on being non-judgemental and affirming the choices that people make, which may be beyond what is considered 'normal'. In many ways, this therapy is client-centred and narrative in nature, but the added element is the awareness of the marginalization of the community. This awareness helps the therapist more acutely to not put the blame on the woman in question. Feminist therapy has a close connection with the lives of marginalized women in the West, and it applies the same assumption of taking into account societal oppression. Lesbian and bisexual women also face systemic and institutional violence. This could be exacerbated because of their not complying with heteronormative expectations of marriage with men. Due to these difficulties, lesbian and bisexual women in therapy might require additional support that primarily should stem from legal and social agencies. However, due to the criminalization of homosexuality, such persons often found themselves completely alone in India earlier, but that should change with the decriminalization of homosexuality and scrapping Section 377.

Oftentimes, women do not recognize their mental health issues in the first place. They are inherently suspicious of mental health personnel due to first-hand negative experiences at the hands of a few professionals who are misinformed about human sexuality and gender and who might also perpetrate violence against such vulnerable individuals. They may thereby have an impression that the larger mental health community is working against their best interests and is therefore unapproachable.

Now, let us turn to menstruation and its importance and impact on women's health and mental health in brief. This has been an important arena for feminist interventions in theory and practice. A lot of ground has been covered in dealing with the menstruation-related taboos and the resultant psychological distress. However, many of the misconceptions, restrictions, superstitions, and negative emotions associated with menstruation continue to prevail. The purity and pollution rituals around them and attempts to delay periods for 'religious/cultural' occasions and ceremonies through swallowing pills are practised even now. This leads to anxiety and panic and has a negative impact on the self-esteem of adolescent and young girls. While on the one hand families in India continue to obsess over girls and menstruation, the discussion about adolescent boys and puberty is mostly ignored. As discussed in earlier chapters, sexuality education is a complex area encompassing biology, psychology, interpersonal relationships, and much more.

My experience of conducting sexuality education workshops in an interactive manner, with freewheeling discussions among young adults, has helped them and me understand the nuances of the sexual, biological, and psychological experience of 'coming of age'. Both young girls and boys want to discuss such things as 'masturbation', 'conception', and 'contraception' and validate and evaluate their beliefs about and attitudes towards pleasure and desire (most of the information is gained from the internet, social media, porn, and peers and ranges from comical, hilarious, unscientific, and old-wives tale to exaggerated, over-the-top, weird, outrageous, and, yes, sometimes scientific, sensible, and accurate!). Diversity is a major factor that influences their access and social and cultural capital index, which in turn has an impact on their knowledge and experience about sexuality.

For instance, in one of our workshops where the discussants ranged from urban and rural poor to international students, their experiential range was 'being regular users of Tinder and Grindr who thought casual hook-ups were de rigueur among young adults' to those 'who were new to the experience of a backslapping approach towards girls'. Thus, the spectrum extends from uber-cool to gauche and naive and those in between, and hence sweeping generalizations are not helpful at all. There is a dire need to unpack the experiential around sexuality, puberty, menstruation, menarche, and sexual maturity of young men and their psychosocial impacts.

156 Gender and Mental Health Challenges

Mid-chapter Exercise

- For girls: Have you wondered whether every woman menstruates? Discuss your experience of menarche. Did your parent give you prior information? What was its psychological impact?
- For boys: Do boys and men need to know about 'periods/chums/menses/monthly period'? How did you come to know about them and from whom/where? What about trans men and periods? Do you know about their experiences?

Just like menarche and the myths and misconceptions around it, menopause too is shrouded in mystery. While the biological knowledge about bodily and hormonal changes is easily available, several women feel that menopause means an end of their 'femininity and desirability'! Along with the hormonal changes that they go through, many of them also experience the 'empty nest syndrome' (grown-up children moving away for education, employment, or both), and this leads to depression among women going through the perimenopause and menopause stages. The phenomenon of menopause is not just biological but also psychosocial. Many women go through a lot of psychosocial distress during perimenopause as well as menopause since their 'femininity is tied up with fertility and is socially constructed', and they feel that after menopause they stop 'being women'! Interestingly, men go through a similar process of andropause/climacteric and experience the empty nest syndrome but can cope better. This happens since andropause is rarely acknowledged and attended to, and the sorrow related to parting from their grown-up children is kept carefully hidden and suppressed by most men.

In the 2000s, the 'hurried woman syndrome', a psychosocial condition that affects women in the age group 25–55, mostly employed women, was identified in the United States, and it is also seen to be prevalent among women elsewhere. It is caused due to distress, and the symptoms are fatigue, low libido, and weight gain. It is connected to perimenopause and, in most cases, leads to depression. If we engage in a feminist psychological analysis of this condition, it is professional and familial pressure, responsibilities, and their burden that lead to this situation. Shared housework, childcare, and empathy in the workplace can help women. A biomedical approach towards this problem is not helpful. What is needed is a psychosocial understanding and a redefining of roles in a gender-sensitive fashion.

Women, fertility, reproduction, and mental health are another area that needs to be explored in more detail. The stigma of infertility for women is huge and creates a lot of mental health issues. In a lot of cultures (especially in South Asia), infertile women are taunted for being 'barren' and are excluded from many cultural and religious functions and ceremonies with the claim that their presence is 'inauspicious'.

Within a year or two of getting married, there are expectations from the extended family that a child would be born to the couple, and when there are problems with this the woman has to constantly face negativity and exclusion. The need to have 'biological children' and social pressure around childbirth have led to the proliferation of 'infertility clinics' in cities, and rural areas too, in India. The ecosystem of assisted reproductive technologies (a problematic term) around infertility and its impact on the mental health of men and women is a subject that needs to be thoroughly explored and researched.

Body image, eating disorders, and gender are also an important area of inquiry. Body image disturbance is a multidimensional construct comprising a perceptual component, like overestimation of one's own body size and body fat and underestimation of one's muscularity, a cognitive–affective component (which includes negative thoughts, attitudes, and feelings towards one's own body, which can manifest as body dissatisfaction, disgust, shame, or sadness) and a behavioural component (such as investment in one's own body in terms of dieting or exercise, appearance fixing, body-related avoidance, and body checking). Women generally have a more negative body image than men, with up to 80 per cent of females reporting dissatisfaction with their own bodies and are also more likely to show eating disorders and body disturbance disorder symptoms, as well as full syndrome eating disorders. Previous studies have shown inconsistent findings regarding body image disturbance and the associated pathology of women of different sexual orientations, and bisexual women have mostly been neglected.

Moreover, previous research on this topic has mainly focused on body dissatisfaction as the cognitive–affective component of body image disturbance, a comprehensive assessment of the broad range of components has not been done, and there has been a disregard of the potential influencing factors. The analyses revealed that heterosexual women reported a greater drive for thinness and leanness and more investment behaviour as compared to homosexual women, but bisexual women did not differ significantly from the others in this aspect. Also, homosexual women reported a significantly lower degree of body checking than did bisexual women, but both preferred a larger ideal body size compared to heterosexual women. Furthermore, discrimination was linked to greater body dissatisfaction, drive for muscularity, and body checking in heterosexual women. For all three groups of women, younger age was associated with more body checking, but even after controlling for age, bisexual women showed significantly more pronounced body checking than did homosexual women. Concerning the behavioural body image component, homosexual women showed less investment behaviour compared to heterosexual women.

Sharan and Sundar (2015) discussed the impact of anti-bisexual discrimination and internalized biphobia on the amount of internalization of sociocultural standards of beauty and body surveillance and how bisexual women might have internalized the beauty standards to a greater extent, since they experienced a higher degree of discrimination. A previous study found that bisexual women with a male

158 Gender and Mental Health Challenges

partner showed a more traditional feminine body ideal, whereas with female partners, they had a less strictly defined body ideal. It is possible that homosexual and bisexual women are more used to discrimination in general and that they attribute these experiences to internal, stable characteristics of their sexual orientation rather than to their appearance. This, combined with their lower degree of internalization of stereotypically feminine beauty ideals evoked by the media, may provide an explanation for this lack of association between discrimination and body image (Henn et al., 2019 in Sharan & Sundar, 2015).

Although recent research has shown that their prevalence in males was previously underestimated, eating disorders do have a clear female preponderance due to various reasons that are mostly psychosocial. An older study conducted by Sharan and Sundar (2015) concluded that 'fat phobia, cross-culturally speaking, is not the *main reason* for all cases of morbid self-starvation and proposed that anorexia nervosa should be conceptualized without invoking the explanatory construct of fat phobia exclusively'.

Sharan and Sundar (2015), in their review of studies in non-Western countries, commented that anorexia nervosa appeared to represent a similar proportion of the general and psychiatric populations, excluding the criterion of weight concerns, in several Western and non-Western nations. The view that eating disorders are causatively related to the internalization of the social pressure resulting from modern female beauty standards holds a dominant position in the current discourse around the aetiology of eating disorders, but Westernization is not the only cultural factor playing an etiological role. Some studies have found an increased prevalence of disordered eating behaviours in ethnic minorities in Western countries, as well as a correlation between disordered eating behaviour and a 'traditional' South Asian cultural orientation.

Much of the early literature on eating disorders has been in the form of case reports and chart reviews, which have demonstrated that various forms of eating disorders exist in our population, but this was not followed by any population-based epidemiological study; hence, the prevalence of these disorders in our country is currently unknown. Recent studies have shown that abnormal eating behaviours and weight concern are common among the student population at a scale that may be nearly equal to that of Western nations. The clinical presentation of eating disorders in India, similar to that of other developing nations, reports the absence of weight concern in most of the cases, and this has both diagnostic and treatment implications, as models of psychotherapy that focus on weight concern may not be applicable for this population (Sharan & Sundar, 2015).

Women, reproduction, and mental health are one more important domain. Several studies help us understand it better. In humans, changes in the reproductive system are regulated by the endocrine system and manifests in women in two ways: in terms of significant reproductive milestones, such as puberty, pregnancy, and menopause; and in terms of smaller, continual fluctuations in hormones across the menstrual cycle. The reproductive hormones are regulated by the hypothalamus and act throughout the brain, causing reproductive functioning to be integrally connected to neural functioning.

In women, epidemiological links between reproductive change and risk for psychopathology are clearly seen at puberty, as girls show steep increases in clinical symptoms across a variety of psychological domains, including internalizing, aggression, delinquency, self-injurious behaviour, substance use, disordered eating, school failure, and interpersonal conflict. Boys also show significant emotional changes at puberty, but all existing research suggests that puberty is more challenging and more widely associated with psychological distress for girls than for boys. Psychological symptoms continue to shift in relation to reproductive events (e.g. menstrual cycle, childbirth, menopause) across women's lives, and this occurs not just in America and other Western nations but all over the world.

Symptoms of depression rapidly increase during the early stages of puberty for girls in a way that it does not for boys, and by the middle of the transition, girls are twice as likely as boys to be depressed. Higher prevalence of depression persists through much of adulthood among females with risk of depression rising drastically during the transition to menopause and then dropping significantly post menopause. For nearly 50 years, medical professionals have noted disproportionately high rates of suicide attempts and deaths during menstruation and early follicular phases of the cycle and dramatically lower rates mid-cycle. One of the perspectives towards studying the link between reproductive and mental health suggests that risk-associated responses to ovarian hormone changes are caused by various individual differences in how a woman's brain and body react to the interactive effects of multiple hormones across multiple tissues and these individual differences that are determined by a complex interplay of sociocultural and biological factors; however, this model is too rarely represented within scientific dialogue.

Men's sexual health and mental health are rarely examined and studied. However, the linkages between low sperm count, impotence, and erectile dysfunction syndrome and the societal pressure of the masculine-gender roles exist. Men must deal with the psychosocial distress that arises due to these problems. Queer men and women, as well as the gender-non-binary persons who have chosen a life outside the ambit of 'reproduction', are also judged and discriminated against by the larger society. Disabled men, women, and queer persons and their sexual and mental health are also rarely addressed in academia and in practice.

For the first time ever, in 2018, the APA came out with 'Guidelines for Psychological Practice with Boys and Men', which takes into consideration their ascribed gender roles; the strain of rigid masculinity; the conflicts that gay, bisexual, and non-binary men face; and their impact on their well-being. Hopefully, more immersive psychotherapeutic practice will emerge because of these guidelines which will help men transcend stereotypical gender roles and yield positive outcomes with them as clients.

160 Gender and Mental Health Challenges

8.4 Narratives Around Gender and Mental Health

Women's experience of 'possession and trancing' has been studied by anthropologists and psychologists. (Men also go through possession and trance but less frequently.) It has been regarded as superstition, but a more nuanced, feminist understanding points out that this is how women negotiate with dominant cultural and religious patterns (Ram, 1992). When women are possessed, they need not bother about many social norms, such as dressing appropriately, doing housework, catering to relatives, and performing tasks in the field or formal sphere. This gives them relief from daily chores, scrutiny, and the pressures of patriarchal households and kith and kin. Hence, very often, possession is prevalent among newly married young women (burdened with domestic and familial chores) or single women (widows, those abandoned by husbands, unmarried women who are otherwise socially excluded and ostracized) – they get attention that rarely comes their way. This ties up with the idea of 'madness' (in this case, possession was diagnosed as hysteria and later as dissociative identity disorder by consequent DSMs) as political protest against discrimination and lack of privilege by those who do not have a voice (Hardiman, 1995).

Another recurring narrative has been around declaring 'women as witches and witch hunting' in the West and in India, other South Asian countries, and Africa. All over the world, even in modern times, very often, widows and single and abandoned women are declared as witches (*dayan* in Hindi) and tortured or murdered. Several Adivasi women in Jharkhand in India have succumbed to these criminal and superstitious practices despite protective laws. Several vulnerable women go through a lot of anxiety, insecurity, and fear due to this targeting and uncertainty. This gender and mental health issue has not been explored satisfactorily.

An important fact that is ignored by interventionists, as well as policymakers, is death by suicide of housewives/homemakers. Since 2001 in India, more than 20,000 homemakers have died by suicide, as compared to 10,349 farmers (National Crime Records Bureau). Both groups deserve attention, intervention, and empathy, but whereas the issue of farmer suicides is addressed, suicides by homemakers are neglected. Politically, homemakers have no clout as a vote bank or a pressure lobby, and no political party thinks of them as a constituent or citizens who need attention. They are also not mobilized as a group. While these are socio-political realities, the causes of housewives'/homemakers' suicides are early marriage and the burden of motherhood, secondary status in the family, burden of housework, son preference, and domestic violence. There is a need to reach out to them and strengthen their narrative.

Inequalities and mental health bring together the problems of caste, class, sexuality, and gender. Rejecting the biomedical paradigm, there is an urgent need to look at the factors like lack of access to resources; social, cultural, and economic capital; and its impact on the mental health of marginalized men, women, queer persons, the disabled, and children. All these factors, humiliation, discrimination, prejudice, and institutional apathy lead to anxiety and depression. In earlier chapters, it has been pointed out that Rohith Vemula and Dr Payal Tadvi are not merely 'victims of death by suicide and the burden of psychosocial distress' but victims of institutional apathy, societal discrimination, and humiliation and hence victims of institutional murder. The larger society is complicit in their deaths and needs to be held accountable. Very often, the 'blame, burden and onus' is shifted to the individual through making mental health and psychological distress an 'individual' problem, which it is not. Mental health is socio-political, psychosocial, socio-economic, and sociocultural. To understand this, the training, approach, and perspectives in mental health sciences need to undergo a sea change.

8.5 Need for Gender, Caste, and Queer Sensitization of Mental Health Professionals and Disciplines

In many of the previous chapters, it has been highlighted how feminists and feminist psychologists have critiqued mainstream psychology, psychotherapy, and psychiatry (the major mental health disciplines of academics, training, and intervention). Have these critiques, research, and protests by women's rights groups, queer rights groups, and Black rights groups (and the emergent Dalit-Bahujan rights groups that are foregrounding mental health justice or psychosocial justice in the Indian context which mainstream disciplines are blissfully unaware of or sidelining) translated into changes on the ground? Not in many cases. What is imperative is the need to gender-sensitize, caste-sensitize, and queer-sensitize mental health professionals (counsellors, psychologists, clinical psychologists, psychiatrists, medical psychiatric social workers, alternative therapists, life coaches, and so on).

Let us look at some of the attempts of examining psychology curricula from a critical lens. Psychology as a discipline, both in India and in the West, has its roots in philosophy. However, 21st-century psychology, in its attempts to be recognized as a 'science' and to achieve professionalism, has borrowed heavily from natural sciences. This has led to a lot of inherent contradictions and tensions within the subject. Though psychology is taught by and large as 'American behavioural science', it does not strictly follow this American model. If this were indeed the case, it would have taken its cue from black psychology and psychology of women, which were introduced as independent disciplines in the United States in the 1970s. Race, colour, and gender discrimination have been debated, discussed, and researched in these two sub-disciplines and within critical, discursive, radical, and cross-cultural psychology in the United States, the United Kingdom, and other European countries.

All this is totally missing in the Indian context. An all-India exercise of curriculum analysis for masters' courses in psychology (Vindhya et al., 2008) underlined the need to bring in critical perspectives, such as the mental health

162 Gender and Mental Health Challenges

perspective, gender perspective, disabilities perspective, and LGBT perspective, into the curriculum. While the curricula did address the areas of psychological testing, clinical practices, and experimental psychology, the need to engage with the larger concerns like 'knowledge building' and 'social justice' were spelt out (Natu, 2011).

In another study, it was found that in 2014 (Kottai & Ranganathan, 2019), a year after the top court recriminalized homosexuality, the then Indian Psychiatric Society president had termed it as a pathology requiring treatment. Examining articles on LGBTIQA+ rights published in two flagship Indian journals in psychiatry and clinical psychology, position statements by professional bodies and international and national developments in human rights mechanisms, this study argued that psychiatry's voice for human rights protection of the marginalized has been akin to whispering sweet nothings in tune with the juridical–penal system. In turn, clinical psychology appears to huddle with biomedical psychiatry without raising its voice against coercive and traumatizing practices within mainstream technocratic psychiatry.

The study sought to explore the troubled relationship between mainstream psy disciplines and LGBTIQA+ persons characterized by psychological evasion: failure of mainstream psy disciplines to take up sensitive, socio-political issues, like same-sex love, in a broader human rights framework, leading to an individualization-pathologizing complex that further sidelines persons living on the margins of society. The study concludes saying that there is an urgent need for clinical psychology to look at mental health from a social justice lens, to respect lived experiences of persons who go through suffering, and to listen to the other side.

Psychologists in India have not raised questions in a concerted manner about how to make psychology training more useful in the struggle for social justice, how conventional micro-level ideas can be scaled upwards to be useful across multiple levels of social analysis, or how we can extend collaboration across and within disciplines to achieve a broader platform to support specific social justice agendas. This lack of a serious engagement with ideas of social justice has obvious implications for gender inequality, as well as its intersections with other layers of inequality, like class and caste inequalities, and their impact on mental well-being (Vindhya, 2008).

The way forward should include more curriculum and training module analysis from a critical psychological perspective, challenging the mainstream practices in therapy and academia; approaching various professional bodies of mental health disciplines with plans for gender, caste, and queer sensitization of those in training, as well as seniors, as part of continuous professional education; and, last but not least, information dissemination, demystification, and myth busting of mental health for all stakeholders and civil society. A multi-pronged strategy like this will help in bringing about change on the ground.

Review Questions

1 Describe how psychology as a discipline is organized in a sexist and gender-biased fashion.
2 Illustrate the gender and queer critique of DSM with examples.
3 Comment on men's and women's mental health in terms of similarities and differences.

Critical Thinking Questions

1 Identify depictions of mental illness in films, web serials, and popular culture which stigmatize mental illness and those that dispel some myths.
2 Chalk out a plan of action for gender, caste, and queer sensitization of mental health professionals.
3 Review a research article on the gender and mental health aspects of Covid-19.

Bibliography

Bento, B. (2018). The review process of the DSM 5: Is gender a cultural or diagnostic category? *Sociology International Journal*, *2*(3), 205–213.

Daley, A., & Mulé, N. J. (2014). LGBTQs and the DSM-5: A critical queer response. *Journal of Homosexuality*, *61*(9), 1288–1312. https://doi.org/10.1080/00918369.2014.926766

Davar, B. (1999). *Mental health of Indian women: A feminist agenda*. SAGE Publications.

Davy, Z. (2015). The DSM-5 and the politics of diagnosing trans people. *Archives of Sexual Behavior*, *44*(5), 1165–1176. https://doi.org/10.1007/s10508-015-0573-6

Hardiman, D. (1995). *The coming of the Devi. Adivasi assertion in western India*. Oxford University Press.

Henn, A. T., Taube, C. O., Vocks, S., & Hartmann, A. S. (2019). Body image as well as eating disorder and body dysmorphic disorder symptoms in heterosexual, homosexual, and bisexual women. *Frontiers in Psychiatry*, *10*. https://doi.org/10.3389/fpsyt.2019.00531

Kottai, S., & Ranganathan, S. (2019). Fractured narratives of psy disciplines and the LGBT-QIA+ rights movement in India: A critical examination. *Indian Journal of Medical Ethics*, *4*(2), 100–110.

Marecek, J., & Gavey, N. (2013). DSM-5 and beyond: A critical feminist engagement with psychodiagnosis. *Feminism and Psychology*, *23*(1), 3–9.

Mendle, J., Eisenlohr-Moul, T., & Kiesner, J. (2016). From menarche to menopause. *Clinical Psychological Science*, *4*(5), 859–866. https://doi.org/10.1177/2167702616650424

Moser, C., & Kleinplatz, P. J. (2005). DSM-IV-TR and the paraphilias: An argument for removal. *Journal of Psychology & Human Sexuality*, *17*(3–4), 91–109. https://doi.org/10.1300/J056v17n03_05

Natu, S. A. (2011). Engendering psychology: Charting a new course. In *Gender studies teacher fellowship project series*. Women's Studies Centre.

Ram, K. (1992). *Mukkuvar women. Gender, hegemony, and capitalist transformation in a South Indian fishing community*. Kali for Women.

Sharan, P., & Sundar, A. S. (2015). Eating disorders in women. *Indian Journal of Psychiatry*, *57*(Suppl. 2), S286–S295. https://doi.org/10.4103/0019-5545.161493

Sharma, P. (2017). How patriarchy and gender roles contribute to mental health issues in Indian women. *The News Minute*. www.thenewsminute.com/article/how-patriarchy-and-gender-roles-contribute-mental-health-issues-indian-women-67688

Vindhya, N., Ravipriya, K., & Kulkarni, N. S. (2008). *Teaching of psychology in India: Mapping the terrain* [Paper presentation]. Symposium presentation at National Academy of Psychology Conference, Guwahati, December.

Vindhya, U. (2008). Towards a public psychology for India: Knowledge translation and social justice perspectives. *Psychological Studies, 53*(2), 97–101.

Vindhya, U., Kiranmayi, A., & Vijayalakshmi, N. (2001, October 27–November 2). Women in psychological distress: Evidence from a hospital-based study. *Economic & Political Weekly, 36*(43), 4081–4087.

Wilkinson, S. (1988). The role of reflexivity in psychology. *Women's Studies International Forum, 2*(5), 493–502.

9

PSYCHOLOGY, GENDER, AND MEDIA

Chapter Highlights

Learning Objectives

After reading this chapter, the students would be able to

- Understand gendered portrayals in the media and their psychological impact.
- Comprehend the portrayal of therapists, patients, patient-mental health professionals relationships portrayed in media.
- Learn about how the impact of psychological conditions or disorders is portrayed in the media.
- Understand the perception of psychology as a subject and diagnosis, which impact the expectations of ordinary persons in media portrayals.
- Study the body image, body shaming, social media connection, and its psychological impact from a gender lens.
- Identify and analyse the gender spectrum representations in media.

Introduction

Both media and social media have a deep impact on the psyche of individuals. Gender stereotypes are portrayed and reinforced through media and social media. There are also the rare sensitive depictions too. In the past, there was a lot of research on whether violence in the real world is depicted in the media or portrayals of violence in media incite more violence in the real world. We acknowledge, nowadays, that this is a two-way street. Similarly, there is an urgent need to understand how gender, media, and psychology are interrelated in myriad different ways. For instance, a perfect 'body type' that is depicted in media and social

DOI: 10.4324/9781003453758-10

166 Psychology, Gender, and Media

media is increasingly influencing millennials and post millennials. A sensitive film or web series showing psychological disorders and their treatment scientifically and rationally can do wonders for awareness building while a film that mishandles the subject does utmost damage to this serious subject. LGBTIQA+ community depictions in popular media and social media have increased. From caricatures, tokenism, and bigotry, to mainstream as well as queer film makers using both these platforms effectively, there is an entire canvas of different kinds of work. For students of psychology, gender studies, and media studies, this is a relevant discourse to decode. This chapter attempts to tease out many such knotty issues and address them systematically.

9.1 Gender and Gender Spectrum Portrayals in the Media and Their Psychological Impact

Mass media or popular media includes, but is not limited to, newspapers, films, radio, television, advertisements, social media, multimedia, and video games. Media platforms play a huge role in informing our view of the world around us while strengthening our opinions, values, and beliefs.

When women are depicted in the media, it is often done in stereotypical and limited ways. Collins (2011) emphasized three patterns: women are often sexualized; subordinated through facial expressions, body positions, and using other factors; and thirdly, shown in feminine roles (such as housewives). This leads to several negative consequences. Objectification of women in ads, films, and web series has dire effects in real life for women. Objectification is internalized by many women; affects body image; leads to body shaming, disordered eating, sexual dysfunctions, and depression (Tiggemann & Williams, 2012).

In the Indian context too, we know that the coveted 'zero figure' for young girls and women became fashionable thanks to media depictions from the glamour industry. For the young boys and men, it was the same with 'six pack abs. The psychological impact of these media trends has been huge: boost for cosmetic products and industry, cosmetic surgeries, eating disorders, depressive disorders, gaslighting of those persons who do not subscribe to such trends, and more.

Key Insight

Recently a skin lightening (fairness) cream ran into a controversy because of its brand name since it promoted prejudices about 'dark skin tones'. The brand name was changed under the pressure of being 'politically correct'. It is ironical that this colourist attitude exists in a country where a huge majority of people are 'brown' and have been pervasive with all kinds of media platforms promoting 'fairness'. But at the same time 'Dark Is Beautiful' campaign launched online in 2009 has morphed into 'India Has Got Colour' in 2019. It started off as an anti-colourism campaign and has now been amplified into a campaign celebrating diversity and myriad skin tones in a country of 135 crore citizens. This proves that media can be used to weaponize discrimination and as a tool for advocacy for social change.

The most recent VFX-fuelled epic franchise to come out of the Hindi film industry (*Brahmastra*, 2022) was ridiculed for its one-dimensional portrayal of women and its lead actress's dialogues that seemed to consist of just shouting out the hero's name and calling out for help: a 'damsel in distress'. Other common tropes are the timid, dedicated housewife, ever sacrificing, shying away from a promising career for the sake of love and children and the woman who passes away to provide a back story for our anti-hero or a cause célèbre for vendetta, vengeance, and a bloodbath.

When we look at studies that did content analysis of substantial representation of women, this is what emerges. In a study (Madaan et al., 2018) 4,000 Hindi movies released between 1970 and 2017 were analysed, based on titles, cast information, plots, soundtracks, posters, and 880 movie trailers between 2008 and 2017. In a span of 50 years, the male characters' name is mentioned over 30 times per plot while female characters are mentioned only 15 times, suggesting that the actress' role is not as relevant or important to the plot. Words that describe physical attributes (beautiful, attractive, and so on) are used to describe women characters whereas the men are described using words like 'strong' and 'successful'. Verbs like 'kills' and 'shoots' are used in context to the men whereas 'marries' and 'loves' are used for the women. This shows that traditional gender role stereotypes are reinforced, and a large section of the audience internalize them as a cultural practice.

Commercial Hindi cinema propagates the impression that the 'good woman' is chaste, submissive, and self-sacrificing, while the 'bad woman' is individualistic, sexually aggressive, Westernized, and is not sacrificing. The study also revealed that the male characters are introduced by their profession, whereas female characters are introduced in association to their physical appearance, emotional state, or their relation to another male. However, despite this neglectful participation in the plot itself, female characters always feature in the trailers and posters as a means of publicity and to draw larger audiences.

Mid-chapter Exercise

Are you aware of the Bechdel or Bechdel-Wallace test?

The usual criteria of the Bechdel test are (a) that in a film or any representation of women in fiction at least two women are featured, (b) that these

168 Psychology, Gender, and Media

> women talk to each other, and (c) that they discuss something other than a man. This is to evaluate biases against women in films and other media.
>
> Have a discussion around this in your group/classroom. Apply Bechdel test to popular Bollywood, Hollywood films, and other media content.
>
> Spin-off versions of the test have been created to measure the representation of sexuality and people of colour, such as the Vito Russo test and DuVernay test, respectively.

In addition to this is the phenomenon on 'item songs' that exist purely for publicizing the movie by objectifying the woman's body. In most cases, the actress featured in the song is not even a part of the main cast but just a special appearance specifically for the song. A few films have tried to break gender stereotypes and binaries, but only a few have been commercially successful or at par with other mainstream masala movies at the box office, such as *Bandit Queen, Mirch Masala, Arth, Fire, Queen, Kahaani, Chandni Bar, Ijaazat, Masaan, Margarita With a Straw, 15 Park Avenue, Lajja, My Brother Nikhil, Lust Stories*, and *Lipstick Under My Burkha* (Mukhopadhyay & Banerjee, 2021).

Indian television soaps on the other hand are tailored for its target audience of homemakers and are more representative of women as far as screen time is concerned. Women are the heroes and the villains; nevertheless, the major theme for soap operas is the power struggle between female family members for absolute authority in the house. It is imaginative with its plots, but the priorities of women seem to remain limited to the house and to her husband. The male members are only seen going to work and coming back from work, or when another female character is attempting to steal him from the protagonist. Most of the women characters are rarely shown employed and their workplace tasks are not fleshed out properly. This has a psychological impact on the niche audience of homemakers and their socialization practices. Some of the regressive content from the daily soaps, films, and web series has both liminal and subliminal psychological impact. Interestingly, avant garde series seem to be taken off air quickly giving less television rating points (TRPs) as the cause.

Advertisements are a separate circus, as it is common discourse about how women are marketed fairness creams (now graciously rebranded as skin-brightening creams) as the one-stop solution for all challenges: romantic, professional, and personal. Domestic products are often shown to be endorsed by women, for women. Men's products are branded as 'macho', 'powerful' and generally come in black packaging.

However, in the last few years, there have been attempts of socially aware and progressive themes and portrayals in media. The most prominent example can be the two-part epic to come from Telugu cinema (*Baahubali*, 2015, 2017), which became a national phenomenon. Even though the protagonist and antagonist were male, and there was undoubtedly a fixation on displays of hyper-masculinity, one would be amiss to ignore the portrayal of powerful women from three separate generations, all of whom were brave warriors and shrewd strategists, having their humane flaws, challenging patriarchal norms, and they had a strong influence on the plot all while being mothers, sisters, and wives. Whether this continues as a trend is yet to be seen.

Issues like rape and sexual assault have seen uneven treatment across media. The Hollywood film *The Accused* (1988) based on a true life story of a gang-raped victim won critical acclaim and an Oscar for Jodie Foster who played the protagonist. Both in terms of content and treatment of the subject it was a sensitive film. *Bandit Queen*, a Bollywood film, on the same theme was also bold and at the same time sensitive. When I watched it in the theatre, the audience reaction was mature and sober.

Pink (2016) brilliantly explored consent as a concept and fought against the stereotype of 'modern', sexually active, independent girls being individuals of dubious character and questioned the prevalent norm of victim-blaming especially in the cases of sexual assault. *Thappad* (2020) raised eyebrows when the protagonist cited 'just one slap' as domestic violence and grounds for divorce, but it mirrored the reality of how married women are conditioned to ignore microaggressions or, in many cases, even physical, emotional, and financial violence within a marriage. However, this film also poses the danger of 'one act of violence, counting as domestic violence' being misinterpreted and trivialized, and since it depicted an upper-middle-class milieu, the character of the married woman may seem 'too distant' for diverse audiences to empathize with.

Television shows can also be seen slowly shifting to different narratives, involving a protagonist navigating her life post-divorce (*Anupama*, 2020), and a middle-aged, unmarried woman falling in love and marrying a widower, while having a healthy relationship with her adult stepdaughter (*Mere Dad ki Dulhan*, 2019), are very refreshing to watch.

Recent ad campaigns have seen detergent powders being endorsed by male celebrity chefs (Sanjeev Kapoor for Ariel detergent) and dish-washing soap being endorsed by male models who urge men to not wait for the product to be in black packaging to buy it (Milind Soman for Vim).

While there seems to be a gradual shift in the portrayal of men and women in media, most of the content found 'palatable' by the masses are a far cry from being sensitive, nuanced, and socially aware. Furthermore, even the 'new age' and modern stories stick to gender binaries, and queer representation is as at best tokenism and at the worst, non-existent. Let us try to understand these forays. One of the first major 'gay' storylines in successful mainstream commercial Hindi cinema was *Dostana* (2008) in which the two men in lead roles were not even gay but were pretending to be gay to find decent housing while trying to win over their landlady's attractive niece. The story and performances were cringeworthy to say the least, with both men portraying their gay personas steeped in stereotypes. Bollywood has

170 Psychology, Gender, and Media

long suffered from the delusion that being gay is synonymous with being effeminate, and this movie played it no differently.

A few commercially successful mainstream Hindi movies that portrayed nuanced queer characters sensitively can be counted on one's fingertips: a movie with the main themes of gay romance and marriage (*Shubh Mangal Zyaada Savdhan*, 2020), another which explored a lavender wedding between a gay man and a lesbian woman, which ended with the protagonists and their respective partners collectively adopting a child (*Badhaai Do*, 2022). A third movie explored a 'macho' man's journey of coming to terms with the knowledge that his girlfriend is a transwoman (*Chandigarh Kare Aashiqui*, 2021). A notable addition to this list is a Tamil film that included a plot of a son and his mother awaiting the estranged father's return after 7 years, only to have the father return as a transwoman, who is eventually accepted by the wife and child and ends up living together (*Super Deluxe*, 2019). *Kapoor and Sons* (2016) followed the story of a dysfunctional family of a husband, wife, grandfather, and two sons, vividly fleshing out each of the characters, and one of the revelations in the third act was that the 'perfect' elder son's 'girlfriend' was a man. The movie did a great job of letting the audience get to know the character as a typical son and brother, not subscribing to any of the gender stereotypes that are associated with being gay, before letting the audience know that he is in fact gay, thus helping the audience connect and relate to him without bias. Such well-made films are indeed a great resource to look at the connections between gender, media, and its psychological impact.

The most crucial fact to be noted is that all the queer characters portrayed in these handful of films are played by cis-gendered, heterosexual actors, which was the cause of severe backlash from the queer community and its allies. The only mainstream exception to this is the web series *Paatal Lok* (2020), where a transwoman character is played by a trans actress. *Paatal Lok* also successfully builds up the back story of the trans character. The queer struggle for acceptance is the focus of these Indian films, and we are yet to see casual inclusion, where being queer is not the central conflict of the story, or even worse, a queer person is portrayed as a villain, or insensitively shown for comic relief.

There are examples from Western television with multiple queer characters in the show, where queerness was not their most notable attribute, although they did address queer-specific challenges in certain episodes (*Brooklyn 99*, *Modern Family*, *Sex Education*, *Never Have I Ever*). *Schitt's Creek* (2015) took this one step further and included a major storyline of gay romance, in a rural setting, where homophobia simply didn't exist, and their queerness was very matter of fact in an ideal egalitarian world. It resonated among many viewers for its depiction of a love story between two men without any of the societal struggles that arise from being gay, providing a stark bittersweet contrast to reality.

Hollywood films such as *Brokeback Mountain*, *Call Me by Your Name*, and *The Normal Heart* stand apart for justifying their content and portrayals of queer persons. An impressive series in print media that is queer inclusive without it being the central focus of the story is Rick Riordan's mythological/fantasy series for teens, the Magnus Chase and Percy Jackson books, which effectively include gender-fluid, non-binary, bisexual, asexual, and pansexual characters that are rarely found even in other queer-allied media content. Closer home, we have Devdutt Pattanaik who has about five published books that explore queer stories in Indian mythology.

Margarita with a Straw (2014) questioned stereotypes regarding ableism, gender, and sexuality in the journey of an Indian woman with cerebral palsy, who falls in love with a Pakistani girl who is blind. Gender, disability, sexuality, and its psychological repercussions are explored extremely well by director Shonali Bose while also being sensitive to real-life Mithu Alur whose life is empathized and celebrated in the film. For the audience, the protagonist's bisexuality; her lesbian lover feeling betrayed; and the protagonist trying bravely to navigate disability, desire, and loss is a psychological tour de force. The intersections of nation, disability, gender, and sexuality and its psychological fallouts are beautifully brought out in this complex, multi-layered film.

Portrayal of female athletes in media in terms of visuals and texts also needs to be analysed from an intersectional approach. For instance, Serena Williams has faced the challenges of being a Black woman in sports and giving up her tennis career after motherhood. Gender, race, maternity versus career were all brought to the forefront, in her case, in international media with very little sensitivity. Sania Mirza has also been a bête noire of media and social media on account of gender, nationality, her choice of attire on the tennis court, and religion, and her personal choices and life have been under the radar of public scrutiny testifying to the gendered representations in media.

9.2 Portrayal of Therapists and Patients

Indian cinema has had its fair share of movies that portrayed characters with mental health challenges. The problem exists in its accuracy as movies have often failed to humanize patients and used their mental challenges for comic relief or horror. In *Khamoshi*, a Hindi film from 1969, the protagonist was a psychiatric nurse who is involved with two of her patients who recover, and the pain that she undergoes was depicted with sensitivity and subtlety. *Paroma* (1985) also effectively portrays how the protagonist is caught in the trap of good versus bad woman while seeking love and desire, and it is ultimately social pressure and not her 'self' that leads to her unravelling and succumbing to mental illness. Both these films are an important resource to understand the interplay between gender and mental health as depicted through media.

Some Hindi movies from recent times that did a fairly good job of portraying mental health issues are *Dear Zindagi* (2016) and *Tamasha* (2015). *Dear Zindagi* portrayed a more general form of counselling to address the protagonist's struggles in connecting with her family and dealing with her feelings of childhood abandonment. It succeeded in destigmatizing help-seeking and focused on how counselling

172 Psychology, Gender, and Media

can be beneficial for everyone going through difficult situations without them having a diagnosed disorder.

Tamasha was a romance-drama that explored the challenges that the protagonist faces in his professional and romantic life due to borderline personality disorder and how he eventually overcomes it with the support of his partner. *Mental Hai Kya* (2019) created a storm by labelling and vilifying mental illness, and after a hue and cry the title of the film was changed to *Judgmental Hai Kya*. This shows that with awareness and advocacy, media can be made to act in a responsible manner. Heroine film showed bipolar disorder, and Anjana Anjani depicted anxiety and suicidal tendencies. *Kartik Calling Kartik* had the protagonist portraying symptoms of schizophrenia and dissociative identity disorder. Mental health being addressed as a topic of conversation and concern in mainstream cinema is a good sign if the story line is real, rational, scientific, and humane.

3 Idiots (2009) highlighted stress, depression, and student suicide. Although the film was not about mental health specifically, it brought conversations about academic stress to the forefront. It is a landmark film, and I use it frequently as a case study in my sessions with young adults.

> Use the discussion points from the film *3 Idiots*: Is success singular (following certain career paths, e.g., engineering, only)? Can parents plan the future of children without their wholehearted willingness and aptitude? How important is the need for social approval when it comes to career choices (the film shows R. Madhavan opting for photography, his passion, instead of engineering which is considered prestigious)? Can youth suicides in premier institutions be prevented by offering safeguards and support, allowing youngsters to explore their choices and drop out when they cannot cope, and offering other options? What do you think?

Devrai (2004) and *Kaasav* (2017) are two films from the Marathi industry that deserved wider recognition among non-Marathi audiences. Devrai sensitively depicted the struggles faced by the sister in the role of a caretaker while supporting her brother through his mental health challenges. The filmmakers had spent a lot of time understanding the underpinnings of persons with schizophrenia and misconceptions about it and handled the subject with the care and caution it deserved. Atul Kulkarni who plays the lead depicted the character with a rare sensitivity, pathos, and gravitas taking care not to go over the top. Kaasav dealt with depression, suicide, treatment, care, and loneliness with a nuanced take on recovery. However, since the milieu was upper middle class, it did not take into consideration major issues such as livelihood of those with psychosocial disability.

A few other movies that portrayed developmental disorders and brought them into the mainstream discourse were *Taare Zameen Par* (2007), *Barfi* (2012), and

My Name Is Khan produced in the year 2010. *Taare Zameen Par* made 'dyslexia' a part of mainstream vocabulary with its portrayal of the eight-year-old protagonist, his academic, and behavioural challenges that arose due to his undiagnosed disorder. The movie accurately depicted how most Indian families react to a child's symptoms of such disorders, and how they resort to strict disciplining rather than remediation and therapy. Even today, dyslexia in India is often referred to by the protagonist or the movie's name.

Barfi was a romance/comedy/drama where one of the three main characters is a girl on the autism spectrum, and the movie follows her love story with the protagonist who is hearing and speaking impaired. While the film does try its best to live up to audience expectations, the female lead seems confused about the difference between a person on autism spectrum and a mentally challenged person. Hence, the portrayal unintentionally ends up being a caricature. My name is Khan also anchored its political messaging around the protagonist's love story with his neurotypical spouse. The movie depicted his difficulty in understanding social cues as well as his challenges with sensory overload.

All these movies, except for *Dear Zindagi*, did not actually show the therapist or the process of therapy. Even in *Dear Zindagi*, the therapist was a charismatic, unconventional practitioner who would be regarded as unprofessional. *Taare Zameen Par* briefly showed remediation activities that helped the protagonist overcome dyslexia.

Some movies have problematic portrayals of mental health professionals and patients. *Bhool Bhulaiya* (2007), although touted at the time as being 'progressive' for dispelling superstition and favouring scientific reasons for the 'hauntings', it still resorted to a religious angle for the 'healing' in the climax. It also perpetuated the stereotype that people with mental illness are a threat to themselves and to people around them. Depictions of persons with dissociative identity disorder hinge between showing it rationally and playing on superstition and the supernatural for pandering to the gallery. *Bhool Bhulaiya* does the latter and, therefore, untold harm.

Tere Naam (2003) was a nightmarish portrayal of how the 'mentally unstable' protagonist is treated in the mental hospital that was comparable to a prison. *Anniyan* (2005), a Tamil movie is comparable to M. Night Shyamalan's *Split* (2016), where it adheres to stereotyping patients and depicts factually incorrect aspects such as the protagonist being able to access drastically increased strength and other physical attributes as a function of their dissociative identity alters.

A film that connects excesses of the state and mental ill health is *Haider* (2014), emphasizing the intersection between identity, nation, and mental health and underscoring the fact that mental ill health is not individual; it is connected to the society and ecosystem in which the individual is located.

Some Hollywood classics such as *A Beautiful Mind* (2001) and *Good Will Hunting* (1997) that portrayed Schizophrenia and PTSD sensitively and empathetically without villainizing the protagonists. They also addressed the misconception in the

174 Psychology, Gender, and Media

minds of laypersons about 'diagnosed persons' never being functional by portraying their productive professional lives albeit with challenges.

The last few years have seen a focus on generational trauma and dysfunctional families, particularly in animation movies such as *Coco* (2017), *Turning Red* (2022), and *Encanto* (2021), where there was no proper 'villain', and the big climax was just children addressing their parents and families about misplaced anger, guilt, shame, and how families can contribute to one's mental health for better or for worse.

Everything Everywhere All at Once (2022), the sleeper hit of the year, incredibly showcased a nuanced metaphor for depression and suicidal ideation due to generational trauma and the difference that love, support, and acceptance from one's family can make.

The most recent *Puss in Boots: The Last Wish* (2022) as well as *The Last of Us* (2023) did a fantastic job of vividly showing what a panic attack looks like and how anxiety can creep into one's life and affect one's decisions.

Films like these are important to highlight the difference between diagnosed mental illness (that some people experience) versus mental health (that is relevant to every individual). They are also important in creating awareness about prevention, promotion, and treatment, and the fact that civil society in the form of audience needs to lend social support to persons with psychosocial disabilities.

The other popular platform for media consumption is OTT, and web series are getting the freedom to publish content-driven work. Most English young adult shows, or shows set in schools/colleges, portray near-realistic versions of counsellors and psychologists with episodes showing some minutes of what a therapy session could look like (*Never Have I Ever*, *Euphoria*, *Sex Education*, *Wednesday*, *The Midnight Club*, and many more). This may largely be due to the target audience (Gen Z) being more aware and informed about mental health challenges, as well as the openness to seek help from mental health professionals. This is a step in the right direction.

Bhugra, D. (2005), in his study, talked about how changing cultural norms affected the portrayal of mental illness in Hindi films. In the 1960s, a political climate of idealism led to gentler portrayals of mental illness, which were globally informed and integrated psychoanalytic methods. The 1970s and 1980s saw an increase in political and bureaucratic corruption as well as political instability, leading to harsher portrayals of mental illness with more depictions of psychopaths. The 1980s saw the rise of female psychopaths and vengeful protagonists to point out the impotence of the judiciary system, whereas the 1990s reflected economic liberalization, and portrayals of stalkers and morbid jealousy increased.

In 28 films released in the last two decades that depicted psychiatric illnesses and found that most of these characters were middle-aged, unmarried, employed, and affluent. The most common symptom shown was aggression; the most common diagnosis – schizophrenia; and the most common outcome – deterioration. Treatment seeking was also low.

Banwari, G. (2011) analysed 28 Hindi films released between 2001 and 2010 that portrayed 33 'psychiatrists'. These characters were found to be male in most cases, middle-aged, and friendly: 42 per cent were clinically incompetent, 70 per cent made inaccurate diagnoses, 39 per cent were unethical, and 53 per cent of the cases treated the patient in an outpatient setting. Prescription drugs were the most common mode of treatment, but positive outcomes were depicted in only 23 per cent of the cases.

This emphasizes the fact that there is a dire need for better content on mental health professionals and the client–professional relationship in media.

9.3 Attitudes Towards Mental Health and Mental Illness

The Live Love Laugh Foundation (TLLLF), an online portal, conducted a study in 2021 to understand how India perceives mental health (knowledge, attitudes, and practices), as well as to compare findings from a previously conducted, similar study in 2018. The sample size was 3,500 people across nine urban Indian cities. Ninety-two per cent (compared to the 54 per cent from 2018) of the respondents said they would seek treatment and would support a person seeking treatment for mental illness. Sixty-five per cent (double of 2018's 32 per cent) of the respondents believed that people with mental illness could find gainful employment and could lead a stable, healthy life. However, while 96 per cent of respondents could name at least one mental illness, the responses were limited to depression, stress, and mood swings with little to no information about conditions like OCD, schizophrenia, personality disorders, eating disorders, Autism Spectrum Disorder (ASD), and Attention Deficit Hyperactivity Disorder (ADHD). The respondents also expressed the unaffordability of mental healthcare, and stigma was still a leading barrier to treatment. A section of the respondents mentioned supernatural forces (24 per cent) and karma (19 per cent) as cause of mental illness, much more than genetic factors (17 per cent). Several respondents reported that they would feel sad, anxious, and even scared if their friends/family were diagnosed with a mental illness.

An article in the World Economic Forum website, in collaboration with the above TLLLF's 2018 study, specified the following perceptions:

1 Although 87 per cent respondents showed awareness about mental health, 71 per cent used terms associated with stigma, showing that stigma and awareness are two separate albeit interlinked issues.
2 Sixty-eight per cent of respondents agreed that people with mental health should not be given any responsibilities.
3 Sixty per cent of the respondents agreed that mental illness was mainly caused by lack of self-discipline and will-power.
4 Sixty per cent believed that people with mental illness should be segregated from groups of healthy people.

176 Psychology, Gender, and Media

5 Forty-six per cent respondents believed it was safer to maintain distance from a person with depression.
6 Forty-four per cent believed that people with mental illness are always violent.
7 Forty-one per cent believed that sitting with or talking to a mentally unhealthy person could negatively affect their own health.
8 Forty per cent expressed fear about the fact that people with mental issues live in their neighbourhoods.

When asked about their feelings towards people with mental illness, 75 per cent of the respondents expressed sympathy but in addition exhibited fear (14 per cent), hatred (28 per cent), and anger (43 per cent) towards them.

Another study conducted in rural Odisha with 400 respondents (Jena et al., 2020) found that lower education level correlated to higher levels of negative attitudes towards mental healthcare and that females had a more negative attitude compared to males. It was also found that respondents belonging to Hinduism had a more negative attitude towards mental healthcare compared to respondents from other religions. Some common perceptions in the community were that psychiatric hospitals are comparable to prisons, and once admitted, it is difficult to get out. They also believed that patients there are merely sedated and not treated. Another major impression they had regarding psychiatric hospitals was that the main form of treatment was electro-convulsive therapy 'as shown in mass media, especially television'. Indeed, depiction of electro convulsive therapy in films, serials and series, most often unscientific and incorrect, has added to misconceptions and fear about treatment.

Some of the barriers to seeking mental healthcare that were qualitatively reported were lack of acceptance or denial about the illness, social stigma, preference of treatment from faith healers, unavailability of specialized services at the local hospitals, economically unaffordability to pay treatment costs in addition to missing multiple days of work, and daily wages to travel to the district hospital.

Another mixed-method study was conducted in Udupi, and district with urban and rural areas in Karnataka, with 212 respondents. The respondents mainly specified unemployment, separation/divorce, and other socioeconomic factors as causes of mental illness. They identified psychiatrists and physicians as the most effective modes of treatment. The respondents were overall found to be more discriminative against people experiencing psychosis (74.8 per cent) as compared to people experiencing depression (25.2 per cent). Male respondents were found to have a stigmatizing attitude (social distancing) as compared to females against people with mental illness. The respondents opined that some of these beliefs are based on real-life experiences and many on depictions in popular media.

Another study conducted in Bangalore with 400 participants by Menon, G. et al. (2012) showed that respondents with lower education levels, lower-income levels, belonging to Hinduism had the least favourable views about people with mental illness. Most of the respondents stated that their extent of awareness about mental illness comes from the internet, television, and movies. Eighty-five per cent of the respondents felt that people with mental illness could be treated within the community, and 86 per cent agreed that prescription drugs were required for treatment. Seventy-nine per cent of the respondents believed that having a mental illness meant that the patient was suffering from a split or multiple personalities. While 66 per cent felt that people with mental illness can hold a steady job, 37 per cent felt that they would be violent and aggressive. The respondents felt that media played an important role in forming impressions about mental illness. Sixty-three per cent felt that mental illness caused public nuisance. Eighty-four per cent felt that physical disability is more acceptable than mental disability. While 91 per cent felt that the best way to treat mental illness was to let the patient stay in the community, 38 per cent maintained that if a mental health facility were to be set up in their community, they would relocate.

In my private practice, I have observed that more and more clients are using the internet and social media to process their symptoms and come in for therapy armed with their 'own diagnosis'! It is an uphill task to help them to clear up misconceptions and anomalies and steer them clear of 'self-diagnosis' and falling prey to cut-paste unscientific, unauthentic stuff on the internet and social media platforms. The other tendency influenced by media and social misinformation, especially during the pandemic, was of catastrophizing by privileged people. This takes away time, efforts, and attention from the vulnerable persons. While stigma about help-seeking persists, coming for therapy and counselling, influenced by media and social media, by the affluent classes has become somewhat faddish these days.

Another cause of concern is the proliferation of mental health influencers on Instagram, some undoubtedly with expertise and skills and some dubious. Since people with distress find them easily accessible, they are turning to them instead of seeking treatment from established and professionally trained experts. Online therapy has also gained more traction since the pandemic. Some of the reasons for using social media influencers for help-seeking can be that the help seeker and/or the service provider get anonymity, can hide, mask, or fake their identities. This creates a false sense of temporary security. Escapism from the severity of the problem is also achieved. Many of the influencers can create trust among the help seekers, monetary gains, and popularity. Hence, licensing, uniformity in training, and regulation in the mental health profession are imperative (Mache and Natu, 2022)

9.4 Body Image, Body Shaming, Media, and Social Media: Psychological Impact

Social media, especially photo-sharing apps, are an undeniable part of the life of young adults in the contemporary world. The youths and adolescents have unchecked access to social media influencers, actors, celebrities, and models. Earlier, the major demographic under attack by unrealistic beauty standards was restricted to women with glorification of fair skin, slim waists, and zero figures.

178 Psychology, Gender, and Media

However, now even men are not spared as everywhere they look; they see media celebrities with muscles, abs, height, well-groomed and styled facial hair, and well-toned bodies.

Social media allows selective self-presentation with the option of photo editing, which has negatively affected body image perception in males and females. Roy, N. et al. (2021) in their study found that body image dissatisfaction is significantly higher in female social media users than in male users. In addition, the social comparison theory shows how females tend to engage in comparisons of upward appearances, causing a negative body image perception for themselves. The causes mentioned in the study that contribute to body dissatisfaction (mainly in females) are negative affect, higher fatness evaluation, altered body perception, body shame, and thin ideal internalization.

Another study found that acute exposure to thin-ideal media images correlates to disturbances in body image, as well as empirically linked body dissatisfaction, self-esteem, and thin-ideal internalization to the thin-ideal endorsed by the media. Another concern is the homogenized standard of beauty that imposes Western standards on non-Western bodies, which contributes to the increase in the global prevalence of eating disorders. Becker et al. (2002) conducted an interesting experiment in a rural community in Western Fiji by introducing a TV. Prior to the TV, being 'thin' was considered unhealthy and unattractive, but after the TV was introduced, the adolescent Fijian girls started to report increasing dissatisfaction with being 'fat'.

Erskine et al. (2016) predicted that eating disorders are going to potentially rise in low- and middle-income countries in a similar way to its current trend in higher socio-economic countries because of cultural change and access to the idealized Western body standard.

Parikh, S. (2019) stated that 90 per cent of women said that body shaming was common behaviour with social media partly to blame. The survey included 1,244 women across 20 Indian cities and found that 76 per cent of women blamed media standards for body shaming. Ninety per cent of the respondents agreed that films and TV shows mocked people who do not conform to these standards of beauty, and 89 per cent of the respondents reported feeling insecure about themselves after reading comments on social media about other people's appearances. Most of the respondents (95 per cent) feel that people don't even realise when they body-shame others.

A study by Mahon and Hevey (2021) found that girls tended to strive for female body ideals, whereas boys tended to strive for functionality ideals. They employed the following three behavioural strategies to manage their consumption of problematic content:

1 Avoidant strategy where they limited platform usage or unfollowed celebrities or people with unrealistic body goal standards. This was not entirely helpful as certain social media algorithms tend to push weight-loss ads/products on profiles and accounts that are listed as female.

2 Active selection of positive content. Boys felt this was a more effective strategy for them; however, girls disagreed as they found that even the body-positive content made them feel dissatisfied. Respondents felt there was a disparity between the body-positive text in the caption versus the image itself, which still showed an idealized body. Only recently, the body-positivity content has started including diverse body types to involve plus-size influencers and models, which is more realistic. However, even then, some respondents mentioned that the diversity is often in extremes with only thin, lean bodies and overweight bodies, and no real representation of the average body types that fall between those two.
3 Active selection of alternative platforms. Girls reported to switching to other platforms that were not as 'serious' or visually edited as Instagram, nor contained feedback options of 'likes', 'comments' or 'followers'. However, Instagram is still the most popular platform by a mile.

Other cognitive strategies included the following:

1 Psychological distancing strategies, used by both boys and girls, to remind themselves that these are actors/models who make a living that depends on them looking a certain way, as well as the financial resources that are available to them to maintain those beauty standards. Girls also reminded themselves that most celebrity pictures use filters or are edited themselves.
2 Reframing strategies such as focusing on goals and achievements, rather than shortcomings, as well as viewing your own bodily differences as a positive, unique thing, rather than something that need to fit in with the ideal.

A recent study mentioned that along with sexism and misogyny, Hindi films have long dictated what the ideal body type should look like. Despite having a vast range of skin colours throughout the country, mainstream media and song lyrics still seem obsessed with fairer tones, and actresses are clearly losing weight from the curvaceous 80s and 90s to the lean and thin actresses since the 2000s.

Rekha and Maran (2012) studied how ads target men and women according to their social beliefs and attitudes, and preoccupation with one's physical appearance has been deemed to be the stereotype for women. Even advertisements focus more on the beauty of the actor/model rather than the product itself. Nearly two-thirds of the respondents in their study agreed that advertisements pressured them to pursue an ideal body shape. When presented with the silhouette figure rating scale, respondents tended to overestimate their current body size while idealizing a much thinner body size, causing a larger discrepancy in body dissatisfaction. In addition, the mean scores for ideal body type, for both men and women, were anorexic.

Other spin-off from the ideal body image obsession is the body positivity movement. While it advocates for diversity in body types and sizes and believes that

180 Psychology, Gender, and Media

women suffer more due to fat shaming and body shaming than men, it is still to be completely mainstreamed. The movement has received criticism from scientists on the grounds that excessive approval of over obese individuals will lead to an increase in lifestyle diseases and dissuade them from making efforts to improve their health. Feminists have criticized the movement for placing undue importance on external appearance and thus leading to negative self-esteem.

All forms of media are ready reckoners for information about health, and illness and some of this information is incorrect, flawed, or exaggerated. Media is responsible for spreading messages about medicalizing everyday experiences such as grieving people need anti-depressants, wrinkles require correction, if you do not like the shape of your nose get rhinoplasty done, thin is in/healthy, fat is unhealthy, and infertile should try their utmost for pregnancy (Markey & Markey, 2015).

Reality television shows have sometimes done untold harm by spreading fear about pregnancy, childbirth, and menopause. Books such as *What to Expect When You Are Expecting* focus on problems thereby priming readers to undergo unnecessary medical tests and interventions. A popular Western sub-genre is reality TV shows based on childbirth. It often focuses on high-risk pregnancies and worst-case scenarios to heighten the drama for the viewers. But if normal scenarios are shown less or rarely it results in creating unnecessary anxiety and stress among pregnant women thereby worsening their birth outcomes (Cole-Lewis et al., 2014).

In conclusion, I am taking note of some positive efforts across the world in creating gender-sensitive content on media that results in psychological enhancement and judicious use of various media and social media platforms for gender and intersectionality awareness. This record is in no way comprehensive. Gena Davis Institute on Gender in Media initiated in 2007 and Sheryl Sandberg's LeanIn.Org aim at increasing the visibility of women in media and depicting women in various roles. Sheryl Sandberg has partnered with Getty Images to create more diverse and less stereotyped images of women. Both feel that if young girls see women in various roles, then they can envision themselves in these varied roles. An interesting example from the Indian context is Khabar Leheriya, a pioneering rural network run by 24 women in eight off-the-map districts of Uttar Pradesh. They write, edit, design, publish, and distribute the newspaper on their own. This is a remarkable effort and needs to be understood and studied.

Review Questions

1 Describe how stereotypical gender roles are perpetuated through media and social media with examples.
2 Comment on the positive and negative aspects of depictions of queer persons' lives across media and social media and its psychological impact.
3 Describe how therapist and client relationship and mental illnesses are depicted in media through a gender lens.

Psychology, Gender, and Media **181**

Critical Thinking Questions

1 Analyse the Hindi film *Raazi* through a gender, psychology, and intersectional perspective.
2 Comment on how the web series *Orange Is the New Black* depicts gay, lesbian, and transgender persons' trials and tribulations.
3 Document some progressive advertisements that portray egalitarian gender roles.

Bibliography

Agarwal, A. (2021). 5 Bollywood movies that brilliantly highlight mental health issues & the stigma around it. *Mens XP*. www.mensxp.com/special-features/features/89925-5-bollywood-movies-based-on-mental-health-issues-in-india.html

Ahuja, K. K., & Pundir, T. (2022). Dreamgirls in Tinseltown: Spotlighting body image stereotypes and sexism in popular Indian media. *Journal of Psychosexual Health, 4*(2), 76–79. https://doi.org/10.1177/26318318221091019

Banwari, G. H. (2011). Portrayal of psychiatrists in Hindi movies released in the first decade of the 21st century. *Asian Journal of Psychiatry, 4*(3), 210–213.

Becker, A. E., Burwell, R. A., Herzog, D. B., Hamburg, P., & Gilman, S. E. (2002). Eating behaviours and attitudes following prolonged exposure to television among ethnic Fijian adolescent girls. *The British Journal of Psychiatry, 180*, 509–514.

Bhugra, D. (2005). Mad tales from Bollywood: The impact of social, political, and economic climate on the portrayal of mental illness in Hindi films. *Acta Psychiatrica Scandinavica, 112*, 250–256. https://doi.org/10.1111/j.1600-0447.2005.00598.x

Chaudhari, S. (2022). Tere Naam to Bhool Bhulaiyaa: A look at how poorly mental health is depicted in Hindi films. *The Telegraph Online*. www.telegraphindia.com/entertainment/tere-naam-to-bhool-bhulaiyaa-a-look-at-how-poorly-mental-health-is-depicted-in-hindi-films/cid/1891191

Cole-Lewis, H. J., Kershaw, T. S., Earnshaw, V. A., Yonkers, K. A., Lin, H., & Ickovics, J. R. (2014). Pregnancy-specific stress, preterm birth, and gestational age among high-risk young women. *Health Psychology, 33*(9), 1033–1045. https://doi.org/10.1037/a0034586

Collins, R. L. (2011). Content analysis of gender roles in media: Where are we now and where should we go? *Sex Roles: A Journal of Research, 64*(3–4), 290–298. https://doi.org/10.1007/s11199-010-9929-5

Erskine, H. E., Whiteford, H. A., & Pike, K. M. (2016). The global burden of eating disorders. *Current Opinion in Psychiatry, 29*, 346–353.

Friedler, S. A., & Wilson, C. (Eds.). (2018, February 23–24). *Conference on fairness, accountability and transparency, FAT* [Paper presentation]. Proceedings of Machine Learning Research, PMLR (Vol. 81, pp. 92–105). New York, NY, USA.

Gayatri, B., Patel, S., & Paladiya, B. K. (2023). Movies and matters of the mind-portrayal of psychiatric illnesses in Bollywood over last two decades: A content analysis. *Asian Journal of Psychiatry, 80*. https://doi.org/10.1016/j.ajp.2022.103398

How India Perceives Mental Health. (2021). *The Live Love Laugh Foundation*. www.thelivelovelaughfoundation.org/uploads/LLLF_Mental_Health_Report_2021.pdf

Iyer, S. 10 Bollywood movies that got mental illness (mostly) right. *Pratisandhi*. www.pratisandhi.com/10-bollywood-movies-that-got-mental-illness-mostly-right/

Jena, S., Sahoo, K. C., Samal, M., Kripalini, P., Shrivastava, C., Anand, H., Mahapatra, P., & Pati, S. (2020). Rural community attitude towards mental healthcare: A mixed-method study in Khurda district of Odisha, India. *Middle East Current Psychiatry, 27*, 48.

Mache, P., & Natu, S. (2022). Pseudo-science versus evidence-based science: Emergence of online therapy by unqualified people. *IAHRW International Journal of Social Sciences Review*, *10*(4), 506–511. ISSN-2347-3797

Madaan, N., Mehta, S., Agrawaal, T. S., Malhotra, V., Aggarwal, A., Gupta, Y., & Saxena, M. (2018). *Analyse, detect, and remove gender stereotyping from Bollywood movies*. Proceedings of the 1st Conference on Fairness, Accountability and Transparency, PMLR 81:92–105.

Mahon, C., & Hevey, D. (2021, May 21). Processing body image on social media: Gender differences in adolescent boys' and girls' agency and active coping. *Frontiers in Psychology*, *12*. https://doi.org/10.3389/fpsyg.2021.626763. PMID: 34093311; PMCID: PMC8175666

Markey, C. N., & Markey, P. M. (2015). Can women's bodies be fixed? Women's bodies, well-being, and cosmetic surgery. In M. C. McHugh & J. C. Chrysler (Eds.), *How medicine and media can create a need for treatment drugs and surgery* (pp. 221–237). Praeger.

Menon, G., Murali, T., & Rao, K. (2012). Public attitude towards mental illness in Bangalore: An exploratory study. *Artha Journal of Social Sciences*, *11*(1), 1–18. ISSN 0975-329X

Motwane, A. (2022). *Gender and sexuality in recent Bollywood films. Perspectives, provocations & initiatives*. Institute of Development Studies, Alumni Network. https://alumni.ids.ac.uk/news/blogs-perspectives-provocations-initiatives/653/653-Gender-and-Sexuality-in-Recent-Bollywood-Films

Mukhopadhyay, S., & Banerjee, D. (2021). Bollywood, popular visual media, and sexism in India: A critical glance back. *Journal of Psychosexual Health*, *3*(3), 256–261. https://doi.org/10.1177/26318318211027312

Nagar, I., & Virk, R. (2017). The struggle between the real and ideal: Impact of acute media exposure on body image of young Indian women. *SAGE Open*, *7*(1).

Padukone, D., Doraiswamy, P. M., & Chandy, A. (2018). 5 charts that reveal how India sees mental health. *World Economic Forum*. www.weforum.org/agenda/2018/04/5-charts-that-reveal-how-india-sees-mental-health/

Parikh, S. (2019, April 12). 89% women face body image issues after reading social media comments: Survey. *Hindustan Times*. www.hindustantimes.com/sex-and-relationships/89-women-face-body-image-issues-after-reading-social-media-comments-survey/story-ARSFGTAnO4nGeh4XyFQhwI.html

Rekha, V. S., & Maran, K. (2012). Advertisement pressure and its impact on body dissatisfaction and body image perception of women in India. *Global Media Journal: Indian Edition*, *3*(1).

Roy, N., Choudhury, N., & Reddy, V. (2021). Body image dissatisfaction in young adults: Impact of social media use. *International Journal of Education and Psychological Research (IJEPR)*, *10*(3).

Sara, H. (2021). 5 Indian films that depict mental health in sensible, realistic ways. *Homegrown*. https://homegrown.co.in/homegrown-voices/5-indian-films-that-depict-mental-health-in-sensible-realistic-ways

Sindhu, M., Phadnis, M., Chouhan, Z., Saraswat, P., & Maheshwari, S. (2021). Awareness and attitudes towards common mental health problems of community members in Udupi Taluk, Karnataka: A mixed method study. *Clinical Epidemiology and Global Health*. https://cegh.net/article/S2213-3984(20)30249-9/fulltext

Tiggemann, M., & Williams. (2012). The role of self-objectification in disordered eating, depressed mood, and sexual functioning among women: A comprehensive test of objectification theory. *Psychology of Women Quarterly*, *36*(1). https://doi.org/10.1177/0361684311420250

10
WAY FORWARD

It is essential to untangle some of the issues, debates, and controversies around psychology and gender to find the way forward. Hence, in this epilogue of the book, I am flagging some important points that need to be unpacked from each chapter.

While we deal with understanding the theoretical underpinnings of gender role stereotypes, thanks to media and social media, what were thought to be prescribed gender roles are 'life skills' that are essential to every human being, such as cooking, caregiving, household chores, learning about repairs, investment, financial literacy, growing of things, and so on. But will mere information translate into attitudinal and behavioural change? Perhaps not. Hence, the need for gender sensitization at all ages and stages, in all spheres of life, has not diminished. Media and social media can play a creative and positive role in bringing about this change in the everyday lives of people. Policymakers, academia, NGOs, and civil society also have to play their role in this transformation.

Gender role development is thought about through the binary of men and women. This has resulted in strengthening essentialism (men are like this, and women are different naturally) and thinking of women (cis women) as deficient and exclusion of LGBTIQA+ persons. While mainstream theoretical canons have been challenged by feminist scholars from various disciplines, these arguments and positions have not percolated to students and ordinary people.

For instance, it is being compellingly argued that world leaders, such as Jacinda Ardern of New Zealand, Angela Merkel of Germany, Sanna Marin of Finland, Tsai Ing-wen of Taiwan, Norway's Erna Solberg, and Iceland's Katrín Jakobsdóttir, have handled the Covid-19 crisis as female leaders. Their success is being attributed to 'feminine qualities of empathy, compassion, humility'! This essentialist argument is fallacious at many levels: These qualities cannot be termed 'masculine' or 'feminine'. These women who got to become leaders are exceptions,

DOI: 10.4324/9781003453758-11

184 Way Forward

and hence, it is difficult to draw generalizations about their success in governance unless we have a pool of many such female leaders to compare with male leaders on parameters of governance. The important conclusion for the field of psychology and gender is that such a flawed line of reasoning is potentially dangerous for women in politics.

Another deeply contentious issue is the widespread misconceptions about feminism. It is important to understand this long-standing history of misconceptions with new additions in every generation. It is necessary to link 'psychology and gender' with feminism, women's studies, the women's movement, the queer movement and queer studies, as well as other social movements, since all its formulations are embedded in the latter. Psychology and gender as a field owes its emergence and growth to these interrelated fields and does not exist in a vacuum. The misconceptions are interesting, since they spell out the resistance to social movements in general and the distancing from women's empowerment. Some of these popular misconceptions are as follows: Feminism is against (anti)men. It is Western. Can men be feminists? Feminism is against (anti)religion. Feminists are not feminine. Feminism wants to replace patriarchy with matriarchy. Feminazis (a derogatory term for 'feminists') are dangerous. Are feminists sympathetic to trans persons? Do they exhibit transmisogyny? And so on.

Added to this, we now have internet/cyber/hashtag/online feminism as well to contend with. This goes to show that there is an acute need to understand the history of the feminist movement in the world, in South Asia, as well as in India. There is also a need to comprehend the connection of feminism with the work that has gone into and is being done currently in the field of psychology and gender that is now engaged in questioning power relations and patriarchies in personal, professional, and political spaces.

Psychology and gender, drawing from feminism, is now about setting right the imbalance and studying the linkages between inequalities and mental health. The initial chapters in this book have given a bird's-eye view about the impact of feminism and the women's movement on psychology and gender as a field, but more in-depth reading and understanding are essential to gauge the nuances and challenges. The emphasis on intersectionality and brief understanding of intersectional feminism in the book has pointers for later chapters of feminist psychotherapies, gender, and mental health. The intersectional perspective is imperative to resolve or at least look for solutions to some of the knotty problems in the field.

Though much work on the psychological problems faced by queer persons is being done by organizations that were started and are being run by LGBTIQA+ persons themselves, the queer movement does need allies and supporters and straight, as well as queer, practitioners of queer-affirmative psychotherapy. It is important for students of both mainstream psychology and feminist psychology to realize this and work in this direction. While support groups for parents of LGB-TIQA+ persons are gaining ground, it is necessary that students of psychology and gender volunteer, intern, associate sensitively, and align with such activities.

It is also important to be mindful of the intersections and hierarchies within queer networks.

Many organizations that are working with queer persons conduct awareness and sensitization sessions, workshops, film festivals, and a range of activities aimed at reaching out to the wider society. This is an opportunity for students to empathetically understand the lives of queer persons, their psychology, and the problems faced by them. It offers a window towards becoming more inclusive in practising psychology and gender.

While the challenge of responding to queer sexualities with confusion, negativity, misconceptions, prejudice, and discrimination continues, it is not as though we in India have become more accepting of heterosexual, intimate relationships. Opposition to all kinds of love is the common refrain. Not willing to respect 'all love as love' is another practice. As theorists, researchers, and practitioners of psychology and gender, it is important to comprehend this reality. While jingoism and the rhetoric of war have a lot of currency, every mention of 'love' is anathema. Depictions of inter-caste, inter-religious, cross-border, and inter-regional love in cinema are denounced, and in real life, such young lovers face ostracism and threats and must elope and even face death.

Both *Sairat*, a film made in Marathi, and *Raazi*, made in Hindi, were big hits. Youngsters across castes, classes, genders, and languages could relate to these films. *Sairat* focused on inter-caste love, and *Raazi* on cross-border love. As depicted in these films, the opposition to transgressive love from family, kinship networks, and the society at large is huge and frightening. It forces youngsters into endogamous relationships and marriages, which is exactly the devious design of orthodox society embedded in patriarchy! It is necessary to discuss such contentious issues and not put them on the back burner, especially when young adults have a choice about whom to fall in love with and whom to marry or not, regardless of caste, religion, region, nation, and sexuality (though same-sex marriages are yet to get the legal nod in India), as important aspects of relationships and psychology and gender. Although the chapter on 'Gender and Social Psychology' talks about marital relationships briefly, it is necessary to engage further in the themes of 'why marry/say no to marriage' and 'singlehood'.

In India, marriage is considered as a given – one must get married. It is also treated as the 'be all and end all', especially for girls. Advertisements until the 2000s spoke about bank loans for a boy's education and a girl's marriage. Though things have improved somewhat, there are other challenges! The event marketing of weddings in the 21st century makes marriage an aspirational badge for millennials and post-millennials. Destination weddings, weddings in a stadium, and those in a helicopter, mid-air, begin to seem like 'choices' to the class that can afford them, and this raises the stake for those down the social ladder. The conundrum of whether marriage (also live-in) is the most intimate relationship in a person's life (psychological perspective) or the most important social institution (sociologically) or both, remains unresolved! Do two individuals get married to one another

186 Way Forward

or do two families, as the typical Indian social order insists? This is another important area that the field of psychology and gender must take on board.

Surveys indicate that many women are embracing singlehood; of course, they belong to the upper middle class or upper strata and are educated and employed. But it is a sign that things are changing, not just in the West but also in India. An increasing number of young men and women all over the world are saying 'no' to marriage. There are many reasons for this, which range from personal choice (did not find a suitable partner), lack of need for economic support (both men and women are self-sufficient financially), facts about marital disasters (divorce rates have gone up), and the ability to lead a full life 'alone' (they have friends, colleagues and family, and sexual partners as well and do not need marriage as a complication!).

Queer individuals are also living together and with less insecurity than during the times when Section 377 was prevalent; they are leading a harmonious and fulfilling life too. Though same-sex marriage is still not legal, some queer rights groups have petitioned that the Special Marriage Act have an amendment and include same-sex marriage as well. Letting young adults choose their partners regardless of sexuality would indeed be a leap for society, but it is essential. Otherwise, a lot of LGBT persons are pushed into heterosexual marriages that are a burden for both partners and often end in divorce – or the couple is forced to lead dual lives. Sometimes, the duplicity is kept under wraps, and in a few cases, it is done taking the other partner in confidence. The psychological cost of this charade is huge, and it is 'marriage at all costs' regardless of the willingness of the couple and the stranglehold of heteronormativity which is the culprit.

Earlier, the term 'eve teasing' was used in place of sexual harassment! The word conjured anachronistic images of the Garden of Eden, while the incident would be one of harassment, assault, or molestation. Thankfully, we are now calling 'sexual harassment' by its right name. However, I want to share an interesting observation (it cannot be generalized but is quite pertinent). Ever since the Sexual Harassment of Women at Workplace (Prevention, Prohibition and Redressal) Act, 2013, came into force, all institutions in the organized sector must have an internal committee (anti-sexual harassment/for prevention of sexual harassment) in place.

Many organizations use the terms POSH committee, POSH issue, and so on, taking a lot of care to avoid using the term 'sexual harassment'. This is indicative of the taboos around sexuality, sexual relationships, and the euphemisms we continue to cling to even when it is 'the businesses' of investigation around sexual behaviour and what is permissible and what is not. The complex issue of 'consent' (which is relevant to all crimes against women, as well as queer persons) is also not unpacked and understood with all its nuances, and cases in the limelight have all pointed to the grey areas pertaining to sexual harassment at the workplace.

Marital rape is still not acknowledged in law and in everyday life. It is not recognized as an issue of violence where the wife goes through psychological trauma and not emphasized in the training of mainstream psychotherapy. Domestic violence, intimate-partner (live-in partner, former spouse, current spouse, or lover) violence, and stalking as events leading to deep psychosocial trauma or PTSD and depression are being unravelled only at present. Hence, there is an urgent need for training in feminist psychotherapy and narrative therapy, which are better suited to dealing with such issues and offering closure and agency to those who face such violence.

Parenting, gender discrimination, and self-esteem are intricately linked. Parents are the primary agents of socialization and hence must take a lot of the credit and blame for how their children turn out! Much can be said and written (and has been said and written) about the need for 'conscious and sensitive parenting'. But here is an attempt to flag what gets left out. What I am writing comes from my engagement with young adults and the experience of conducting parenting workshops for parents whose offspring are 18–22 years old. First of all, in India, we have a curious mix of old-fashioned 'parents who know it all and are the best judges of what their children should do, should become and so on' (authoritarian), those who just completely leave their kids alone (albeit a small number – laissez faire/status quo), and a handful who engage as 'authoritative' parents (lead by example, are democratic, accessible, non-judgemental, and so on) as well as 'helicopter parenting'. As a result of this, we come across youngsters who are absolute rebels, resistant, or completely traditional and conservative in their choices, and a handful who are open, accepting, and liberal.

Most parents are politically correct and do not accept in public that they discriminate between their sons and daughters. However, the crux of the matter is the freedom in the latter's choice of career and choice of friends, partners, and lifestyles. Daughters are firmly shown their place, and the willingness to spend on their higher education (even among the upper middle class and upper class) is seen to be less than that on sons' higher education. In the case of marginalized communities and classes, the dropout rate of girls in higher education is much more than that of boys. Parents' attitudes and acceptance of their children's sexuality and intimate partners (live-in, marriage) remain a critical factor. Even in contemporary times, many parents want to control and micromanage their young-adult children's lives. This must change, and for that, parents must be willing to participate in parenting workshops with experts. Parenting requires thoughtful decision-making, which in turn requires training and discussion. We must create an ecosystem where more and more parents are willing to attend such trainings at all ages and stages of their child's life, to do well by the latter. It is also imperative for parents to let and prepare their children to become independent and self-reliant and gain life skills. There is a reluctance on the part of many Indian parents to 'let go' off their children, to train them in life skills, or to give them exposure that prepares them to face the world.

Aptitude testing has become par for the course in urban areas in India, and with well-meaning NGOs working for rural development, it has also percolated to rural and semi-urban areas. But sadly, this does not take care of 'gendered perceptions'

188 Way Forward

about careers and fields, affordability versus aspiration, and stereotypes about successes. These hurdles, challenges, and reality checks are not addressed by career counsellors and vocational guidance experts (most of whom are looking at this field as a lucrative profession, barring some wonderful exceptions, of course).

Let me share some of the insights that I have gained from my many years of imparting vocational guidance. One, for a long time now, medical education has been clearly outside the ambit of poor students in India since it is exceptionally expensive (more so in private colleges). Statistics shows that women get 51 per cent of the admissions for MBBS courses in India, but this figure reduces to one-third at the PG and doctoral levels, and only 17 per cent of these female doctors practise (allopathic medicine). This skewed ratio is attributed to women having to balance their career and household responsibilities. If this is the case with the 'hallowed' field of medicine, where almost 9–10 years are spent in specialization and super-specialization training, then not being able to practise what you are trained for, it is such a tragedy!

Though there are efforts across all sectors – government, corporate, NGO, STEMM – to get 'women' back into a field after a break for marriage and/or motherhood, or care of young children, such efforts are meagre and not focused. Moreover, women require support and encouragement at all stages, from the entry point to career advancement, in taking up leadership positions and carving a niche for themselves, and the road is uneven. It is also not a level playing field in workplaces for marginalized and excluded communities such as Dalit Bahujans, Adivasis, and LGBTIQA+ persons. They continue to remain underrepresented in all fields of work.

Glorification of motherhood has been critiqued by various feminist scholars, but most mainstream social sciences, including psychology, are still attached to the idea of 'mother as the sole and better nurturer'. Not only does this take away from the need for parenting (instead of mothering), but it also increases the social expectations from mothers. This creates a 'double bind' for many women, both full-time homemakers and mothers, as well as women who try to straddle the world of paid employment, home, and motherhood. While the former end up feeling 'I am just a housewife' and that mothering is a thankless job, the latter carry tremendous guilt that they are not doing justice to their home, children, and job while bearing the double burden.

The solution lies in getting fathers to 'participate' in fatherhood and co-parenting, not just 'support' mothers. There is a qualitative difference between the two. With merely supportive fathers, the major responsibility remains with the mother, and she gets most of the blame and hardly any credit for parenting. But when the joys and challenges are shared equally and fathers become active participants, it means two heads, two hearts, and four hands at work! This is good for the child, as well as the parents. Fathers can be sensitive, sensible, and creative and contribute, since none of the so-called nurturing traits are either feminine or masculine – both parents can acquire the necessary life skills and adapt to the parenting role.

There is enough impressionistic data to suggest that children benefit from co-parenting and when both parents are equal participants in the process of a child's personality development. As I have noted in the chapter on 'Gender and the Workplace', several outliers, such as house husbands (who take care of nurture too) and couples who take turns at major responsibilities of parenting and employment, have done well and turned the belief of 'mothers as better parents' (a gender stereotype) on its head. Such social transformation all over the world and across cultures, besides better day care facilities, more paid maternity and paternity leaves and other benefits, flexitime, and work from home with shared household chores and parenting tasks, would go a long way in helping women attain their goals and contribute more fully to national development.

Another irony that continues to prevail even in the 21st century in India (and many other parts of the world) is that women are forced to make a choice between marriage and career and, later, between motherhood/household chores and career! Those who enter the workforce are asked demeaning personal questions about their marital status, pregnancy, plans about having children, and so on under the presumption that they will leave their job at all these junctures. This reinforces the existing stereotypes about women and paid work (home, marriage, and children should come first for them). There is a need for a paradigm shift in the ways in which parents and families socialize daughters, the ways in which young men think about women's right to employment and their willingness to participate in household chores and childcare. Only positive changes in social attitudes will create a level playing field for women in the world of paid work.

An example would suffice to illustrate the gender differences in perceived adult roles. My work in a reputed IT (information technology) company as an external expert for hiring entry-level engineers, computer scientists, and freshers from allied fields was an eye-opening experience. When I asked questions pertinent to professional life management and goals, there was no difference among the male and female candidates, but when it came to questions of personal life management, such as whether they would choose a life partner from the same IT field (long hours, gruelling work, many challenges), how would they both achieve work–life balance (work–life balance is thought to be a feminine domain, since male employees do not have to bother about homes!), if they had thought about sharing household chores, if they would choose their own partner or go for an arranged marriage, what were their thoughts about fatherhood and parenting, and so on, the majority of the male candidates were stumped and ill-prepared, and the female candidates sounded defensive.

This led me to conclude (after achieving data saturation) that there was a need to sensitize young men about personal life management and their adult roles, which included being a partner, father, and householder and treating their spouse as an equal. It is amazing how these young men have clearly demarcated between women in their workspace (classmates and colleagues) and those in their personal sphere (would-be life partner and, later, wife). While the women in the workspace

190 Way Forward

could be treated collegially (sometimes as part of political correctness and in exceptional cases genuinely), women at home were to be viewed and treated traditionally, conventionally, and in an orthodox fashion! A lot of work needs to be done in masculinity and traditional male-gender roles. My research on male gender roles also corroborates that we in India (as also the rest of South Asia and the rest of the world) are a long way off from achieving gender equality in the private and public space, and the field of psychology and gender has a whole lot to contribute to achieving this.

Homophobia and transphobia and discrimination and injustice meted to queer persons need to be addressed in myriad different ways. Most of it has been signalled in the chapters on 'Understanding Feminist Psychotherapies' and 'Gender and Mental Health Challenges'. Hence, I am just sharing some insights gained from workshops that I have conducted with the corporate sector on gender-spectrum sensitization. For most companies, after separate departments and verticals were created catering to D&I, the D&I seemed to start and end with hiring cis women and setting the gender ratio right; then came some pinkwashing as in hiring token LGBTIQA+ persons (mostly lesbian, gay, and bisexual people), of course with some notable exceptions. In the last few years, however, there have been more efforts for hiring, as well as giving more visibility to, queer persons.

Being aware of this positivity and change, I conducted some workshops for senior managers aimed at creating a more congenial atmosphere for hiring LGBTIQ individuals. We navigated the spaces of misconceptions, curiosity, and trepidation and went on to address 'what a queer-friendly workplace would look like and how it would function', and what straight people would have to do as seniors, bosses, colleagues, and juniors. Many of the participants were receptive, empathetic, and open to the idea of hiring queer persons, recognizing the needs and dignity of queer persons who were working in the organization (but may not have 'come out'), and becoming aware of the needs of 'persons who are different but equal' and how queer-inclusive workplaces would be more 'creative' and 'productive' workplaces in the real sense.

Another contentious issue that needs to be highlighted further (it has been flagged in Chapter 7 on 'Understanding Feminist Psychotherapies') is the mantra used by mainstream practitioners of asking women to 'adjust' with husbands and marital families in marital homes where they are facing violence, conflicts, and exploitation. Despite all the work of gender sensitization of mainstream mental health professionals done by feminist activists, feminist scholars, and practitioners in the last four decades, not much has changed. There is an urgent need for curricular changes where domestic and intimate-partner violence is not brought in only as a social issue but is also understood in terms of violence that happens in homes and intimate spaces. The approach in intervention and therapy, gynagogy should also speak to processes of child sexual abuse, domestic and intimate-partner violence, and violence against LGBTIQA+ communities. While the vibrant women's movement in India has brought in a sea change in the domains of redressal for domestic violence in terms of laws, one-stop crisis intervention centres, shelters for battered women and children, and much more, it is not reflected in the academic or therapeutic training in mainstream psychology. Disciplines of social work, sociology, and women's studies are more aligned to these issues and practices, and psychology needs to follow suit.

The terms such as 'intact homes' and 'broken homes' are deeply problematic and stigmatizing for those who are dealing with challenges of familial conflicts. Clinging on to the ideals of 'intact or normal families', which could well mean facing ongoing, long-term conflict but living under the same roof, needs to be challenged. Many studies have shown that children whose parents have separated or obtained divorce amicably fare much better in life than those from conflict-ridden (so-called intact) homes. However, the 'D' word (divorce) continues to be stigmatized in mainstream psychology literature and practice, though social acceptance has in fact increased in the last decade. Single parents and children of single parents are no longer a rarity, and not making them stigmatized identities is important for all mental health practitioners. In fact, the term 'dysfunctional' is also pejorative, since functional automatically corresponds to a higher-stratum, upper-caste person, family, or group! It is a dominant group that is the norm against which all others are compared and an authority from a dominant group who defines, diagnoses, and treats!

The shift from a completely biomedical approach to mental health towards a bio-psychosocial approach has taken place gradually all over the world, thanks to the relentless advocacy and push from the women's movement, queer movement, and user and survivor movement, and several other allies and supporters, such as caregivers and sympathetic mental health practitioners. However, in many instances, the primacy to 'bio' (medical is inherent) over psychosocial is obvious. Sometimes, it is merely paying lip service to psychosocial while remaining completely biomedical. There is a visible hierarchy among mental health professionals where the biomedical psy disciplines such as psychiatry gain precedence over clinical psychology, medical anthropology, medical sociology, health psychology and sociology, medical and psychiatric social work, and so on. In India, we have yet to realize fully that it is a team of mental health practitioners – clinical psychologist, medical psychiatric social worker, psychiatrist, psychiatric nurse, counsellor, health psychologist, alternative therapist, and so on – who can together and perform the task of 'healing'. There is also a strong need to locate the distress/illness/disorder within the social context (region, nation, caste, class, gender, sexualities = hierarchy) rather than 'within the individual'.

Covid-19 has underscored this need for healing spaces that recognize the connection between bio-psychosocial contexts emphatically. This humanitarian crisis has been exceptionally challenging for marginalized communities and has exposed the existing inequalities in societies all over the world. It is a clarion call for mental health professionals to move beyond solely 'individual'-centric work to community mental health and people-centred, diversity-centred psychology, something

192 Way Forward

that has been the mainstay of feminist psychology and feminist psychotherapy all along.

Another critical concern is the use of aversive therapy with LGBTIQ clients. While it has received censure and reprimand from various bodies, many mental health practitioners continue to use it. There is a welcome move from aversive therapy to queer-affirmative therapy all over the world, but it must gain universal recognition and acceptance. There is a need to create more awareness and popularize its training among students and professionals.

It was not in the scope of this book to focus on problems of the homeless mentally ill and those who recover and find families averse to having them back. A few dedicated individuals and organizations are working on these issues in India which fall well within the ambit of psychology and gender, since there are many women, queer persons, and disabled persons among either of these groups. As students of psychology and gender, we need to engage more with both these issues critically, being mindful of intersectionality.

Understanding neurodiversity and neurotypicality from a bio-psychosocial perspective would be advantageous for the field of psychology and gender. It is a relatively new area, but since it questions pathologizing conditions, just like feminist psychology, there is a lot in common which needs to be explored further. Similarly, including caste-, gender- and queer-sensitive approaches in academics, research, and practice in the field of psychology will bring it closer to feminist and critical psychology and create a more just and humane psychology. In the Indian context, dominant narratives of all social sciences engage very often in the 'othering' of minorities (religious and sexual) and marginal castes hence there is a need to pay attention to domains like Muslims and mental health, and caste and mental health in theory and practice. Organizations and individuals working with Muslim minorities on economic, educational, employment opportunity and familial, marital, and other issues have been voicing concerns about dealing with their mental health issues. Feminist psychologists need to take this on board and work with such organizations, and mainstream psychology also needs to be more empathetic. Persons and organization working on livelihood issues of persons from marginalised castes are also flagging off mental health issues. Solidarity and collaboration and learning with them are also essential.

Finally, decoloniality/decolonialism and decolonization, in the context of psychology and mental health, have been major fields of work and engagement for many years. Embracing both these paradigms would mean moving away from 'individual-centric' approaches and 'EURAM (Europe and America)-centric canons', and moving towards the philosophy of feminist psychology. Hence, as students of psychology and gender, we need to work with these paradigms more closely and use them in our everyday lives. Decolonization paradigms create more possibilities for social transformation. They also draw from political psychology – like feminist psychology – and believe that mental health is deeply political.

Knowledge production then becomes a collective activity rather than being top-down and authoritative.

To make sense of the field of psychology and gender, it is important to recognize that this field draws from feminism, intersectionality, critical psychology, decoloniality, and decolonization and contributes to these fields as well. To move from mainstream frames to psychology and gender would be a leap of faith, and liberating. It would mean doing away with disciplinary silos and accepting multidisciplinary knowledge systems, practices, and praxes. The SDGs of the United Nations and other global policies and practices also emphasize the need for engaging with the field of psychology and gender. Both in theory and in application, it is a critical and significant field. We need to recognize the need to study and engage with transnational feminism in psychology which implies moving beyond difference and engaging with deconstructing processes of power at the intersection of the local and global.

To build more consistent academic and applied work in this field, it is essential to promote it among professional bodies and research organizations within academia and NGOs and mentor students and early career professionals. Concerted efforts, like those undertaken by a Special Task Force of APA Division 35 in partnership with the APS, are crucial. APA Division 35, Society for the Psychology of Women, constituted a Special Task Force called 'Educating Through Feminist Research', with the APS pitching in through symposia on 'Gender Beyond Difference'. This endeavour aimed at building fora on research on gender across sub-fields of psychology and invited young researchers and early career professionals to engage with innovative, theoretically driven research on gender, which culminated in the strengthening of efforts of individual researchers and documentation in the form of a pathbreaking book that will serve as a template for those who want to initiate, strengthen, and give direction to their work on psychology and gender. There is a dire need to undertake such projects in India and South Asia and build more networks and collaborations to do this. A more open and equal dialogue between Global North and Global South with all stakeholders also needs to be strengthened.

INDEX

Note: Page numbers in *italics* indicate a figure and page numbers in **bold** indicate a table on the corresponding page.

ABVA *see* AIDS Bhedbhav Virodhi Andolan
Accused, The (film) 169
adolescence 32, 42, 59, 63–68, 111; closing gender gaps 68; depression and 64; gender roles 63–64; LGBTIQA+ adolescents 67–68; peer and societal pressure 64; physiological changes and 65; sexuality education workshops 66; social conformity restrictions 64, 65; surveillance and moral policing 64–65; unequal gender norms and 64
adolescents 48, 64, 66, 68, 108–109, 115, 155, 177
adoption 73–74, 96–97, 107, 121
adoptive parents 95
adulthood challenges and gender 68–74
advertisements, gendered portrayals in 168, 169
ageing 74–75, 77, 152
'agents of socialization' 31–33; media 32–33; parents 31–32; peers 32; school and college 32
age-related decline 74
aggression 7, 24, 28, 33–34, 47–48, 60, 92, 159, 174; aggressive behaviour and testosterone, link between 24; gender gap in 34; and social learning theory 28–29

aggressive feminists 17
AIDS Bhedbhav Virodhi Andolan 120
alpha bias 37–38
alpha error 37
ambitions 10, 57, 59, 82, 114
ambivalent sexism 11
American Psychological Association 15, 19–20, 113, 125, 138, 146, 148, 150–151, 159
androgyny 9, 30, 38
anger 47, 138, 141, 176
anthropological understanding, of gender roles 34–35
anxiety 103, 153, 155, 160–161, 174
APA *see* American Psychological Association
Arden, Jacinda 88
arranged marriage 45
artistic personality-type persons 83
assault 11, 102, 153
Association of Psychological Sciences 20
'attachment theory' 86
attachment to primary caregiver 60
attitudes 8, 10, 27, 44, 46–47, 49–50, 58–59, 61, 63–64, 88, 110, 112, 118, 139, 147–148, 155, 157, 166, 175, 179

Bandit Queen (film) 169
Barfi (film) 173
beauty treatment for women 14

Index 195

behaviours 5, 7–12, 24, 27–29, 32–34, 36, 44–46, 53, 61, 63, 96, 103, 111–113, 125, 139, 141, 148, 151, 178; feminine 24, 32–33, 150; gender-appropriate 28, 32; gender differences in 33–34; gendered 12; gender-inappropriate 32; gender-related 60; hysterical 125; societal role structures shaping 33
beliefs 8, 43, 65, 70, 86–87, 93–94, 128, 148, 151, 153, 155, 166, 176
benevolent sexism 11
beta bias 37
beta error 37
Bhool Bhulaiya (film) 173
biological determinism 26, 130
biological essentialism 36
birth, infancy, childhood, and gender 62–63
birth spacing 65
bisexual women 154, 157–158
body dissatisfaction 157, 178–179
body image 64, 157–158, 165–166, 177–178
body shaming 64, 165–166, 177–178
body types, ideal 179
borderline personality disorder 149, 172
BPD *see* borderline personality disorder
brain 74, 159; development, sex differences in 25; gendered 25; male and female 25–26
'breaking the ice' between males and females 52
British Psychological Society 20
bullying 11, 32, 67
Butler, Judith 6

Canadian Psychological Association 20
career 9–10, 31, 45, 57, 63, 69–70, 81–86, 88–91, 93–95, 99, 101, 120, 137, 167, 171; advancement 97, 99; development 81–82, 85, 95–97; dreams and aspirations 82; gender bender 70; male-dominated 70; *vs.* marriage 89–95; professional 84, 94, 99
career and work, challenges in 97–104; access of women to STEMM careers 99–101; access to professional careers and sectors 99; discrimination against women 98; domestic workers and 98; representation of women on boards 99; sexual harassment 101–104; women and LGBTIQA+ persons,

career advancement for 97–98; 'work from home' 98
career choices 32, 59, 63, 83, 89, 91, 172; dilemmas of women 81–82; influencers of 78–79
career development, models of 82–83; gender analysis of 83–85; Holland's model 83; Super's model 84–85
caregiver 60, 67, 92
caregiving demands 74
caretaker 51, 134, 172
caste 2, 5, 8, 14–16, 29, 42, 44, 58, 61, 63, 65, 72–73, 81, 84, 91, 101, 103, 107, 112–113, 118, 120–121, 124–125, 127, 129–130, 137, 145–147, 160–163; biases 82; domination 49; inequalities 162; marginalized 58, 69, 82–83, 103; patriarchy 153; privilege 116; privileged 86
castration anxiety, in boys 27
child: development 86; identification with same-sex parent 26–27; rearing 43, 86, 92, 94–95, 137; relationships 59, 76
childbirth 87, 90, 94, 153, 157, 159
childcare 7–8, 10, 86–87, 91–95, 99, 133, 153, 156; role of father in 90–95; social responsibility for 87
childhood 60, 62–64, 68, 82, 132; early 42, 62, 132; gender sensitizationsince 63
Chodorow, Nancy 15, 27–28, 133–134
civil rights movement 18
clinical psychology 2, 146–147, 162
cognitive development theory of gender role development 29–31; feminist ethic of care 31; Gilligan's work 29–31; Kohlberg's theory of moral development 29–30, *30*; postulates of 29
cohabitation *see* live-in relationships
collegiality 46, 103
'coming out' 116, 118–119
Committee on the Status of Women in India 14
commodification of women 32, 45, 110
conflicts 30, 42, 48, 58–59, 90, 97, 119, 125, 137–138, 153, 159
conformity 32–33, 59, 138
consciousness raising 125, 128, 152
consent 49–50, 103
counselling 72, 121, 126–128, 139, 171, 177

196 Index

CR *see* consciousness raising
Crenshaw, Kimberlé Williams 13
crimes committed against women 48
cultural differences 33
cultures 7, 12, 25, 27, 31, 33–36, 50, 60,
  62–63, 65, 90–91, 106, 108, 112,
  115, 130, 133, 135, 156

D&I 44, 82, 95, 97
dating apps 112
day care services 94
Dear Zindagi (film) 171–172, 173
deconstruction technique 141–142
decriminalization of Section 377 19, 44, 73,
  114, 154
Delhi rape case of 2012 53
depression 50, 60, 64, 67, 74–76, 103, 153,
  156, 159, 161, 166, 172, 174–176
derived identity 91–92
developmental disorders, portrayal of
  172–173
developmental psychology, 'mother-
  blaming' studies in 87
Devi, Bhanwari 102
Devrai (film) 172
Diagnostic and Scientific Manual (DSM)
  classifications 125, 145, 148–149,
  151–152; DSM-5 149–151;
  feminists objecting to 149; queer
  analysis and critique of 149–152
In a Different Voice (Gilligan) 29, 31
disciplines 5, 14, 18, 26, 31, 66, 94–95,
  101, 113, 145, 147
disclosure 61, 119
distress 59–60, 64, 76, 98, 120, 127,
  150–153, 156, 177
domestic chores 51, 90, 92, 94, 98, 101
domestic labour 61, 85, 90, 94, 137
domestic-labour debates 90–95; 'adoptive
  parents' 95; 'compromise' 91;
  derived identity 91–92; devaluation
  of housework 90; domestic chores
  and childcare 90; industrial society
  and 92; nurturing responsibility
  92–93; 'queer couples as parents'
  95; 'single parents' 95
domestic tasks 34, 91
domestic violence 10, 15, 17, 29, 48–49,
  62, 136, 153, 160, 169
Dostana (film) 169–170
'double drudgery' 85
dysfunctional families, portrayal of 174

eating disorders 157–158, 166, 175, 178
education 8, 11, 14, 16, 18, 32, 58–59, 61,
  67–74, 84, 90, 92, 94–96, 99, 101,
  107, 109, 121, 148, 156; higher 19,
  32, 59, 69, 72, 81, 95–96; sexuality
  and gender 108; transgender 71
egalitarian individuals 8–9
egalitarian parenting 93–95
Ek Ladki Ko Dekha Toh Aisa Laga (Hindi
  film) 118
Electra complex 27
emotional burnout 51
emotional development of child 86
employed mothers 85–88, 93
employed women 9, 30, 88–89, 93, 98, 156
employment 11, 14, 18–19, 59, 68, 71,
  73–74, 81, 84–86, 88, 90, 95–96,
  98, 101, 107, 121, 156, 175
empowerment 128–129
'empty nest syndrome' 75–77, 84, 156
enculturated-lens theory 36
endocrine disorders 24
engendering psychology 123, 146
enterprising personality-type persons 83
equality 18, 53, 121, 128, 148
ethics 31, 139
Everything Everywhere All at Once
  (film) 174
evidence 16, 24, 27, 64, 71
evolutionary psychology 33–34
existentialism 142–143
externalization technique 141

families and gender 58–62; bonds between
  family members 62; children's
  divergence from parents' attitudes
  59; discrimination against girl 61;
  dissimilar parents and children
  59; family patterns of attitudes
  58; gender role attitudes 58;
  LGBTIQA+ persons 60; parent–
  child relationships 59; queer young
  adults 59–60; sexual-orientation
  disclosure 60–61; stigma related
  to gender nonconformity 60; youth
  homelessness 60
family systems therapy *see* gender-sensitive
  family therapy
fear 50, 62, 67, 96, 115, 117, 120, 131, 138,
  160, 176
female athletes, portrayals of 171
female education and marriage 72

Index 197

female employees, discrimination against 11–12
female hormones 24
female moral development, stages of 30
'female voice' 30
feminine behaviour 33
feminine gender roles 7–8
femininity 27, 35–36, 63, 132, 150, 156
feminism 6, 13–16, 27, 123, 125, 127, 129–132, 137, 149, 152; definition of 14; feminist ethic of care 31; and gender 16; and men's movement 16–18; and psychoanalysis 130–135; and women's movement 14–16, 15
feminist psychologists 31, 85, 87, 121, 125, 132, 137, 147, 153, 161
feminist psychology 146
feminist psychotherapies 123–126, 128–130, 138–139, 146, 153–154; feminist practice 127–130; history of 124; initiatives of **126**
feminist theory 128, 149
fertility 110, 156
financial incentives, to have daughters 61–62
Freidan, Betty 15, 131, 153
Freudian psychoanalysis 27, 130–132
Friends (sitcom series) 42
friendships 47, 65, 103; and gender 42–43; opposite-gender 32, 42–43; same-gender 32, 42

gatekeeping 43
Gawde, Durga 111–112
gay/lesbian/bisexual/transgender 112
gay persons 6, 8, 13–14, 18–19, 67, 108, 111, 113–114, 116–118, 120–122, 135, 159, 169–170
gay rights movement 18
gender: analysis 20, 75, 81–82; attitudes 64; atypical behaviour 32; based division 58, 61, 85, 92; based value system 29; bias 11, 125, 129, 145–147; binaries 44; Butler's theorization of 6; definitions of 5; as demographic variable 5–6; as difference 61; disparity 63–64, 99; equality 14, 17, 32–33, 65, 86; and friendships 42–43; gap 34, 68, 101; identity 6, 10, 12–13, 36, 41, 44, 57, 60, 67, 71, 73–74, 106,

139, 149–150; inequality 11, 52, 64, 68, 83, 162; lens 6, 23, 83, 89, 165; neutrality 17; nonconformity 60; norms 41, 57, 64, 135, 138, 150; parity 53; polarization 36; as process 61; and psychology 6; regulating interaction between 32; sensitivity 52, 135, 148; sensitization 52–53, 63, 82, 109, 135; and sex, difference between 4–7; social construction of 33, 36, 131; as structure 61; terms related to **6**; three-dimensional theoretical structure of 61
gender differences 5, 23–25, 28, 37, 42, 69, 72, 92, 97, 145, 152, 154; in behaviour 33–34; evolutionary analyses of 33–34; old age and 74–78
gender discrimination 9–11, 10–12, 18–19, 42, 46, 48, 52, 58, 59, 60–61, 65, 67–68, 71–72, 74, 86, 98, 113, 119, 121, 123, 136, 145–146, 152, 157–158, 160, 161; female employees 11–12; LGBTIQA+ community 11; prevalence of 10, 11; sexism 10–11
gender-discriminatory social sanctions and social control 63
gendered behaviour, normative patterns of 12
gender exceptionalism 61
gender-fluid 6, 12–13, 67, 96, 111–112, 171
gendergrams 138
gender harmony 32, 41, 51–52; 'breaking the ice' between males and females 52; complex factors of 54; gender sensitization 52–53; marital harmony 51–52
gender identity disorder 149
'gendering' of professions 8
gender-just society 10
gender role 4, 7–9, 12, 31–38, 58–59, 61, 86, 92, 108, 127, 136, 150, 159; adolescence and 63–64; attitudes 7–8, 58; development 2, 23–24, 26, 28, 31, 36; drive to adhere to 7–8; in gender-differentiated practices 28; learning and internalization of 7; meaning of 7; prenatal hormones effect on 24; and sexual desire 25; socialization 8–9,

198 Index

129; stereotypes 7–10, 16, 29, 46, 57, 63, 64, 94, 159, 167; traditional 9; typing 28, 35; understanding of 4
gender role development, biological influencers of: hormones 24–25; nervous system and neurotransmitters 25–26
gender role development, theories about 23; alpha and beta bias 37–38; biological influencers 24–26; cognitive development theory 29–31; gender schema theory 35–37; 'nature' theories 23; 'nurture' theories 23; psychoanalytic theory 26–28; psychological anthropology 34–35; social learning theory 28–29; social role theory 31–33; socio-biology and evolutionary psychology 33–34
gender schema theory 35–36, 35–37, 132
gender-sensitive family therapy 37, 123, 135–138
gender similarity hypothesis 24
gender stereotypes 8–11, 9, 25, 32, 36, 46, 63, 69, 81, 84, 92, 111, 126, 128, 135, 165, 170; families reinforcing 62–63; peers and 32
gender-typed occupations 82
generational trauma, gendered portrayals of 174
Generation Z 43
GID see gender identity disorder
Gilligan, Carol 29–30
girl–boy friendships 42

Haider (film) 173
harassed husbands 17
harassment 17, 33, 50, 63, 67, 71, 99, 103, 107, 119–121, 123
health 14–16, 18, 61, 64, 67–68, 71–72, 74–75, 96, 121, 124, 146, 155, 176; gender and mental 2, 127, 145, 160, 171; sexual 109, 114, 119, 159
hegemonic masculinity 60
heterosexual 13, 16, 44, 60, 67–68, 108, 111, 113
Hindi movies, gendered portrayals in 167–175
HIV/AIDS pandemic 18, 50, 52, 113–114, 117–118, 120, 125
Hollywood films, gendered portrayals in 168–171

homelessness 60
homophobia 18, 50, 106–107, 114, 118–119, 139, 170
homosexuality 19, 60, 87, 113, 116–117, 119–120, 154; decriminalizing 19, 44, 73, 114, 120–122, 154; psychological impact of 120–122; Section 377 of IPC criminalizing 19
hormones 24–25
Horney, Karen 15, 27, 131–132
hostile sexism 11
'house husband or stay-at-home dad' 94
housework 9, 85, 90, 92, 98, 160
Humsafar Trust 18, 114–115, 121

IAWS *see* Indian Association of Women's Studies
'identification' process 28
identity, gender 6, 12, 14, 27, 36, 60, 63, 71–72, 75, 86, 91, 107, 111–112, 120–121, 124, 128, 130, 132, 141, 148, 173, 177
'imitation' process 28
Indian Association of Applied Psychology 20
Indian Association of Clinical Psychology 20
Indian Association of Women's Studies 20
Indian Council of Social Science Research 15–16
Indian Penal Code: decriminalization of Section 377 19, 44, 73, 114, 154; fight against Section 377 of 19; misuse of Section 498A of 17
Indian television soaps, gendered portrayals in 168, 169
infancy and gender 63
'infantilization' 54
infertility 110, 157
information 4, 15, 28, 35, 45, 66–67, 73–74, 82, 100, 108–109, 138, 155, 175
institutional discrimination 11
International Union of Psychological Science 19
Internet 110, 126, 155, 177
interpersonal relationships 2, 30, 41, 64, 107, 120, 155; friendships 41–43; gender harmony 51–54; relationships at workplace 46–47; romantic relationships 41, 43–46; and violence 47–51
intersectional feminism 13–14, 17, 129
intersectionality 2, 4, 6, 13–14, 16, 18–19, 23, 53, 95, 101, 103,

112, 128, 130, 137, 162, 171, 173; career development, gender, and 95–97; concept of 4; and feminism, linkages between 13–14; and gender sensitization 53; implications for psychology and gender 14, 16; meaning of 13–14; within queer communities 36
intersex person 13
intimate relationships 42, 44, 47, 66, 73, 107, 111, 113, 118–119, 121, 153
investigative personality-type persons 83
IPC *see* Indian Penal Code
'item songs' of films, gendered portrayals in 168
IUPsyS *see* International Union of Psychological Science

jobs 53, 82, 84, 86–87, 90, 93, 97–98, 141, 170

Kaasav (film) 172
Kartik Calling Kartik (film) 172
Kaur, Harnaam 111
Khairlanji (Maharashtra) case 53
Khamoshi (film) 171
Kohlberg's theory of moral development 29–30, *30*

labour 32, 34, 58, 61, 85, 90, 92, 94, 137
language 10, 37, 44, 69, 112, 132–133, 135, 140, 146
leadership in workplaces 47
leaves, reasons of taking 92–93
lenses, kinds of 36
lesbian 8, 13, 18–19, 42, 72, 108, 111–112, 116, 118–120, 154
LGBT community: depression among 67; romantic relationships 44
LGBTIQA+ adolescents 64; family acceptance of 67; and gender disparity 67–68; isolation and alienation of 68; sexuality and gender 67
LGBTIQA+ child 57
LGBTIQA+ persons 11, 18, 32, 45, 60, 68, 84, 96–97, 107, 112, 114–115, 121, 162; discrimination against 11; experiences with parents 114–117; gendered portrayals of 166; interpersonal relationships of 107; and media 32; relationships across lifespan 114–117; relationships

and psychology 113–114; underrepresentation in corporate sector 96–97
LGBTIQ persons 8, 42, 95, 121; sexual harassment at workplace 104; sexual violence against 50
LGBT issues 116–117
LGBTQ people 150–151
LGBT students 60–61, 67
The Live Love Laugh Foundation 175
live-in relationships 41, 43–46, 49, 73, 110
loneliness 76, 117, 119, 172
love marriage 45

mainstream psychology 2, 82, 87, 106–107, 114, 123, 146, 149, 152–153
mainstream psychotherapies 107, 123–126, 129–131, 138, 149
male brain and the female brain 25–26
male-centeredness 36
male–female opposition 37
male hormones 24
'male voice' 30
Maras, Pam 19
Margarita with a Straw (film) 171
marriage 10, 43–45, 61, 72–74, 77, 84–85, 88–91, 96, 99, 110, 116, 131, 154, 169–170; arranged 45, 91; changing patterns of 72–73; choice of 72–73 73; early 65, 72–73, 160; gender differences and gender discrimination impacting 72–73; inter-caste/-community 119; LGBT youngsters and 73; marriageable age 73; problems faced by transgender persons 73–74; as social institution 72
marriageable ages 65, 73
masculine gender roles, drive to adhere to 7–8
masculinity 7, 9–10, 12, 17, 27, 30, 35–36, 47, 50, 60, 63, 70–71, 75, 111, 132, 135, 150, 159
mass-based women's organizations 14–15
maternal employment 85–89; acceptance of 88; changing patriarchal attitudes towards 94–95; conflicting views on 85–86; discrimination in workplaces 86; factors impacting 94; impact on children 85–88; theoretical underpinnings of 88
MAVA (Men Against Violence and Abuse) 17

200 Index

media: as agents of socialization 32–33; media and social 31, 165, 171, 177; popular 45, 110, 166, 176
media and social media, gendered portrayals in: advertisements 168, 169; developmental disorders 172–173; dysfunctional families 174; female athletes 171; generational trauma 174; gradual shift in 169–170; Hindi movies 167–175; Hollywood films 170–171; Indian television soaps 168, 169; 'item songs' of films 168; LGBTIQA+ community 166; mental health challenges 171–172, 174–175; mental health professionals and patients 173, 175; 'mentally unstable' protagonist 173; 'new age' and modern stories 170; OTT and web series 174; panic attack and anxiety 174; perfect 'body type' 165–166; psychological impact of 165, 166, 177–180; queer characters 170–171; rape and sexual assault issues 169; schizophrenia and PTSD 173–174; socially aware and progressive themes 168–169; stress, depression, and student suicide 172; therapists and patients 171–175; violence 165; Western television 170; women 166–168
men and women: differences between 5; similarities between 24
menopause 156, 158–159
men's liberation movement 16
men's mental health 152–159
men's movement 18; classification of 16; in India 17; masculinity studies 17–18; in West 16–17
men's rights group 16–17
men's studies 17–18
menstrual cycle 65, 124, 159
menstruation 65–66, 155, 159
Mental Hai Kya (film) 172
mental health 2, 20, 92, 124–125, 127, 135, 139, 141, 145–146, 145–147, 149, 152–153, 155–163, 171–175; challenges, gendered portrayals of 171–172, 174–175; disciplines 161–162; intersectional understanding of 145; issues 50, 73, 115, 154–156, 160, 171; of men and women 152–1599; and

mental illness, attitudes towards 175–177; of men and women 152–159; narratives around gender and 160–161; narratives in post-globalization world 145–146
mental health professionals 68, 113–114, 127, 161, 173–175; and disciplines 161–162; and patients, gendered portrayals of 173, 175; queer sensitization of 146, 161
mental illness 152, 154, 171–177
'Me Too' movement 102
Mirza, Sania 171
misogyny 11
moral development, stages of 29
moral policing 32, 43, 64–65
motherhood 9, 27, 85–86, 88–90, 92, 99, 130, 160, 171
mothering 15, 31, 86–87, 89, 92, 132–134
multifactorial gender identity theory 36
My name is Khan (film) 173
mythopoetic movement 16

NAOP *see* National Academy of Psychology
narrative therapies 123, 139–143, 146, 149; deconstruction technique 141–142; existentialism 142–143; externalization technique 141; non-blaming 140; overview of 139–140; principles of 140–141; 're-authoring' technique 141; respectful 140; unique-outcomes technique 142
National Academy of Psychology 20
natural selection 33
nature *versus* nurture debate, points of view in 12
Naz Foundation 121
neurosexism 25
'new age' and modern stories 170
NGOs *see* non-governmental organizations
non-governmental organizations 15, 46, 52, 97, 102, 108–109, 112, 120
nurturing 9, 12, 23, 25, 31, 34, 41, 92–95

objectification and commodification of women 45–46, 110, 147, 166, 168
occupational development 84
occupational tests 82
occupations 83
Oedipus complex 27
old age and gender differences 74–78; andropause 77; cardiovascular

diseases 74–75; climacteric and its psychological effects 77; elderly women 74; 'empty nest syndrome' 75–76; financial stability 78; health 75; healthy ageing 75; perimenopause and menopause 77; remarriage 77–78
opposite-gender friendships 42
oppression 13–14, 53, 126, 128, 148
OTT and web series, gendered portrayals in 174

Paatal Lok (Hindi series) 63, 170
panic attack and anxiety 174
parent–child relationship 76
parenting 9, 73, 84, 88, 92–95, 133
parents 9, 19, 27, 31–33, 42, 45, 50–52, 58–65, 68, 72, 75–78, 87, 92, 94–95, 107–109, 114–120, 133, 135, 156, 174; adoptive 94–95; as agents of socialization 31–32; gender-conforming 60; queer couples as 94–95; same-sex 26–28, 37; single 94–95
Paroma (film) 171
passive–aggressive behaviour 29
patriarchy 5, 9, 16–17, 31, 46, 48, 83, 93–94, 98, 103, 125, 132, 153–154
PCOS *see* polycystic ovary syndrome
peer pressure 32, 64
peers 28–29, 31–34, 59, 64, 81, 109, 112, 155; as agents of socialization 32; gender-congruent 29; and parents, shaping gender norms 64
perfect 'body type' 165–166
perimenopause and menopause 77
personality 12, 25, 33, 83
personal-life management 91
physical aggression 47–48
Pink (film) 169
PMDD *see* premenstrual dysphoric disorder
PMS *see* premenstrual syndrome
polycystic ovary syndrome 111
pornography 110
poverty 29, 71, 74, 84, 117
Prabal programme of Humsafar Trust 114
prejudice and discrimination against queer persons 119
premenstrual dysphoric disorder 124
premenstrual syndrome 124
prenatal hormones 24
primary caregiver, attachment to 60
primary caretaker 51
pro-feminism 16, 17

professional-life management 91
'protectionism' 54
Protection of Women from Domestic Violence Act of 2005 48, 102
pro-women laws, rampant misuse of 17
psychiatry 114, 124–125, 149, 152
psychoanalysis 123, 127, 130–131, 134
psychoanalytic feminism 132–134
psychoanalytic theory of gender role development: child's identification with the same-sex parent 26–27; Chodorow's work 27–28; criticism of 27
psychodiagnostics 148
psychological anthropology 34–35
psychological distress 107, 125–128, 131, 153, 155, 159, 161
psychological guilt, employed mothers 93
psychological impact of 165, 166, 177–180
psychology: engendering 2, 123, 146; feminist 106, 132, 146–147, 152–153; intersectionality implications for 14
psychopathology 148
psychotherapy 19, 114, 123–124, 126–127, 148, 152, 158, 161
puberty 64
Puss in Boots: The Last Wish (film) 174

queer-affirmative therapies 68, 120–121, 123, 138–139, 146
queer characters, gendered portrayals in media 170–171
queer communities 18, 45–46, 50, 72, 83, 121, 170
queer couples 18, 46; gender identity 44; romantic relationships 43–45
queer groups 19, 114, 139
queer movement 18–19, 113, 120–122
queerness 36, 67, 112, 170
queer persons 2, 18–19, 44, 51, 59–60, 68, 73, 82, 96–97, 106–108, 111–118, 120–122, 124, 128, 139, 159–160, 170; prejudice and discrimination against 119; taboo around and social ostracism of 68; underrepresentation in corporate sector 96

RAHI Foundation 108
rape 15, 48, 71, 102–103, 125, 153; and marital rape 49; and sexual assault issues, portrayal in media 169
realistic personality-type persons 83

202 Index

're-authoring' technique 141
relational harmony 52
relationships 31, 41–48, 52, 57–59, 61,
    72, 75, 77, 113–114, 116, 119, 128,
    135–137, 142; egalitarian 126,
    128–129; familial 43; marital 41,
    52, 76; violent 117, 119
reproductive sexuality 110
Rights of Persons with Disabilities Act
    (2016) 96
RISE (Reimagining Inclusion for Social
    Equity) 97
role conflicts 31, 88
role models 28, 87, 99–100
romantic relationships 41, 43–44, 43–46,
    50; attitudes and behaviour of
    youth 44; close relationships
    online 45; emphasis on aspects
    of 43; formation of 43; forms of
    44; gender binaries 44; LGBT and
    intersex person 44, 45; One-sided
    attraction 45; premarital sexual
    relationships 45; queer couple
    43–44; statistics related to 45;
    taboos and inhibitions 43–44;
    violence against women 45

Samatesathi Amhi Pursush 17
same-gender friendships 42
same-sex marriage, battles across world for
    120–122
Samyak 17
Save Indian Family Foundation 17
schizophrenia and PTSD 173–174
school: and college, as agents of socialization
    32; gender sensitivity at 53
Section 377: criminalizing homosexual
    acts 120–121; scrapping of
    121–122
self-categorization 29
self-concept, gender-based 29
self-esteem 8
self-images 8
Seth, Leila 59
Seth, Vikram 59
sex 4–7, 10–12, 27, 36, 67, 106–108, 110,
    112, 115, 128, 131–134; definitions
    of 5; differences 23, 25; education
    52, 108, 113, 170, 174; and gender,
    difference between 4–7; within
    marriage 110
sex/gender reassignment surgery 6

sexism 32, 154, 179; definition of 10,
    11; level of severity 10–11; in
    psychology 146–147; types 11
sex-typed individuals 35
sexual assault 49–50, 169
sexual desire: expression by women 25;
    social and cultural factors role in
    25; testosterone role in 25
sexual harassment at workplace 46,
    48, 50–51, 50–52, 58, 82, 96,
    101–103, 101–104, 125, 153–154;
    and assault 11; law framed to
    prevent 102; salient points of
    101–102
sexuality 2, 5–7, 10, 12–14, 16–18,
    23–24, 28–29, 44–45, 50, 59,
    65–67, 65–68, 72–73, 81, 84,
    106–121, 125, 127–133, 137,
    146, 148, 150–151, 155, 160,
    168, 171; acceptance of 112;
    children's 114–117, 119; definition
    of 107–108; discussion of
    nuances of 66; double standards
    in overt expression of 110; and
    gender education 108; and gender
    identities 112; and genders
    7, 67, 73, 112–113, 118; and
    intersectionality 112; monogamy
    111; one-night stands and hook-ups
    110; pathologizing 113; polyamory
    111; queer 2, 59, 112; references on
    110; regulating 32; sex and gender,
    confusions between 108; and sexual
    orientation 111–112; and social
    learning theory 28–29; as taboo 112
sexuality education and awareness
    workshops 66, 108–110, 155
sexual minorities 7, 60, 69, 102, 107,
    121, 147
sexual orientation 7, 13, 45, 51, 60, 67, 74,
    97, 106–107, 111, 113–114, 116,
    148, 151, 157–158
sexual-orientation disclosure 60
sexual permissiveness 110
sexual violation 112–113
sexual violence 49–50, 112–113
shared child rearing 86
shared parenting issues 90–95
Shubh Mangal Zyada Saavdhan (Hindi
    film) 118
sibling dyads 58
SIFF *see* Save Indian Family Foundation

single parents 95
sisterhood, mechanical and automatic
assumptions of 16–17
social change 13–14, 29, 128, 167
social conformity restrictions 64, 65
social construction of gender 36
socialization 2, 7, 12, 24–26, 46, 95; agents
of 8, 31; concept of 26; definitions
of 2; gender role development 26;
gender roles and stereotypes with
9–10; primary and secondary 63
social learning theory 28–29
socially aware and progressive themes
168–169
social media 29, 31–33, 42, 102, 112, 117,
155, 165–166, 171, 177–178
social personality-type persons 83
social pressure and social conformity
restrictions 64
social psychology 36
social responsibility for childcare 87
social role theory of gender role
development 31–33
societal evolution 51
societal pressure 93
societal reformation 53
Society for the Psychology of Women
19–20
socio-biology 33–34
stereotypes 7, 8–12, 31, 42, 58, 69, 94–95,
99, 108, 124, 147, 149, 169, 173, 179
stigma 19, 60, 62, 66, 71, 113, 116–117,
119, 149, 152, 156, 175, 177
stress, depression, and student suicide 172
structural and relational harmony 52
suicides of Rohith Vemula 53–54
Super's model of career development 84;
decline stage 85; establishment
stage 84; exploration stage 84;
growth stage 84; maintenance stage
84–85
'super women' 88
Sweekar: The Rainbow Parents 114

Taare Zameen Par (film) 172–173
Tamasha (film) 172
tensions 107, 114, 137, 149, 161
Tere Naam (film) 173
testosterone: and aggression, link between
24; role in sexual desire 25
Thappad (film) 169
therapists and patients 171–175

TLLLF *see* The Live Love Laugh
Foundation
tokenism 6, 10, 82, 96, 98–99, 166
Towards Equality report 14
transgender boy identity 63
transgender persons 50, 60, 63, 67, 71–73,
96, 98, 108, 116–117, 120;
discrimination against 12; lives of
12–13; marriage problems faced
by 73–74
Transgender Persons (Protection of Rights)
Act, 2019 96
transgender teenagers, sexual and romantic
behaviours among 50
transphobia 12–13, 18, 106–107, 114,
118–119
tribal cultures 118
Truth, Sojourner 13

unique-outcomes technique 142
Unnao rape case of 2017 53

victimization 60
violence, in relationships 9–10, 12,
15, 17, 24, 28, 41, 45, 47–48,
47–50, 47–51, 52–56, 60, 62,
66, 71, 107–108, 110, 116, 119,
121, 125, 137, 152–153, 165,
169; aggression 47–48; crimes
committed against women 48;
domestic violence 48–49; gendered
portrayals of 165; LGBTIQ
community 50; misogynistic views
contributing 49; rape, sexual
assault, and marital rape 49–50;
sexual harassment at workplace
50–51; violence against women 45,
49; against women 153

Western television 170
white/heterosexual/ableist/upper caste/
upper class, dominant ideas of 13
Williams, Serena 171
women 14, 61, 88; content analysis of
substantial representation of 167;
gendered portrayals of 166–168;
and men, differences between 5; in
politics 88; primary responsibility
of 51; 'women as deficient model'
29; women's/gender studies 5;
'women and stir approach' 6
women's mental health 152–159

204 Index

women's movement 14–17, 29, 48–49, 101–103, 124, 126, 147, 152; definition of 14; and feminism in India 14–16; in West 16–17
women's organizations 14, 16, 66, 102
Women's Reservation Bill 98
women's safety 54
women's studies 4–5, 14–15
workforce and gender 81–82
'working mothers' debate' 85–87
work-life balance 89
'work–life balance' 9
workplace 8–12, 37, 43, 46–47, 50, 52–55, 61, 63, 69–70, 73, 81–105, 82, 119, 153–154, 156; gender as structure in 61; gender sensitivity at 52; mechanism of hiring in 82; relationships 46; relationships and gender 46–47; sexual harassment at 50–51
workshops 17, 44, 52, 66, 109, 155

youth challenges and gender 68–74; choice of courses, streams, and careers 69; feminine discourses 69, 70; gender differences, in employment 68–69; higher education 69; marriage patterns 72–73; option to join armed forces 69; transgender education 70–71; vocational education and training (VET) 69–70, 70